"Information through Innovation"

Henry D. Crockett

Gillian R. Hall

Mark E. Wheeler

Portland State University
Portland, Oregon

boyd & fraser

boyd & fraser publishing company

Publisher: Thomas K. Walker
Acquisitions Editor: James H. Edwards
Production Editor: Barbara Worth
Manufacturing Director: Dean Sherman

A division of South-Western Publishing Company
Boston, MA 02116

Manufactured in the United States of America

ISBN: 0-87835-883-8

Stock Number BF8838

1 2 3 4 5 6 7 8 9 10 DH 5 4 3 2 1

Excelerator System Component Types and Codes

Code	Type	Code	Type
CAT	Category	PRG	Presentation Graph
CHG	Change Request	PGC	Presentation Graph Connection
CTF	Control Flow	PGO	Presentation Graph Object
CSA	Control Store	PPS	Primitive Process Specification
CTT	Control Table	PRC	Process
CTA	Control Transformation	PRM	Prompt
DAE	Data Entity	REC	Record
DAF	Data Flow	REF	Reference Document
DFD	Data Flow Diagram	REP	Report
DMD	Data Model Diagram	RED	Report Design
DNR	Data N-Ary Relationship	SDE	Screen Data Entry
DAR	Data Relationship	SDR	Screen Data Report
DAS	Data Store	SCD	Screen Design
DEL	Deliverable	SIG	Signal
DOF	Document Fragment	STA	State
DCG	Document Graph	TRD	State Transition Diagram
DOC	Document Group	STC	Structure Chart
ELE	Element	STD	Structure Diagram
ERQ	Engineering Requirement	SGC	Structure Graph Connection
ELS	Entity List	SDT	Structured Decision Table
ERA	Entity-Relationship Diagram	SDV	System Device
EXT	External Entity	TAB	Table of Codes
FUN	Function	TST	Test
ISS	Issue	TVA	Transition Vector
MOD	Module	USR	User
NTE	Note	URQ	User Requirement
		WBS	Work Breakdown Structure

ACKNOWLEDGMENTS

Portland State University
School of Business Administration
Equipment and Office Support

Apple Computer, Inc.
Kevin D. Hurst
Loan of Apple Equipment

Intersolv, Inc.
Educational Grant for Excelerator Release 1.9
Permission to Reproduce Copyrighted Material

Arthur H. Weisbach
Copy Editor

Gloria Oman and Jeff Hathaway
Accuracy Verification

Pages in Print
Gail Hall
Editing

Computer Applications Group, Inc.
Jim Hall
Document Layout Concepts

Kyle Lee Wheeler
Dragon Artwork

This book was produced on Apple Macintosh computers using Quark Express v3.0 and Aldus Freehand v3.0.

T

TABLE OF CONTENTS

Preface — Using this Book

Excelerating Systems Analysis & Design is specifically intended as a first-step learning tool for Excelerator Release 1.9, a computer-aided systems engineering (CASE) product for the IBM PC.

Although it does not cover all of Excelerator's many functions, this tutorial provides a solid foundation in using Excelerator for structured systems analysis and design. To get the most value from the exercises, it may be helpful to have a set of Excelerator manuals and a systems analysis text available for reference.

An example project for a company called Anonymous Autos is used throughout the book to help you understand how Excelerator's functions fit together in the context of a real project.

The Anonymous Autos project is completely developed in a step-by-step process using Excelerator's integrated tools for process modeling, physical and logical data modeling, prototyping, and structure design.

This tutorial was written using the following conventions:

- Section names and new terms (both general and Excelerator specific) appear in **bold type**.
- References to Excelerator manuals (supplied with each purchased copy of Excelerator) appear in *italics.*
- Lists and instructions are bulleted and indented like this.
- When we want you to type something, the characters you are to type **`LOOK LIKE THIS.`**
- When we want you to press a key, we'll show you a picture of it. For example [F3], [↵] (for Enter or Return), [Pg Up], and [Tab].

- Mapmakers in other times often used fearful and fanciful beasts to warn of dangerous or unexplored places. They said, "Beware! Here there be dragons!" We use a dragon to denote advanced features of the product that may not be suitable for beginning students.

- Menu options appear in boxes. **THEY LOOK LIKE THIS.**

Exercise

Exercises are in boxes like this one.

We use the side bar for figure descriptions, hints, and warnings.

Excelerating Your Skills ...

Advanced exercises appear at the end of some sections. They look like this.

Learning new software can be fun. We guarantee frustration, joy, agony, and satisfaction in your travels through Excelerator's many facets. Relax and enjoy learning to use this powerful tool.

1

INTRODUCING THE SYSTEMS DEVELOPMENT PROCESS

1.1

The Systems Development Life Cycle (SDLC)

The **Systems Development Life Cycle (SDLC)** is a methodology providing a structure for tasks involved in developing a computerized information system. There are as many slightly different versions of the SDLC as there are authors who discuss it. The following seven-phase version of the SDLC is used as a basis for our discussion:

- Investigation Phase
- Analysis Phase
- Design Phase
- Development Phase
- Installation
- Review Phase
- Product Maintenance Phase

The **Investigation Phase** includes an examination of the scope of the new system and a feasibility study to determine whether or not the project should be undertaken. The **Analysis Phase** includes a review of the previous system (if any), a determination of the requirements of the new system, and a selection among competing alternative system solutions. The **Design Phase** incorporates a blueprint of the hardware and software required to provide the new system requirements. During the **Development Phase**, programming and testing of system hardware and software occur. They are followed by the **Installation Phase** which includes all conversions required from the old system and physical installation of the new system. The **Review Phase** is an examination of the process used to develop the new system, the purpose being to identify problems which might be avoided on future projects. Finally, the **Product Maintenance Phase** ensures that the installed system functions properly and that any enhancements are documented. Near the end of the useful lifetime of the system, a new SDLC is begun.

Many businesses develop and maintain SDLC documentation called the **project encyclopedia** (sometimes called a **repository**). The project encyclopedia is an expanded version of the **project dictionary**. It is compiled throughout the SDLC phases and contains all accumulated project information. The encyclopedia provides information which helps in the initial development, maintenance, and enhancement of the system. It also provides a basis for the development of a replacement system at the end of the current system's useful life. For each SDLC phase, the project encyclopedia contains one or more of the following:

- **Investigation Phase**
  Executive Summary
  System Overview
  Feasibility Study
  Recommendations
- **Analysis Phase**
  Physical Data Flow Diagrams
  Process Descriptions
  External Entity Descriptions
  Data Store Descriptions
  Data Flow Descriptions
  Logical Data Flow Diagrams
  Entity-Relationship Diagrams
  Data Entity Descriptions
  Data Element Descriptions
- **Design Phase**
  Request for Proposal
  Screen and Report Designs
  Terminal Dialogues
  Physical Data Design
  Table Descriptions
  Data Element Descriptions
  Table of Codes
  Program Module Design
- **Development Phase**
  Program Coding
  Test Data
  Program Evaluation Method
  System Evaluation Method
  Verification Test (alpha test)
  Validation Test (beta test)
  Physical Data Description
- **Installation**
  File Conversion
  Installation/Conversion Plan
  EDP (Electronic Data Processing) Audit
- **Review Phase**
  System Operation Evaluation
  Development Process Evaluation
- **Product Maintenance Phase**
  Enhancement Log

1.2

Integrating Computer-Aided Systems Engineering (CASE)

In the past, the development of computer information systems was perceived as an art form. The programmer-artist came in and discussed requirements of a new information system with the end-users. Then, without further input from users, the programmer went away and designed the new system. The resulting system, delivered months or years later, was rarely what the end-user really wanted.

As the complexity and size of new information systems increased, development took longer and longer and resulting systems were not satisfying user needs.

Finally, the idea of structuring the systems development process like a science rather than an art-form emerged. The result, it was hoped, would be a much more consistent and satisfactory end-product. The science which arose, called **systems engineering**, required a cohesive design methodology.

Even using the new methodologies, the systems development process was still too slow and system documentation was often insufficient. The idea of computerizing the systems engineering process itself has resulted in a wide range of **computer-aided systems engineering** tools like Excelerator. These automated tools are used to describe and document the entire Systems Development Life Cycle.

Excelerator provides the following functions supporting the SDLC:

- **Investigation Phase**
  - Work Breakdown Structure
  - Presentation Graph

- **Analysis Phase**
  - Data Flow Diagrams
  - Entity-Relationship Diagram
  - Data Model Diagram
  - Extended Analysis
  - Graph Verification
  - XLDictionary

- **Design Phase**
  - Report Design
  - Screen Design
  - Structure Charts
  - Structure Diagram
  - State Transition Diagram
  - Table of Codes
  - XLDictionary

- **Development Phase**
  - Code Generation
  - Presentation Graph

- **Installation**
  - Work Breakdown Structure
  - Presentation Graph

- **Review Phase**
  - Work Breakdown Structure
  - Presentation Graph

- **Product Maintenance Phase**
  - XLDictionary

The XLDictionary is the repository for all SDLC information. It contains details of Excelerator-described data structures and the relationships between them. XLDictionary tools help analyze and report on defined structures. Examination of project documentation generated by Excelerator helps ensure a consistent and well-documented system definition.

2 INTRODUCING EXCELERATOR

Excelerator is a computer-aided systems engineering (CASE) product. Its integrated tools are used in the systems analysis and design process to define, verify, and document a system prior to code generation. Among these tools are the following:

- **Graphics** facilities are used for creating charts and diagrams which provide a visual representation of the system.

- The **data dictionary** (XLDictionary) stores information about system components. The data dictionary also facilitates the examination and revision of system components.

- **Screen and report prototyping** facilities allow the designer to define screen and report designs completely .

- **Analysis** facilities provide information about defined system components and the relationships among them.

A complete list of Excelerator system components and their three letter identification codes is located inside the front cover of this book for quick reference.

2.1

Using the Mouse

In Excelerator, the **mouse**, shown in Figure 2.1, is used differently depending on the type of screen being worked with and the task being performed:

- On menu screens, the mouse may be used to select menu options.
- On description screens, the mouse may be used to select a position for the **insertion point** before entering text.
- On graph and chart drawing screens, the mouse is used to position graph objects, labels, and text blocks.
- In screen and report design, the mouse is used to position fields and text on the drawing screen.

The mouse cursor appears as an arrow on graph and chart drawing screens, as a flashing box on menu screens, and as a flashing underline character on description screens.

To select a menu option, text insertion point, or an item from a selection list,

- Move the mouse until the cursor displays on the item to be selected.
- Press the left button on the mouse.

To cancel an action or selection,

- Press the right button on the mouse.

To display a selector list or to save current work and then exit from a description screen,

- Press both buttons on the mouse together.

Figure 2.1
Typical PC Mouse

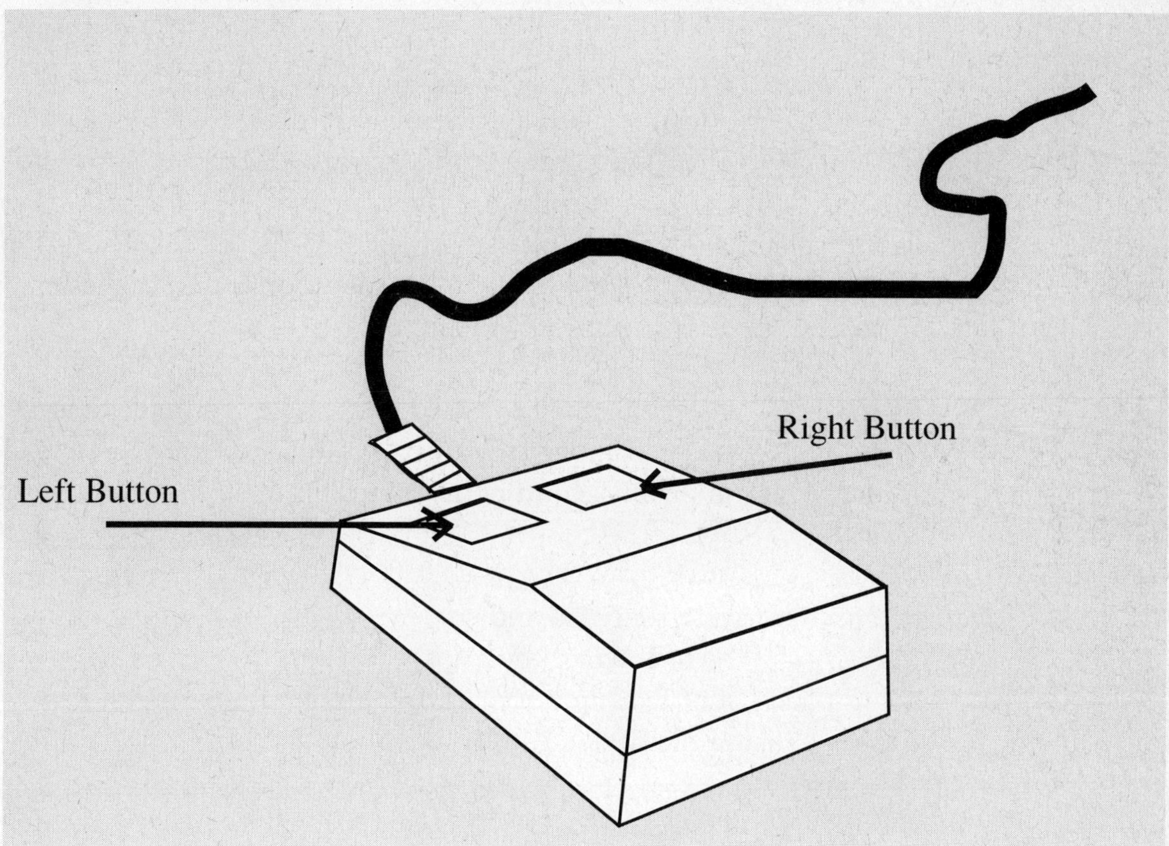

2.2

Using the Keyboard

In Excelerator, the keyboard, shown in Figure 2.2, is used to select menu options and items from lists, to complete and modify description screens, and to navigate from one entity to another.

On menus and selector lists, the keyboard cursor is the highlighted option or item. This cursor is moved using the ↑ ↓ ← → keys. Once the desired option or item is highlighted, it is selected by pressing F3 or ↵ (the Enter or Return key). Menu options and selector list items are cancelled by pressing Esc. Menu options may also be selected by simply pressing the corresponding **selector**. The selector is usually the first letter of the menu option or the letter preceding the option name on the menu.

On description screens, the keyboard cursor/insertion point is a small flashing box. When you begin typing, it is at this point where text will appear. This cursor/insertion point may be moved using the these keys: ↑, ↓, ←, →, Tab, Shift + Tab, Backspace, and Spacebar.

Text on description screens and screen and report designs may be edited using the following keys: Ins, Del, Backspace, and Spacebar. A complete list of Excelerator's editing keyboard commands is available inside the back cover of this book.

Excelerator provides three special function keys which are useful throughout the product. They are as follows:

F2 — **Help** provides a short explanation of the menu option or field on which the cursor is positioned.

F3 — **Save** stores your description screen entries and screen and report designs. This key also has limited navigational functions. For example, it can be used for making menu selections.

F4 — **Browse** allows movement between related entities.

Figure 2.2
Typical PC Keyboard

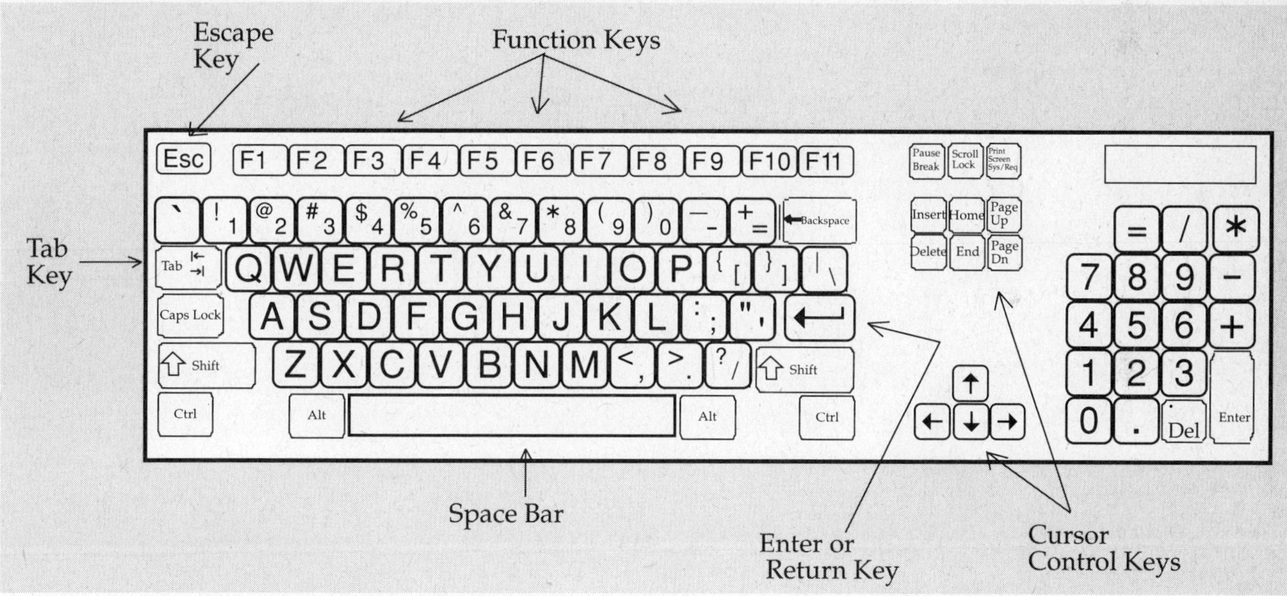

2.3

Accessing Excelerator

Before Excelerator can be accessed, it must first be installed. The installation process is described in the *Excelerator Installation Guide,* Chapter 2, Installing Excelerator (documentation provided with the purchase of Excelerator). Once it is installed, follow these steps to access the program:

- Turn on your computer.

Wait for the operating system prompt to display. This is usually a C>. This means you are in the C drive where Excelerator is normally installed. At the C>,

- Type `excel` as shown at the top of Figure 2.3.
- Press ↵, and the Excelerator **Copyright Screen** appears.
- Press ↵ again, and the **Log-on Screen** appears.

You are now ready to log-on to Excelerator. If users, passwords, and projects have not yet been assigned,

- Type `user` in the **Username** field. (Be sure to use lowercase letters as Excelerator is case-sensitive in this field.)
- Press ↵, and the insertion point moves to the **Password** field.
- Press ↵ again, and one **Project** is displayed called Demo.
- Press ↵ again, and Excelerator's **Main Menu** is displayed.

User, password, and project assignments may then be made from the **Housekeeping** option on the Main Menu. Detailed instructions on making these assignments are found in the *Excelerator Facilities and Functions Reference Guide*, Chapter 8, Housekeeping.

If users, passwords, and projects have already been established (this is often the case in classroom applications where an instructor makes these assignments prior to student involvement),

- Type your assigned log-on name in the Username field on the Log-on Screen.
- Press ⏎, and the insertion point moves to the Password field.
- Type your assigned password.
- Press ⏎, and all Projects to which you are assigned are displayed.
- Select a project with the mouse or keyboard, and the Main Menu appears.

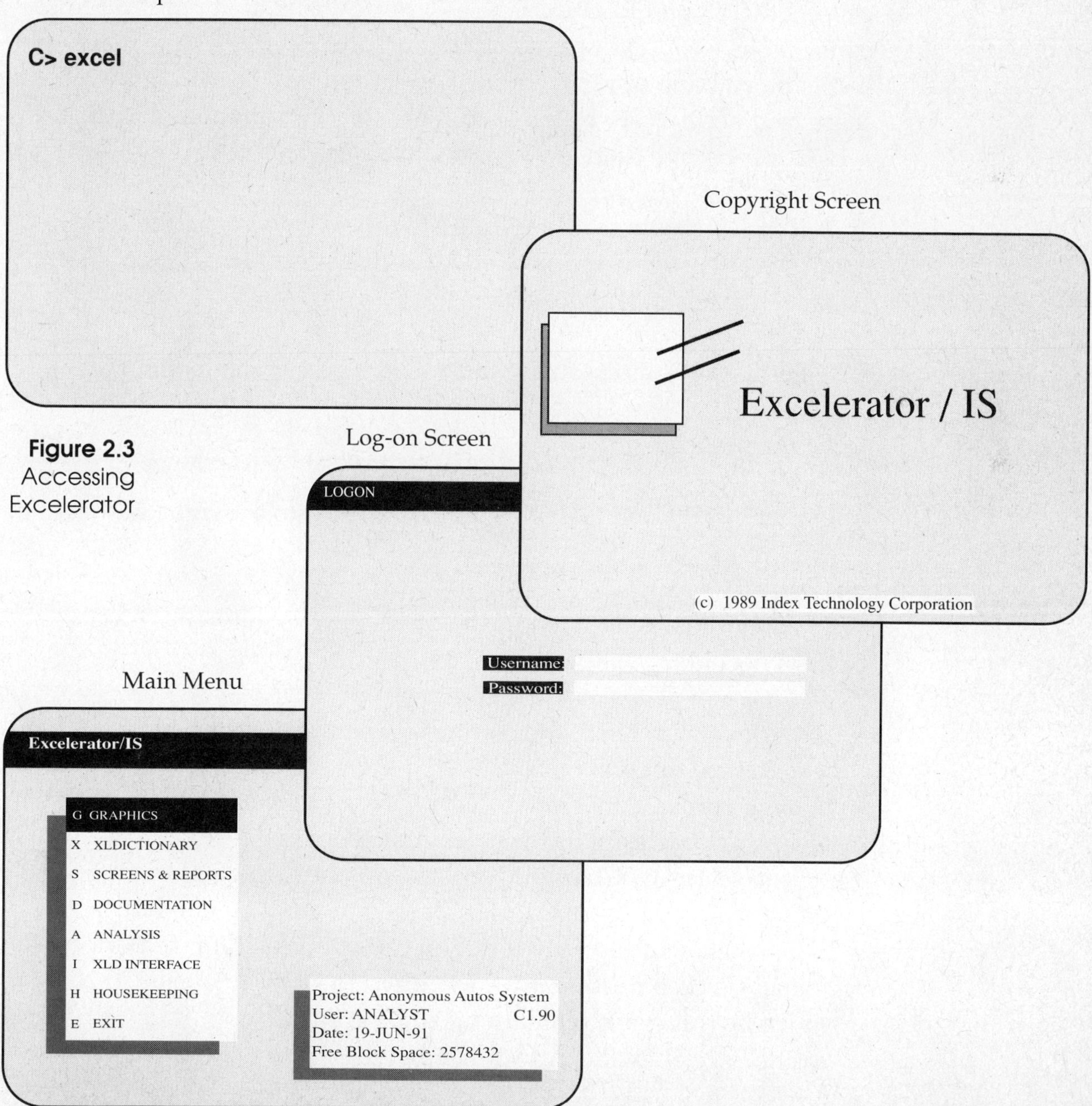

Figure 2.3
Accessing Excelerator

2.4

Exiting Excelerator

Before turning off your computer, it is imperative that you exit from Excelerator. Failure to exit properly will result in corruption of your files. Such corruption can be remedied using Excelerator routines called **FIXSYS** and **FIXPROJ**. Be aware, however, that in rebuilding connections within your project, FIXSYS and FIXPROJ may make some information unrecoverable. Excelerator will let you know when these routines need to be invoked. For more information on their use see *Excelerator Facilities and Functions Reference Guide,* Page A-3.

To exit from anywhere in the product, first save your current work by pressing F3 or selecting save and exit from graphics menus. When you arrive back at a menu screen,

- Select **Exit** until you are returned to Excelerator's Main Menu.

From the Main Menu,

- Select **EXIT** and the EXIT options appear to the right as shown in Figure 2.4.

When you select EXIT from the Main Menu, the following EXIT options become available:

- Exit directly to DOS (the computer operating system) by selecting the **Return to DOS** option.
- Change projects by selecting the **Change Projects** option and then selecting the desired project from the list displayed.
- If you select the **Change Users** option, the Log-on screen will appear. A new Username and Password are then entered.
- The **Analysis Prep & Exit** option causes Excelerator to perform its Analysis Prep routine prior to exiting to DOS. Analysis Prep must be run prior to renaming some graph objects or generating some Excelerator reports, but is not used in this tutorial.

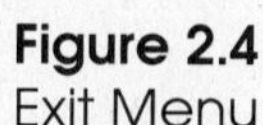

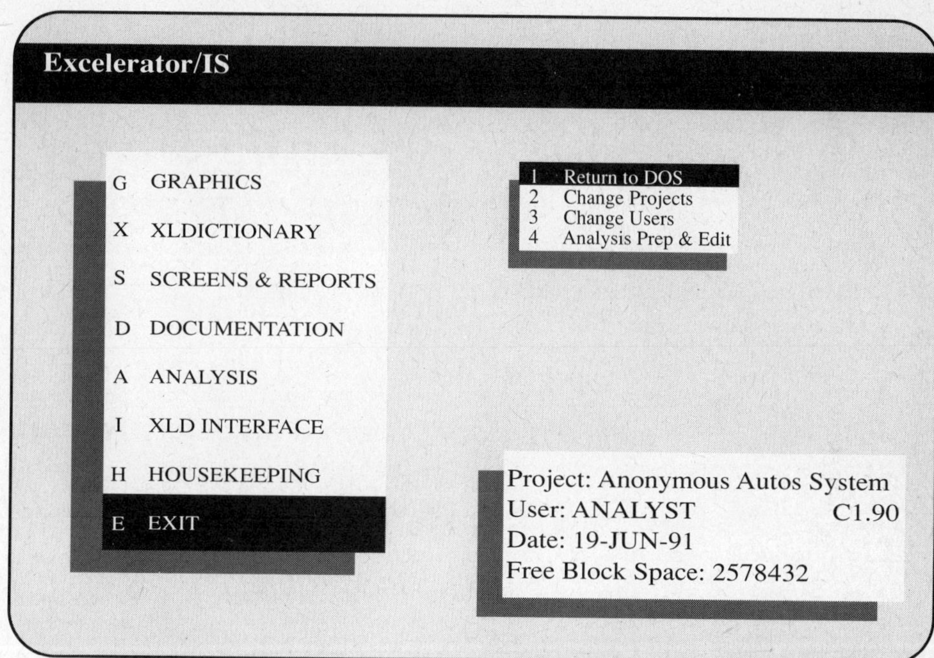

Figure 2.4
Exit Menu

3

THE ANONYMOUS AUTOS PROJECT

The Anonymous Autos project is presented in this tutorial to illustrate the use of CASE in the context of a systems development project. In each chapter, you are shown Excelerator functions in the context of this project. The exercises presented in some sections ask you to perform tasks which further develop the Anonymous Autos project.

In completing this tutorial, you complete both the analysis of the existing system at Anonymous Autos and design of a replacement system. During this process you generate printed documentation for the project encyclopedia as follows:

- Physical Data Flow Diagrams and Descriptions
- External Entity Descriptions
- Process Descriptions
- Data Flow Descriptions
- Data Store Descriptions
- Record Descriptions
- Element Descriptions
- Entity-Relationship Diagram and Description
- Data Entity Descriptions
- Data N-ary Relationship Descriptions
- Screen Designs and Descriptions
- Report Designs and Descriptions
- Structure Charts and Descriptions
- Function Descriptions
- Structure Graph Connection Descriptions

It is important not only to learn how Excelerator works, but also to experience its use in the context of a project. The purpose of the Anonymous Autos project is to give you that experience.

3.1

Physical System & Inventory Procedures

Rich Royce, the owner of an auto dealership called Anonymous Autos, would like to install a computerized information system at his dealership. Rich believes that computerization will improve customer satisfaction and reduce the time between agreement on price and the actual sales contract signature.

Rich tries to maintain a staff of five salespeople. The turnover in the sales staff is about three salespeople per year. On the average, this means there are eight different people in sales every year. Salespeople are paid on a commission basis.

Since Rich deals exclusively with new foreign sports cars, sales are highly seasonal and can be affected by slumps in the local economy. All cars sold are purchased from inventory; Rich does not special-order cars. All trade-in vehicles are immediately sold for cash and are not maintained in inventory.

The first step in computerizing his dealership is the automation of vehicle inventory, sales, and reporting procedures. Rich would like the system to retain inventory data concerning cars sold and cars currently on the lot.

The accounting department at Anonymous Autos now maintains the Vehicle Inventory Record (VIR) for all newly arrived cars. An example VIR is shown in Figure 3.1a on the next page. The accountant obtains the PURCHASE DATA on each car from the shipping source document. The BASE COST recorded on the VIR includes all options installed by the factory. The STICKER PRICE marked on the car is determined by summing the BASE COST and FREIGHT, then multiplying the result by 1.23. This reflects a 23% dealer mark-up.

If options purchased by the buyer are supplied by the Anonymous Autos shop, then each shop installed option is listed on the VIR at cost. The total DEALER COST of the vehicle is the sum of the BASE COST plus FREIGHT plus the sum of all of the newly installed OPTION COSTs.

Figure 3.1a Current Vehicle Inventory Record (VIR) Form

Vehicle Inventory Record

PURCHASE DATA:

Manufacturer: ____________	Man. Invoice #: ____________
Make: ____________	Year: ____________
Model: ____________	Serial #: ____________
Exterior Color: ____________	Trim: ____________
Freight: ____________	Base Cost: ____________

(Base Cost + Freight) * 1.23 = Sticker Price: ____________

Options Installed by Shop

Code	Description	Cost
____	____________	____
____	____________	____
____	____________	____

Base Cost + Freight + Sum New Options = Dealer Cost: ____________

3.2

Sales Procedure

The procedure for making a sale at Anonymous Autos has been developed and formally documented to instruct new sales people. This procedure has been used by the sales staff for the last nine years and is summarized as follows:

1. Salesperson encourages customer interest in high-priced cars and identifies the most expensive car the customer can afford.
2. Salesperson contacts the used car dealer and obtains the market value of the customer's trade-in vehicle (TRADE-IN ALLOWANCE).
3. Salesperson discusses with the customer options already installed on the new car and additional options available through the shop.
4. Once the details concerning options have been agreed upon, a Sales Invoice is filled out on the new car.
   a. Customer fills out SOLD TO and TRADE-IN sections.
   b. Salesperson fills out sold-by, new car, and options sections.
   c. Salesperson calculates TOTAL PRICE and TOTAL DUE.
5. If necessary, the salesperson has the customer make an offer to be presented to the sales manager.
6. Salesperson returns the counter-offer to the customer.
7. If the counter-offer is not acceptable, the customer meets with the sales manager to close on a negotiated SALES PRICE and TOTAL DUE.
8. The remaining information on the invoice is completed by the salesperson, and both BUYER SIGNATURE and SALES MANAGER SIGNATURE are obtained.

The TOTAL PRICE on the Sales Invoice, shown in Figure 3.2 is the sum of the STICKER PRICE and total OPTION PRICE. The PRICE of each shop-installed option is determined by multiplying the OPTION COST (from the VIR) by 1.23 for a 23% mark-up factor.

The TRADE-IN ALLOWANCE is the market value of the customer's car as determined by the used car buyer. None of the Anonymous Autos trade-ins are inventoried. They are sold directly to the used car buyer.

Figure 3.2
Current Sales Invoice Form

Sales Invoice

Invoice #: ______________ **Date:** ___/___/___

SOLD TO: Name: ______________________
Address: ______________________
____
City: ______________ State: ____ Zip: ________
Telephone:(___) ___ - _____

SOLD BY ______________________

NEW CAR: Make: ______________ Year: ______________
Model: ______________ Serial #: ______________

OPTIONS:

Code	Description	Price

TRADE-IN: Make: ______________ Year: ______________
Model: ______________ Serial #: ______________

Sticker Price + : ________
Total Option Price + : ________
Discount - : ________
Total Price = : ________
Trade-In Allowance - : ________
Tax & License Fee + : ________
Total Due = : ________

BUYER SIGNATURE ______________

SALES MANAGER SIGNATURE ______________

The DISCOUNT shown on the Sales Invoice is determined through negotiations with the customer. It is used to reduce the cost of the new car to the customer. It is in the salesperson's interest to keep the DISCOUNT as low as possible because the DISCOUNT has a direct affect on sales profit and commission, which is 17% of sales profit. Sales profit is calculated by subtracting the DEALER COST and DISCOUNT from the TOTAL PRICE.

TOTAL DUE is the TOTAL PRICE minus TRADE-IN ALLOWANCE minus DISCOUNT plus TAX & LICENSE FEE. The LICENSE FEE is currently $50, but it is subject to change. The TAX is also variable and is currently 5% of the TOTAL PRICE minus the DISCOUNT.

3.3

Reporting Procedures

Accounting produces several reports for Rich Royce at the end of each two week period. The first is a summary report of sales by make of car. An example of this report is shown in Figure 3.3a. This report helps Rich decide which make of car to purchase to replace sold cars. The second report, shown in Figure 3.3b, displays itemized and total commissions earned by each salesperson. This report allows the accounting department to maintain correct payroll information.

To help track time and parts used in the repair shop, Rich would also like a listing of options installed in each car by Rich's own shop. This new requirement will result in a new report not currently being produced.

Anonymous Autos has budgeted $50,000 to cover the purchase of a computer, software, and project development costs.

Commissions Report

Salesman: D.J. Anders

Serial #	Profit	Commission
1078834	1,458	247.86
4077654	5,040	856.80

Total= $1,104.66

Salesman: J.R. Carlston

Serial #	Profit	Commission
4674575	10,465	1,779.05
1020034	1,570	266.90

Total= $2,045.95

Salesman: H.I. Hanley

Serial #	Profit	Commission
4098333	6,860	1,166.20
7639736	8,770	1,490.90

Total= $2,657.10

Salesman: F.R. Williams

Serial #	Profit	Commission
6576767	5,455	927.35
4025056	4,305	731.85

Total= $1,659.20

Figure 3.3a
Current Commissions Report

Auto Sales by Make

Make: Lotus

Serial #	Total Price	Dealer Cost	Discount	Profit
4674575	55,965	45,500	0	10,465
6756767	47,355	38,500	3,400	5,455
7939736	60,270	49,000	2,500	8,770
				24,690

Make: MG

Serial #	Total Price	Dealer Cost	Discount	Profit
1020034	11,070	9,000	500	1,570
1078834	11,808	9,600	750	1,458
				3,028

Make: Porsche

Serial #	Total Price	Dealer Cost	Discount	Profit
4025056	28,905	23,500	1,100	4,305
4077654	34,440	28,000	1,400	5,040
4098333	39,360	32,000	500	6,680
				16,005

Total Profit: $43,723

Figure 3.3b
Current Auto Sales by Make Report

MODELING PROCESSES

Developing a quality information system in today's computer environment requires a tremendous amount of planning and project management. Developers must understand the processing needs of their end-users. Process models are developed to communicate the desired system functionality. In this chapter **process modeling** is accomplished using a graphical method called **Data Flow Diagramming**.

The DFD is a graphical representation of processes, data flows, data stores, and entities in the systems environment. DFDs are excellent tools for communicating systems specifications to people interested in the new system. End-users can, with a short description of graphical representations, read, understand, and evaluate DFDs.

DFDs also allow systems professionals to expand each item represented to a high level of detail. This is done by creating a layered structure of diagrams through the explosion of DFD objects.

In this chapter, you use process modeling to analyze the current system described in **3. The Anonymous Autos Project**. You learn to draw and describe DFDs and DFD components by creating physical DFDs for the Anonymous Autos current system.

4.1

Introducing Drawing Functions

Excelerator provides the following graphical methods for modeling system design, examples of which are shown on the opposite page in Figure 4.1:

- Data Flow Diagram (DFD)
- Entity-Relationship Diagram (ERA)
- Structure Chart (STC)
- Data Model Diagram (DMD)
- State Transition Diagram (TRD)
- Structure Diagram (STD)
- Presentation Graph (PRG)
- Work Breakdown Structure (WBS)

The graphical models addressed in this book are Data Flow Diagrams, Structure Charts, and Entity-Relationship Diagrams. The drawing techniques for all graph types are basically the same. Differences for Entity-Relationship Diagrams and Structure Charts are discussed in Chapters 6 and 8 respectively.

Some graphical models can be exploded to show additional detail through layering. All graphs are linked to the XLDictionary providing further textual detail of the model. This link to the XLDictionary means that changes to a graph may affect other aspects of the project dictionary.

It is important to remember that all of these graphical models are developed to communicate ideas. To do this effectively, the printed graph must be readable. Excelerator users should take time to draw graphs which fit on one page, have no crossing lines, and show labels which are clearly associated with objects and connections.

In this section, you learn to use Excelerator's drawing functions through the development of a physical context Data Flow Diagram for the Anonymous Autos project.

Figure 4.1 Graphical Modeling Facilities in Excelerator

Data Flow Diagram

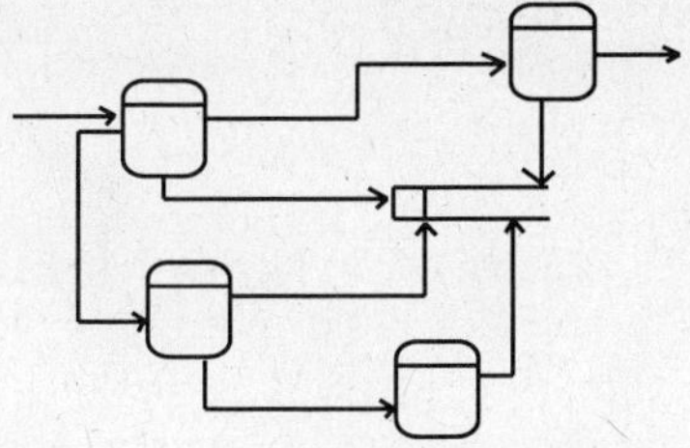

Entity Relationship Diagram

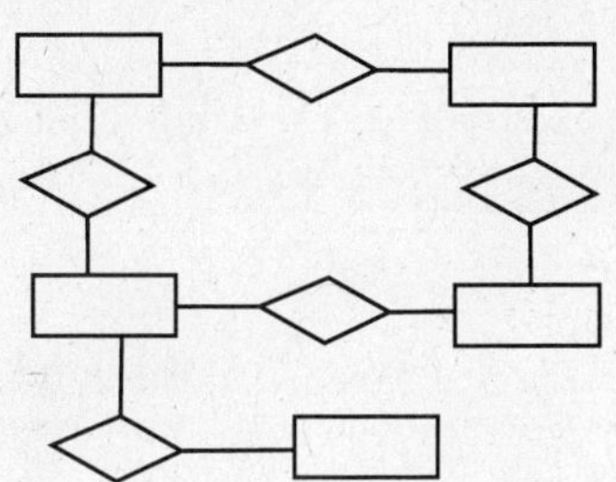

Structure Chart

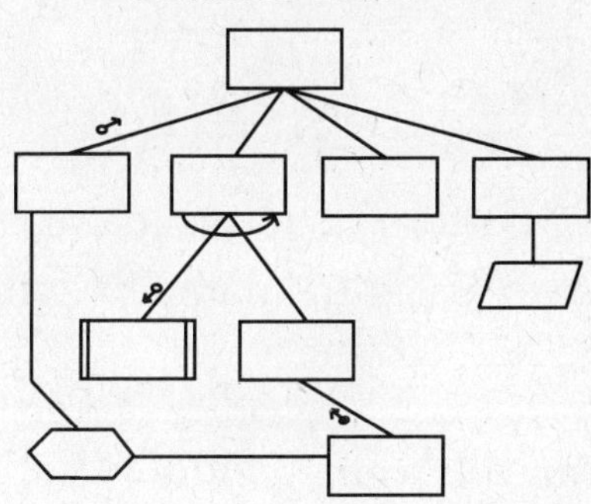

Data Model Diagram

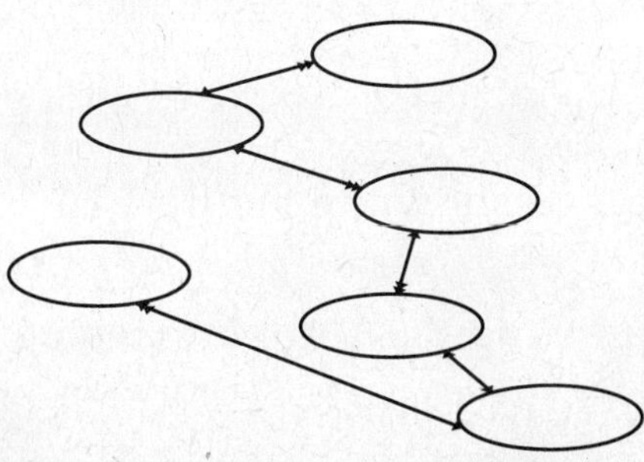

State Transition Diagram

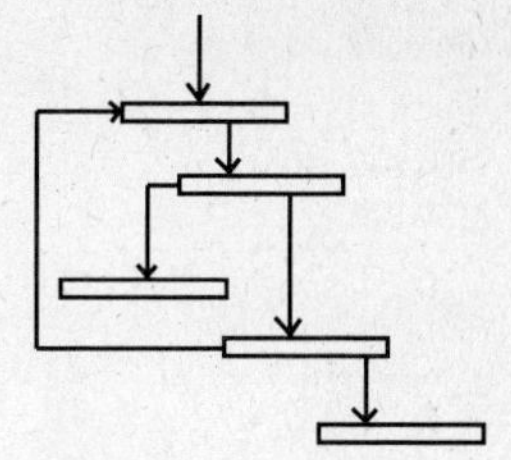

Structure Diagram

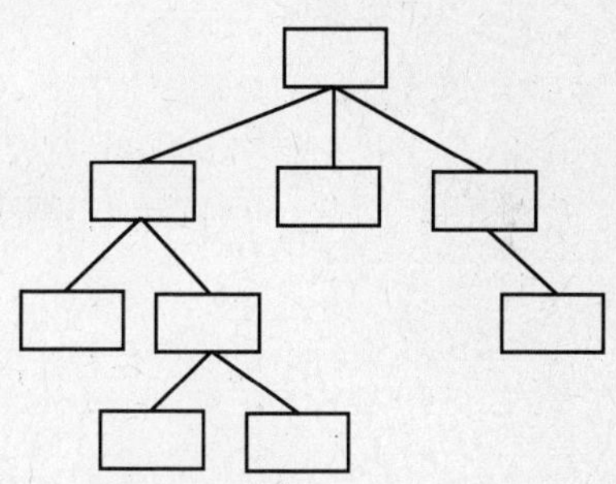

Presentation Graph

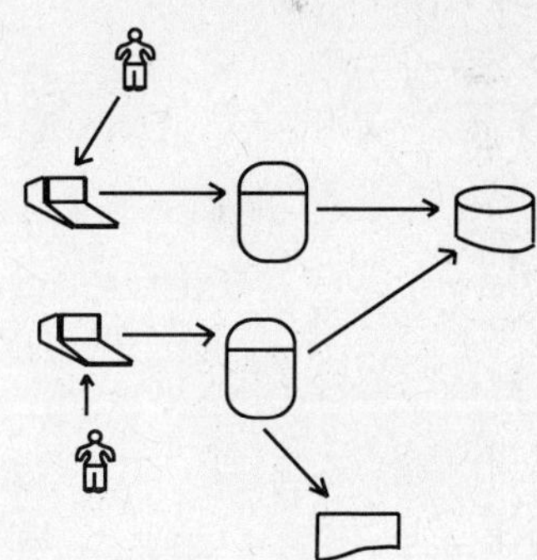

Work Breakdown Structure

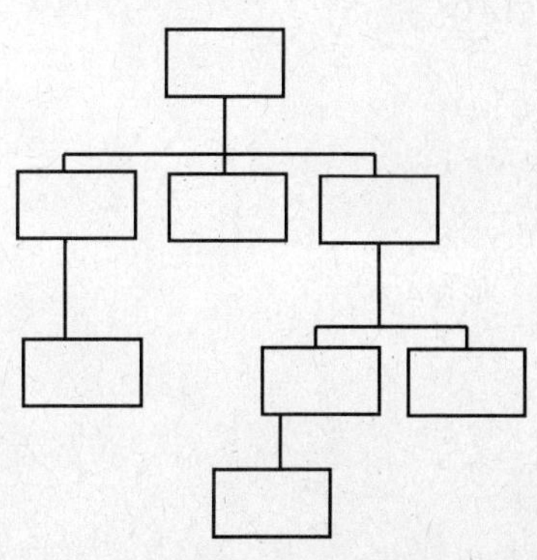

4.1.1 Initiating Drawings

To begin drawing a chart or graph using Excelerator's graphics facilities,

- Select **G GRAPHICS** from Excelerator's Main Menu as shown in Figure 4.1.1a.

The **Graphics Menu** appears. You are given a choice of eight chart and graph types from which you may choose the graph type you desire.

Because the development of Data Flow Diagrams (DFDs) is discussed in this chapter,

- Select **F Data Flow Diagram** from the Graphics Menu.

The **Graphics Action Keypad** appears to the right of the Graphics Menu. Because we want to initiate a new graph,

- Select **Add** from the Graphics Action Keypad.

The **Name** field appears at the bottom of your screen as shown in Figure 4.1.1b. Excelerator is requesting the name by which this new graph will be identified in the XLDictionary.

- Type **AA CONTEXT DFD** in the Name field.

This will be the context level physical Data Flow Diagram for the system currently in place at Anonymous Autos.

- Press ↵.

The **Drawing Screen** appears as shown in Figure 4.1.1c.

The next section, **4.1.2 Introducing the Drawing Screen**, explains the drawing screen in detail.

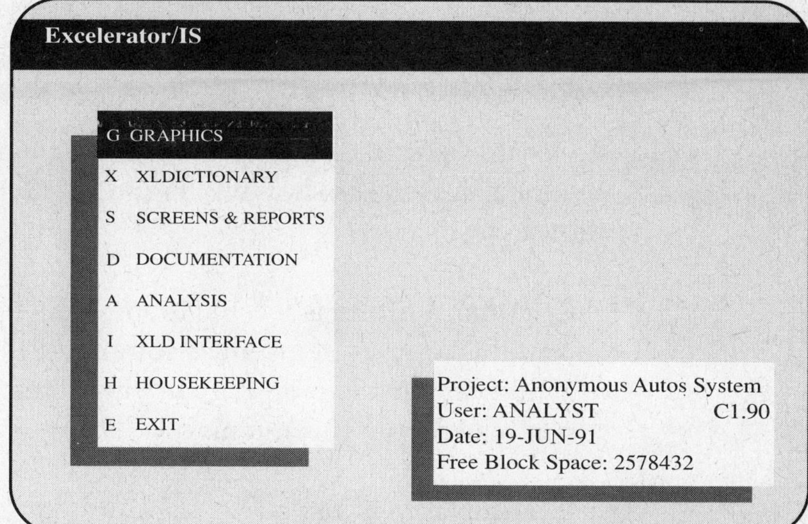

Figure 4.1.1a Excelerator's Main Menu

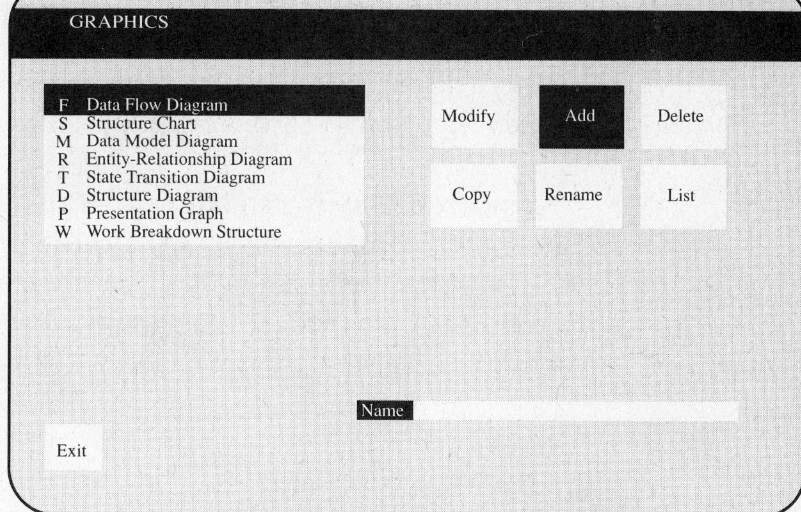

Figure 4.1.1b Graphics Menu

Figure 4.1.1c Drawing Screen

4.1.2 Introducing the Drawing Screen

Excelerator's chart and graph drawing screen is made up of several functional regions as shown in Figure 4.1.2. These regions are as follows:

- **Command Menu** is located along the left side of the screen. It contains a series of graphics commands and sub-menus. No action can be taken on the drawing screen without first selecting a command from this menu.

- **Graph Name** is just below the Command Menu. Only the first ten characters of the graph name being worked on are displayed.

- **Explosion Level Number** is displayed just below the graph name. The explosion level number is the hierarchical level of the current graph in relation to the top-level graph.

- **Orientation Map** is a square box located below the level number showing a miniature view of the entire drawing area. Each object appears as a single dot. The orientation map shows the position of the portion of the graph being viewed with relation to the entire graph.

- **Status Line** is located at the bottom of the screen. Excelerator provides prompts or message information on this line, which is also used for entering object identifiers during object description.

- **Drawing Area** is located to the right of the Command Menu. It is the largest portion of the screen. The graph or chart is actually created in this area.

- **Title Block** is located in the bottom right corner of the drawing area. The title block contains the graph name, date, and user information.

Figure 4.1.2
Drawing Screen Components

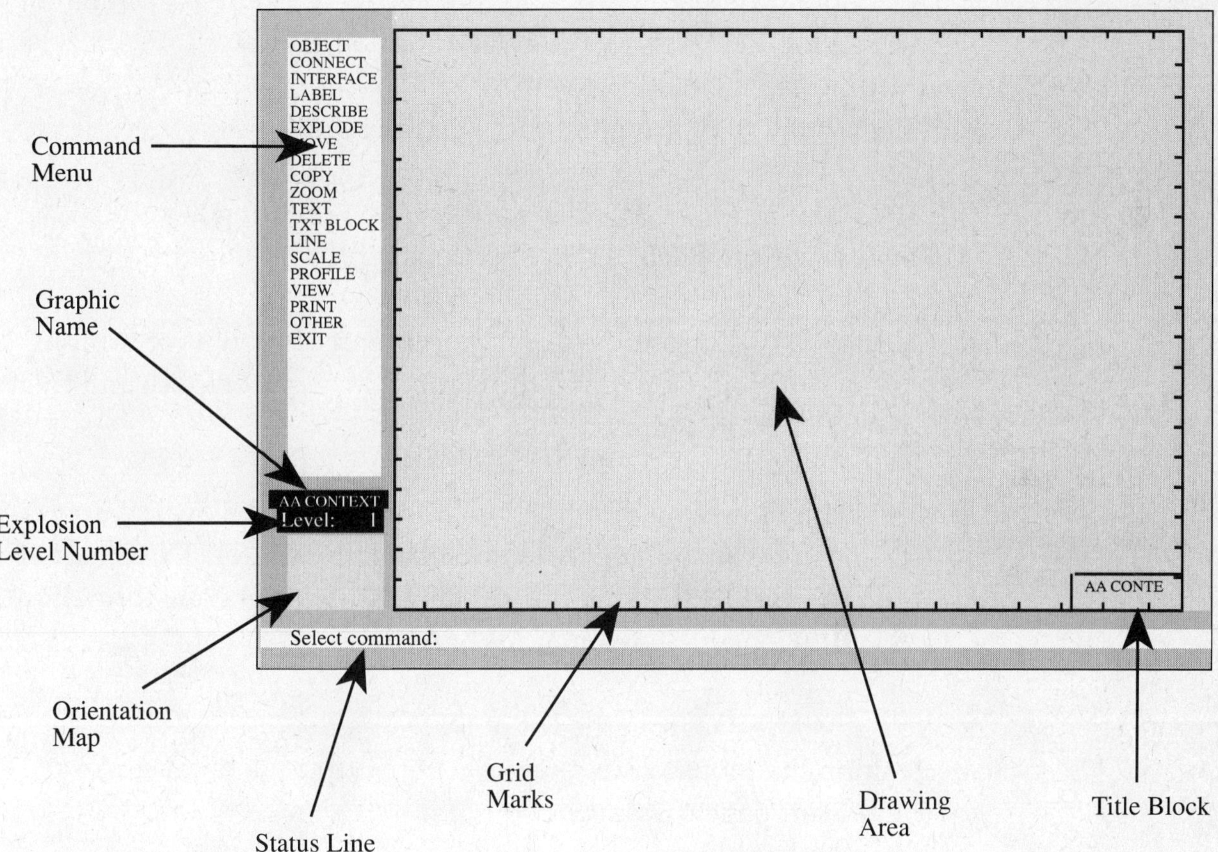

4.1.3 Placing Objects on the Screen

The blank drawing area initially displayed represents six pages of printed output. Before placing objects on the screen, it is helpful to see the delineation between displayed pages. To display delineating lines,

- Select **PRINT** from the Command Menu.

PRINT options appear below a double dotted line on the Command Menu: **FULL GPH**, **WINDOW**, **DRAFT**, and **SETUP**.

- Select **FULL GPH** from the PRINT options.

As shown in Figure 4.1.3a, lines appear in the drawing area breaking it into six sections. Each of these sections represents a page.

- Select **OBJECT** from the Command Menu. (If you have trouble making this selection, press the right mouse button once and then try the selection again.)

A list of Data Flow Diagram (DFD) objects appears below the double dotted line in the Command Menu: **PROCESS**, **X-ENTITY** (External Entity), **DAT STOR** (Data Store), **CTL TRN** (Control Transformation), **CTL STOR** (Control Store), and **OFFPAGE**.

- Select **X-ENTITY** from the list of DFD objects.
- Position the mouse cursor (arrow) in the upper left hand area of the top left page displayed.
- Press the left button on the mouse.

An External Entity appears on the screen. Until you make another menu selection, each time you press the left mouse button an External Entity will appear on the screen.

- Place the other External Entities on the screen as shown in Figure 4.1.3b.
- Select **PROCESS** from the list of DFD objects.
- Position the mouse cursor in the center of your drawing.

- Press the left mouse button to place a Process in the center of the drawing as shown in Figure 4.1.3b.

Don't worry if objects appear in the wrong place. You will learn to move and delete objects in the next section.

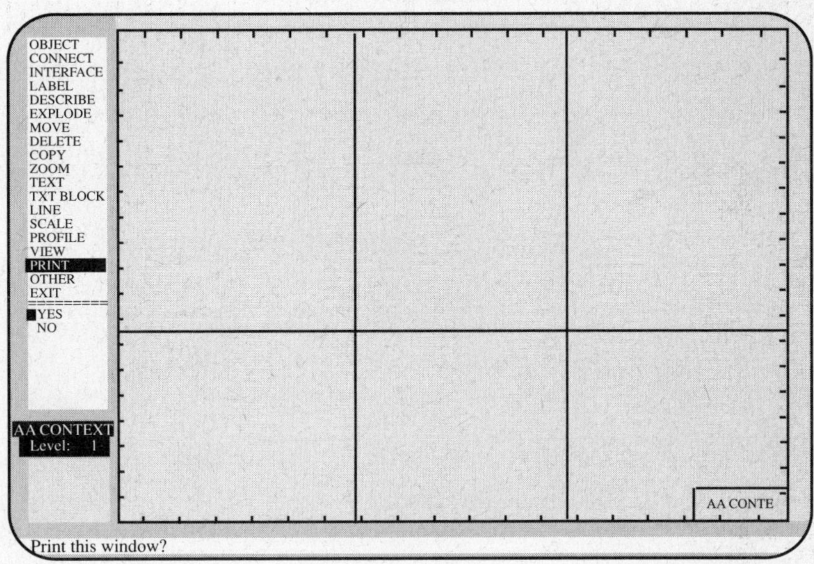

Figure 4.1.3a
Page Delineation in Drawing Area

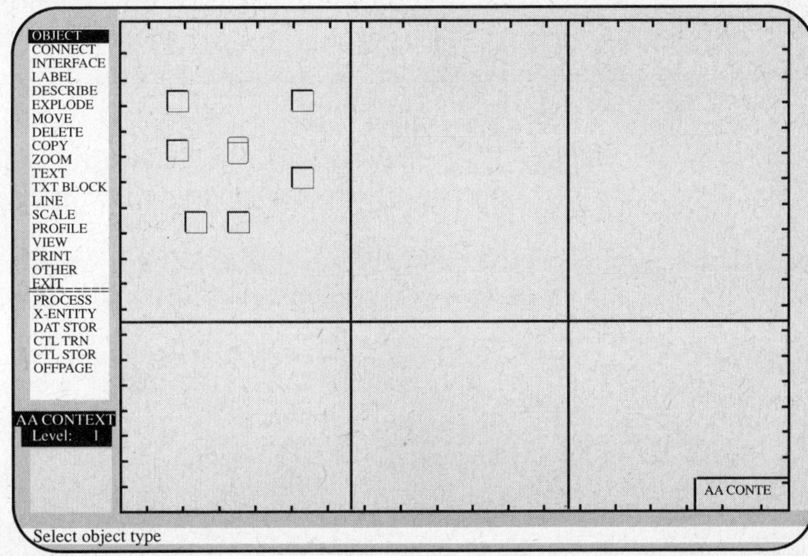

Figure 4.1.3b
DFD Objects Placed in Drawing Area

4.1.4 Moving, Deleting, and Copying Objects

Anything you place in the drawing area can be moved, deleted, or copied. The **MOVE, DELETE,** and **COPY** commands are shown in the Command Menu in Figure 4.1.4.

To move or copy an object in the drawing area,

- Select **MOVE** or **COPY** from the Command Menu.
- Position the mouse cursor over the object to be moved or copied.
- Select the object by pressing the left button on the mouse.
- Position the mouse cursor where you want the object to appear.
- Select the position by pressing the left button on the mouse.

Hint
Objects will often stubbornly resist placement in a desired location. See **4.1.6 Adjusting the Grid**.

If you are using the MOVE command, the object will appear in the new location you selected. It may take several attempts to get the object positioned exactly where you want it. The object must be re-selected prior to every move attempt.

If you are Copying, an exact duplicate of the object will appear in the location selected.

The DELETE command works in the same way as MOVE and COPY:

- Select **DELETE** from the Command Menu.
- Position the mouse cursor on the object to be deleted.
- Select the object by pressing the left button on the mouse.

The selected object disappears. (Note: If the object has been described, you are asked if you want its description deleted from the XLDictionary. If the object is connected to other objects on the drawing, Excelerator asks if you want to delete it and all attached connections. Your response to either question is made by selecting **Yes** or **No** from the bottom of the Command Menu.)

Figure 4.1.4
MOVE, DELETE, and COPY Commands

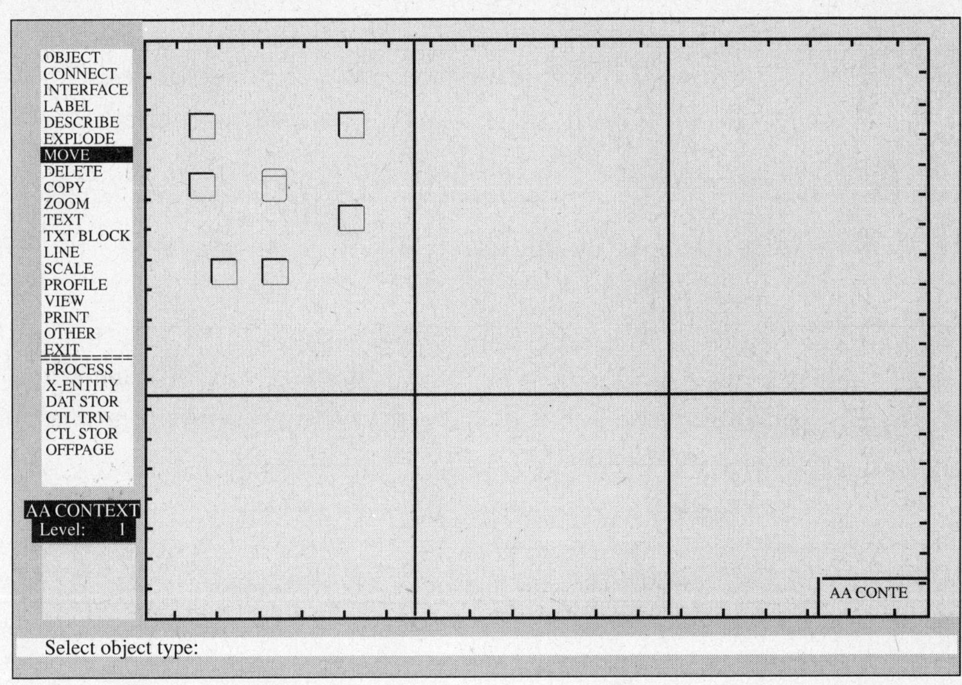

4.1.5 Using ZOOM Options

ZOOM is used for adjusting the magnification and position of your drawing on the screen.

- Select ZOOM from the Command Menu.

Three ZOOM options appear below the double dotted line on the Command Menu: **CLOSE UP**, **MEDIUM**, and **LAYOUT**.

- Select MEDIUM from the ZOOM options.
- Position the cursor on the orientation map shown in Figure 4.1.5a.

The orientation map represents a miniature of your drawing area. Dots on the orientation map represent objects in the drawing area.

- Select any location in the orientation map by pressing the left button on the mouse.

As shown in Figure 4.1.5a, the selected portion of the drawing area is displayed at **MEDIUM** magnification. The box shown in the orientation map tells you what part of the drawing area you are viewing.

To get an even closer look at your drawing,

- Select CLOSE UP from the ZOOM options.
- Place your cursor on the part of your drawing you wish to view.
- Select the location by pressing the left button on your mouse.

The selected portion of your drawing area will be displayed at **CLOSE UP** magnification as shown in Figure 4.1.5b. The orientation map again shows the part of the drawing area you are viewing.

As shown in Figure 4.1.5c, **LAYOUT** displays your full six page drawing area without page delineation lines. To use this command,

- Select LAYOUT from the ZOOM options, and the graph is displayed in LAYOUT format.

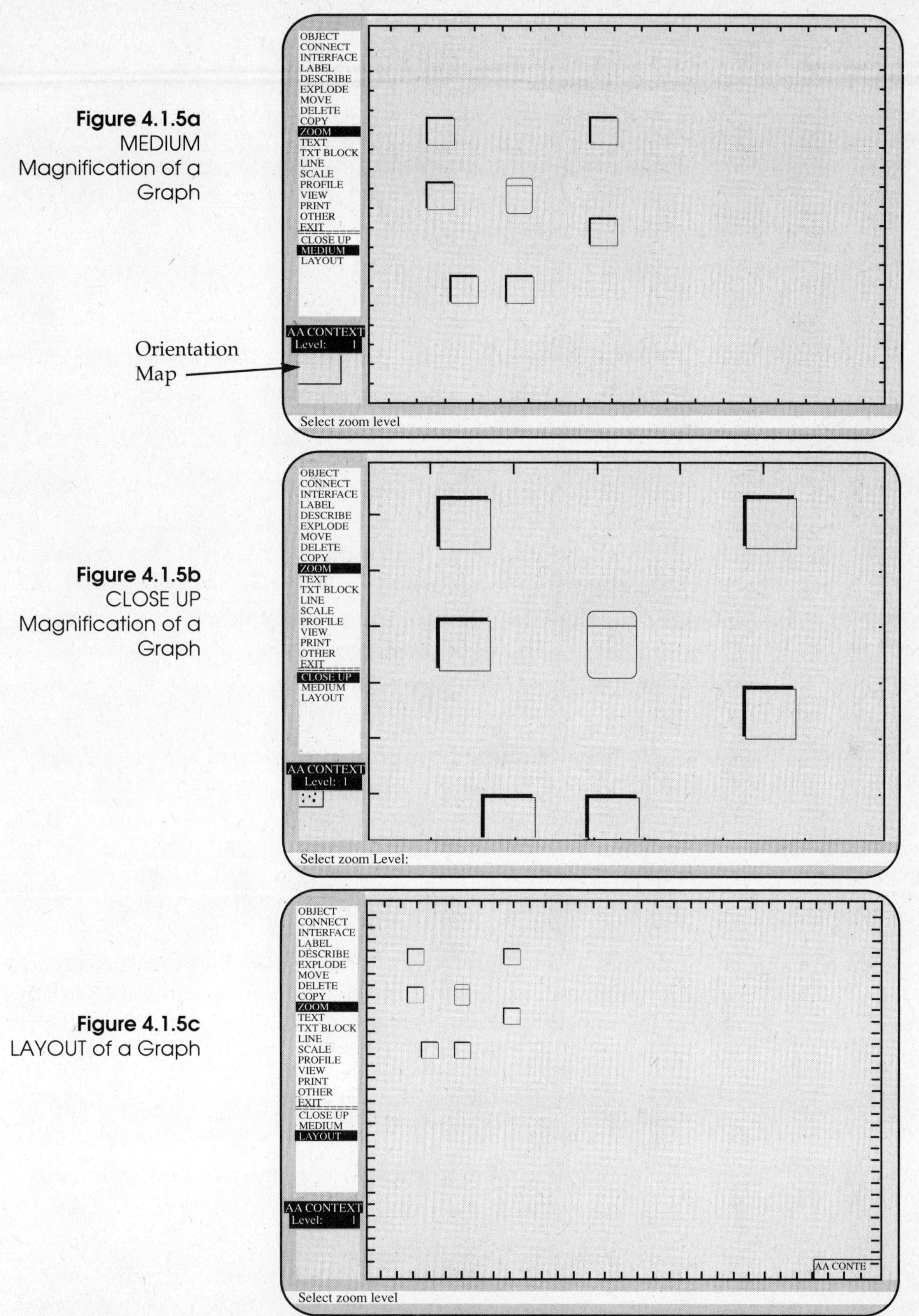

Figure 4.1.5a MEDIUM Magnification of a Graph

Figure 4.1.5b CLOSE UP Magnification of a Graph

Figure 4.1.5c LAYOUT of a Graph

4.1.6 Adjusting the Grid

GRID settings determine the spacing of grid marks in the drawing area. These grid marks control object placement in the drawing area. When an object is placed on the screen, Excelerator centers it over the nearest intersection of vertical and horizontal grid marks.

- Select **PROFILE** from the Command Menu.

The **PROFILE** options as shown in Figure 4.1.6a. GRID is the first option listed. The other PROFILE options are discussed in the following sections.

- Select **GRID** from the PROFILE options.

The GRID options appear in the Command Menu as shown in Figure 4.1.6b. Six options are listed: **NO GRID**, **FINE**, **SMALL**, **MEDIUM**, **LARGE**, and **COARSE**. Try selecting each of these settings. Notice how the spacing of the grid marks around the edges of the drawing area change as you choose each setting.

- Select **FINE** from the GRID options.

The FINE option allows you the most flexibility, while still producing tidy results. If you ever have difficulty placing an object in a desired position, the trouble may be due to the grid setting. Figure 4.1.6c shows objects placed using each of the six GRID options.

When the GRID setting is changed, the placement of objects already on the screen is not affected. When new objects are added or existing objects are moved, however, the new GRID setting will affect their placement.

- Press the right button on your mouse to return to the PROFILE options.
- Press the right mouse button again to return to the Command Menu.

Figure 4.1.6a
PROFILE Options Displayed on the Drawing Screen

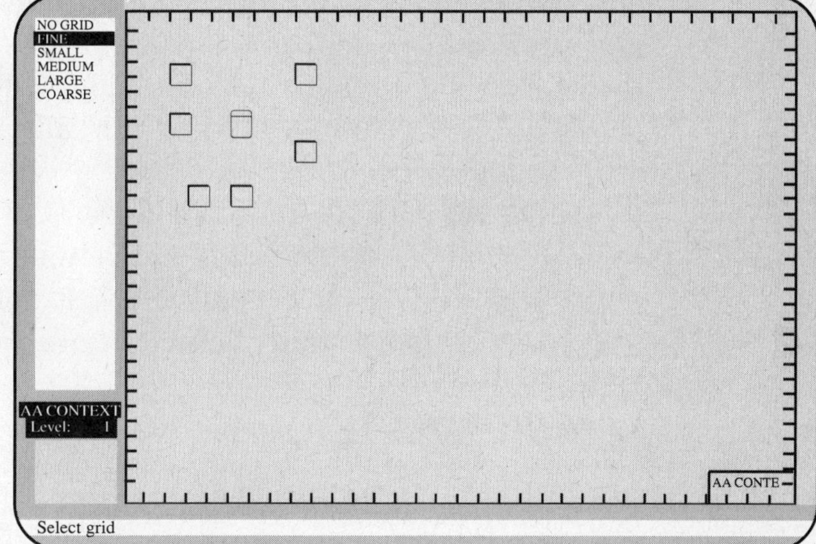

Figure 4.1.6b
GRID Options Displayed on the Drawing Screen

NO GRID
FINE
SMALL
MEDIUM
LARGE
COARSE

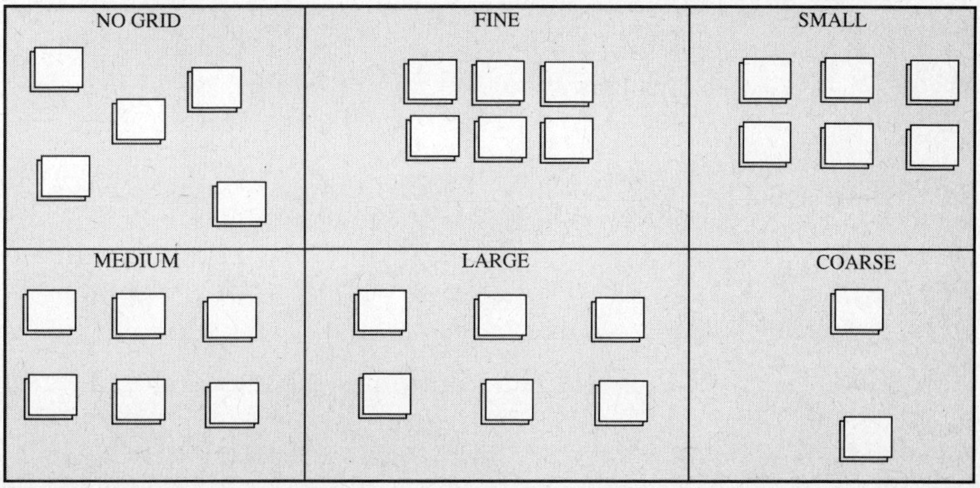

Figure 4.1.6c
Excelerator's Six GRID Options

4.1.7 Customizing Connections

When drawing Data Flow Diagrams (DFD), connections are called **Data Flows**. They are lines connecting DFD objects and represent the flow of data through the system. Before you begin drawing Data Flows, it's a good idea to customize your connections by specifying how you want them to look. These connection specifications affect only the current graph. Settings return to default values on new graphs.

- Select **PROFILE** from the Command Menu, and the PROFILE options appear.

ONE WAY and **PIPE** are both default selections to leave alone for now. ONE WAY means connections will have an arrow only at the terminating end. PIPE means connections will have rounded angles. Figure 4.1.7a and Figure 4.1.7b show the alternatives to these defaults.

SYSPORT is a default setting to change. SYSPORT gives Excelerator complete control over the shape and location of connections. **USER-PORT** gives you control of connections. Examples of connections drawn with SYSPORT and USERPORT are shown in Figure 4.1.7c.

- Select **USERPORT** from the PROFILE options.

SAVECONN is another default selection affecting connections. SAVECONN forces Excelerator to maintain selected connection ports when you move connected objects. **CHGCONN** allows Excelerator to pick new connection ports when connected objects are moved. An example is shown in Figure 4.1.7d.

SAVECONN is the best choice when moving connected objects only slightly. Although there is no sure-fire way to move connected objects very far without creating a mess, if gross position changes become necessary, CHGCONN usually works best.

- Press the right button on your mouse to return to the Command Menu.

Figure 4.1.7a
ONE WAY, TWO WAY
and NO ARROW
Connections

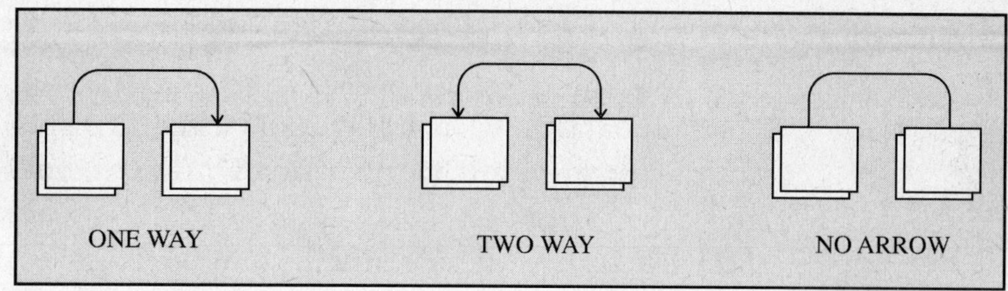

Figure 4.1.7b
PIPE, STRAIGHT, and
ARC Connections

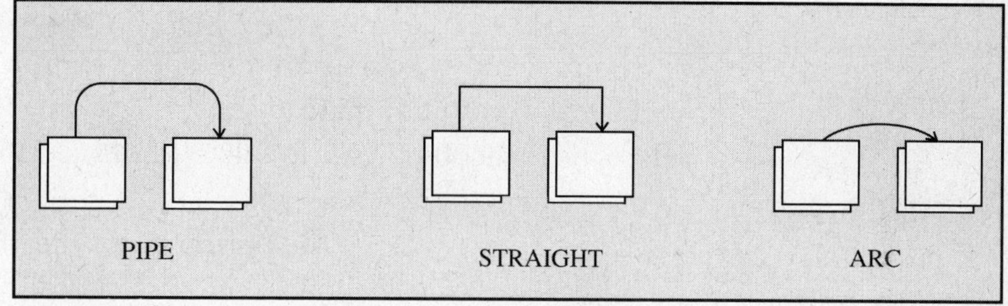

Figure 4.1.7c
SYSPORT and
USERPORT
Connections

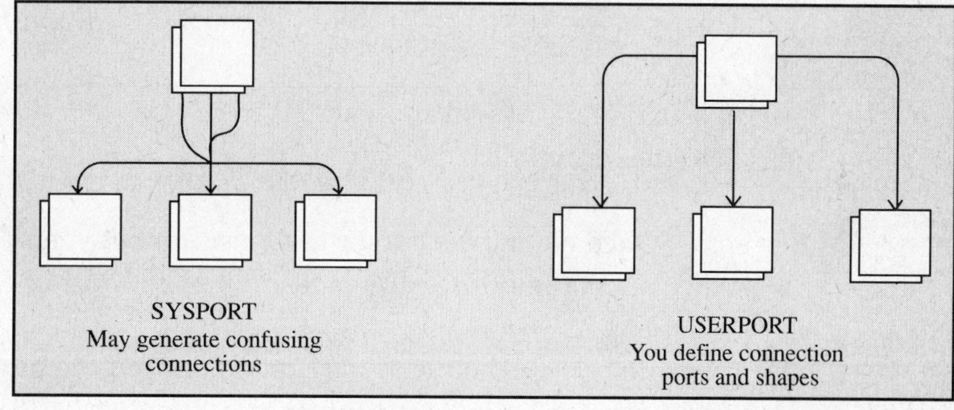

Figure 4.1.7d
Object Moved Using
SAVECONN and
CHGCONN

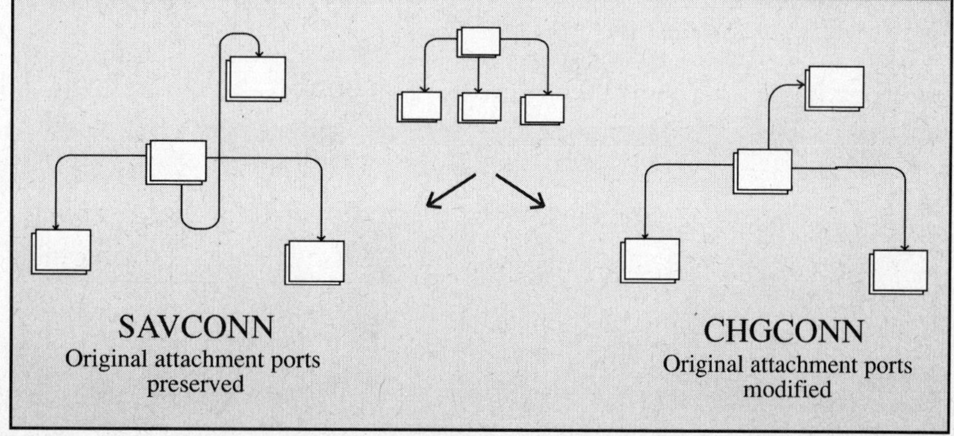

4.1.8 Connecting Objects

If your Data Flow Diagram is not currently displayed, retrieve it using the instructions in **4.1.1 Initiating Drawings**, but select **Modify** instead of **Add** from the Graphics Action Keypad. Refer to **4.1.5 Using ZOOM Options** to magnify the graph using the MEDIUM option.

- Select **CONNECT** from the Command Menu.
- Select **DAT FLOW** (Data Flow) from the connection choices.
- Position the mouse cursor on the object from which the Data Flow (connection) is to originate.
- Select the object by pressing the left button on your mouse.

A tiny arrow appears along the perimeter of the object as shown in Figure 4.1.8a. This arrow allows you to select **connection port** for the Data Flow. Using your mouse, you can move the arrow around.

- Select a connection port with the left button on the mouse.

If you feel you will need angles in the Data Flow in order to connect it to the terminating object neatly,

- Place the mouse cursor in a position between the two objects.
- Select the position by pressing the left button on your mouse.

A line appears between the first object and the intermediate point. You may select as many intermediate points as you want. If you want to erase an intermediate leg of the Data Flow, press the right button on the mouse one time for each leg to be deleted.

When you are ready to connect the Data Flow to the object at which it will terminate,

- Select the termination object and the desired connection port in the same way as you did for the origination object.

The Data Flow terminates with an arrow at that object.

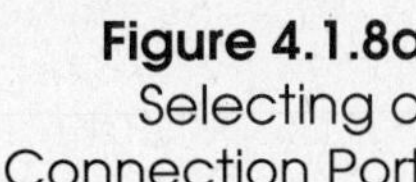

Figure 4.1.8a
Selecting a Connection Port

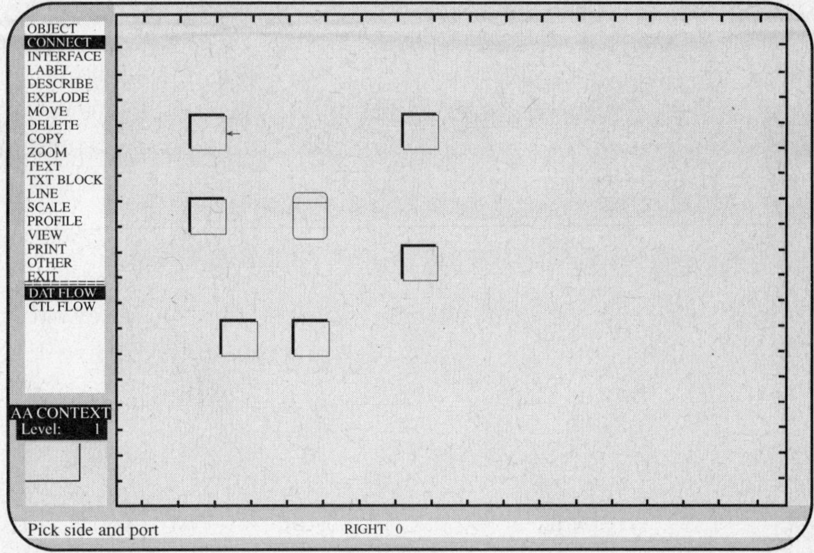

Figure 4.1.8b
Connections Completed for AA Context DFD

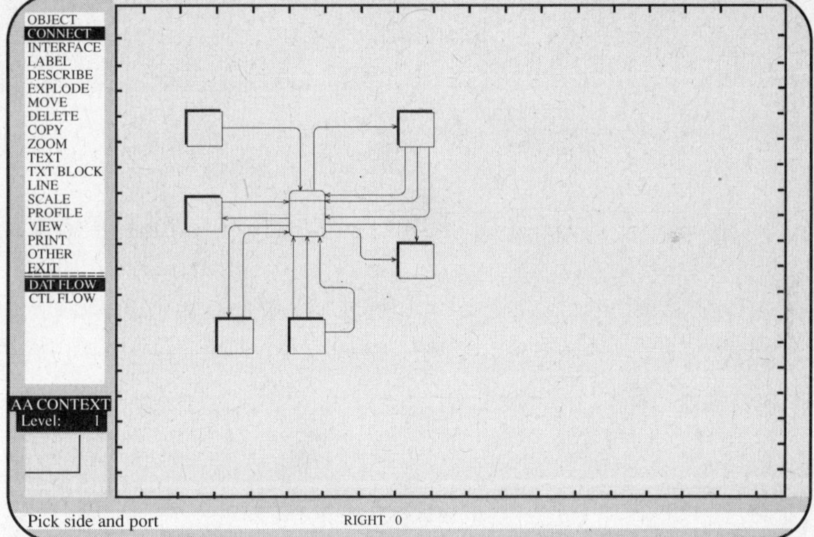

Exercise 4.1.8

On your AA CONTEXT DFD, create Data Flows resembling the ones in Figure 4.1.8b. Remember, the Data Flow arrow points to the last object selected.

If you need to move or delete connections, go to the next section where those processes are explained.

4.1.9 Moving and Deleting Connections

As with objects, connections can be moved and deleted. The process for moving and deleting connections differs from objects.

- Select **DELETE** from the Command Menu.

Excelerator places a small square box near the center of each connection on your graph as shown in Figure 4.1.9. This box is called a **handle**. It is used for selecting connections you wish to modify.

Handles appear on the screen when **LABEL, DESCRIBE, EXPLODE, MOVE**, or **DELETE** is selected from the Command Menu. They never appear on printed output.

To delete a connection after selecting DELETE,

- Place the mouse cursor on a Data Flow (connection) handle.
- Press the left button on the mouse to select the Data Flow.

The Data Flow disappears. (If the Data Flow has been described, you are asked if you want the description deleted from the XLDictionary. Respond to the question by selecting YES or NO from the options which appear at the bottom of the Command Menu.)

To move a connection,

- Select **MOVE** from the Command Menu.
- Place the mouse cursor on a Data Flow (connection) handle.
- Press the left button on the mouse to select the Data Flow.

Excelerator places new handles on the Data Flow, one at each end.

- Place the mouse cursor on the handle at the end of the Data Flow you wish to move.
- Select the end you wish to move by pressing the left button on the mouse.

The Data Flow disappears.

- Place the mouse cursor on the object to which you want the selected end of the Data Flow to connect.
- Select the object by pressing the left button on the mouse.

A tiny port selection arrow appears.

- Position the arrow with the mouse.
- Select the desired port location with the left mouse button.

The selected end of the Data Flow moves to the new connection port.

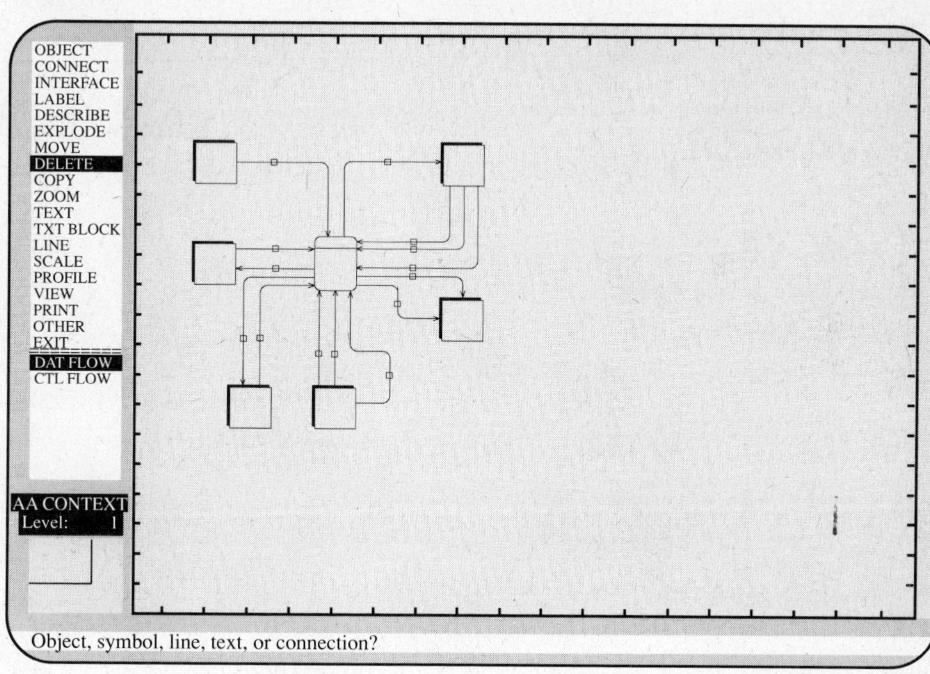

Figure 4.1.9 Connection Handles Displayed on the AA CONTEXT DFD

4.1.10 Creating Interface Connections

The purpose of the **INTRFACE** (Interface) command on the drawing screen Command Menu is to create connections with one free-standing end. It is used for showing connections to objects not displayed on the current graph.

INTRFACE offers three connection types:

- **INPUT** — an arrow appears at the object end of the connection. This connection represents data coming in from another graph.
- **OUTPUT** — an arrow appears at the free-standing end of the connection. This represents data leaving the current graph.
- **UPDATE** — arrows appear at both ends of the connection. This represents data traveling both to and from the current graph.

- Select **INTRFACE** from the Command Menu.
- Select **DAT FLOW** from the connection types displayed.
- Select **OUTPUT** from the list of INTRFACE options which appears in the Command Menu.
- Position the mouse cursor in the drawing area near any one of your graph's objects.
- Select the position by pressing the left button on the mouse.
- Position the mouse cursor on the object to which the INTRFACE connection is to attach.
- Select the object with the left mouse button.
- Select the connection port with the mouse.

The INTRFACE connection appears as shown in Figure 4.1.10. This connection indicates data flowing from this graph to another graph.

INTRFACE connections are commonly used when drawing low-level DFDs on which data is often shown leaving or entering the graph.

- Select **DELETE** from the Command Menu.
- Select a handle on the INTRFACE Data Flow you just drew.

The INTRFACE Data Flow disappears.

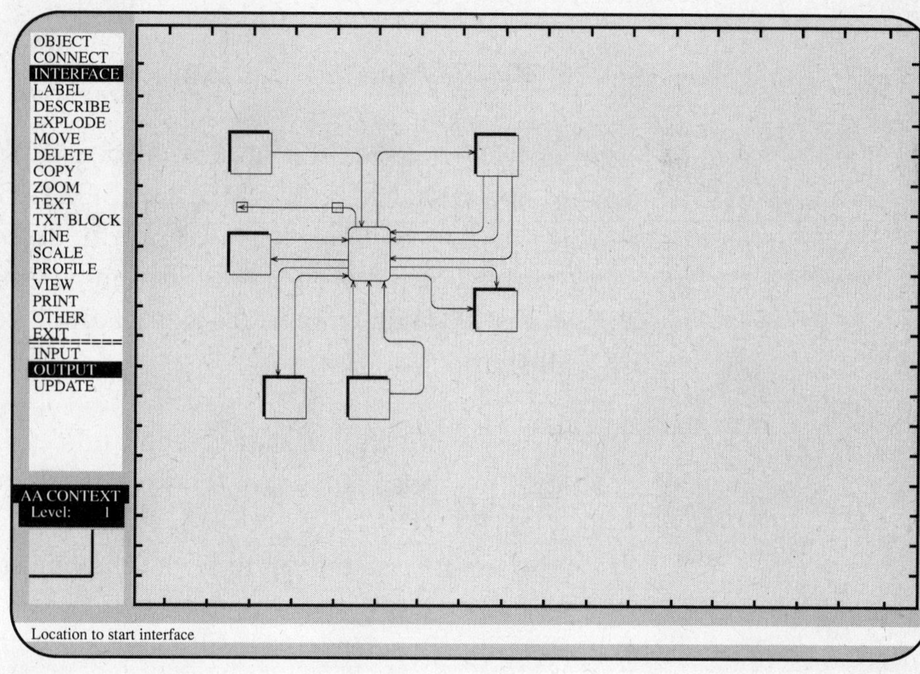

Figure 4.1.10
INTRFACE Options Displayed in the Command Menu and an INTRFACE Connection Drawn on the Graph

4.1.11 Scaling Objects

The **SCALE** command allows you to change the size of objects in the drawing area. SCALE is only an option for Data Flow Diagrams, Presentation Graphs, State Transition Diagrams, and Work Breakdown Structures.

The difference between SCALE and ZOOM is that while ZOOM can change the apparent size of drawings by providing magnified or reduced views, SCALE changes the actual size of objects.

- Select **SCALE** from the Command Menu.

In Figure 4.1.11, three SCALE options appear at the bottom of the Command Menu: **X AXIS**, **Y AXIS**, and **BOTH**. These commands determine the direction you wish to scale an object. X AXIS can make an object wider or narrower, Y AXIS can make an object taller or shorter, and BOTH can change the size of an object while preserving its original shape.

- Select **X AXIS** from the Scale Commands.
- Position the mouse cursor on the upper left External Entity on AA CONTEXT DFD.
- Press the left mouse button to select the object.

In the status line, Excelerator prompts you: *Touch location to scale to.* This means select a position, either outside or inside the object, to scale the object up or down. Selecting a position inside the object makes the object smaller, while selecting a position outside the object makes it larger.

- Position the mouse cursor outside the selected object.
- Press the left mouse button to select the position.

The object is scaled-up.

You must re-select the object each time you scale it. If you wish to return the object to its original size,

- Select the object with the left button on the mouse.

- Position the mouse cursor inside the object.
- Press the left mouse button.

The object is scaled-down. You may find it necessary to scale objects several times before achieving the size desired.

Leave the upper left External Entity on your graph scaled-up on its X-axis.

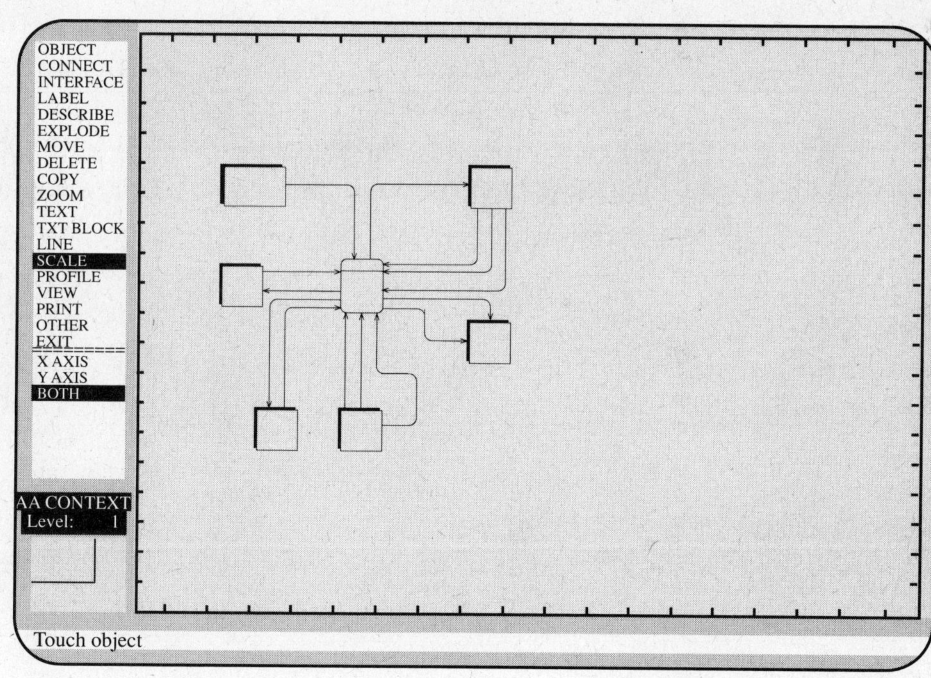

Figure 4.1.11 SCALE Options Displayed on the Command Menu and External Entity Scaled-Up

4.1.12 Labeling Objects and Connections

The **LABEL** command allows you to attach descriptive text to objects, symbols, and connections on your graph.

Refer to **4.1.5 Using ZOOM Options** to view the upper left area of the AA CONTEXT DFD using the ZOOM command and CLOSE UP option.

- Select [LABEL] from the Command Menu.
- Position the mouse cursor on the upper left External Entity.
- Press the left button on the mouse to select the External Entity, and a label text box appears near the middle of the drawing area.
- Type **MANUFACTURER** in the text box as shown in Figure 4.1.12a.
- Press [↵], or press the left button on the mouse.

The label appears in the selected External Entity. (Note: If the word MANUFACTURER is too long to fit on one line, you should scale-up the External Entity and re-label it as shown in Figure 4.1.12b.)

- Select [LABEL] from the Command Menu.
- Position the mouse cursor on the handle of the Data Flow leaving the External Entity labeled MANUFACTURER.
- Press the left button on the mouse to select the Data Flow.
- Type **SHIPPING** in the label text box which appears.
- Press [Tab].
- Type **DOCUMENT** on the second line of the label text box.
- Press [↵], or press the left button on the mouse.

Hint
When moving labels, select the new position where you want the label's upper left corner to be positioned.

The Data Flow label may not appear in an ideal location. If this is the case, use the MOVE command to change the location as shown in Figure 4.1.12c.

Exercise 4.1.12

On your AA CONTEXT DFD, finish labeling the objects and connections as shown in Figure 4.1.12d.

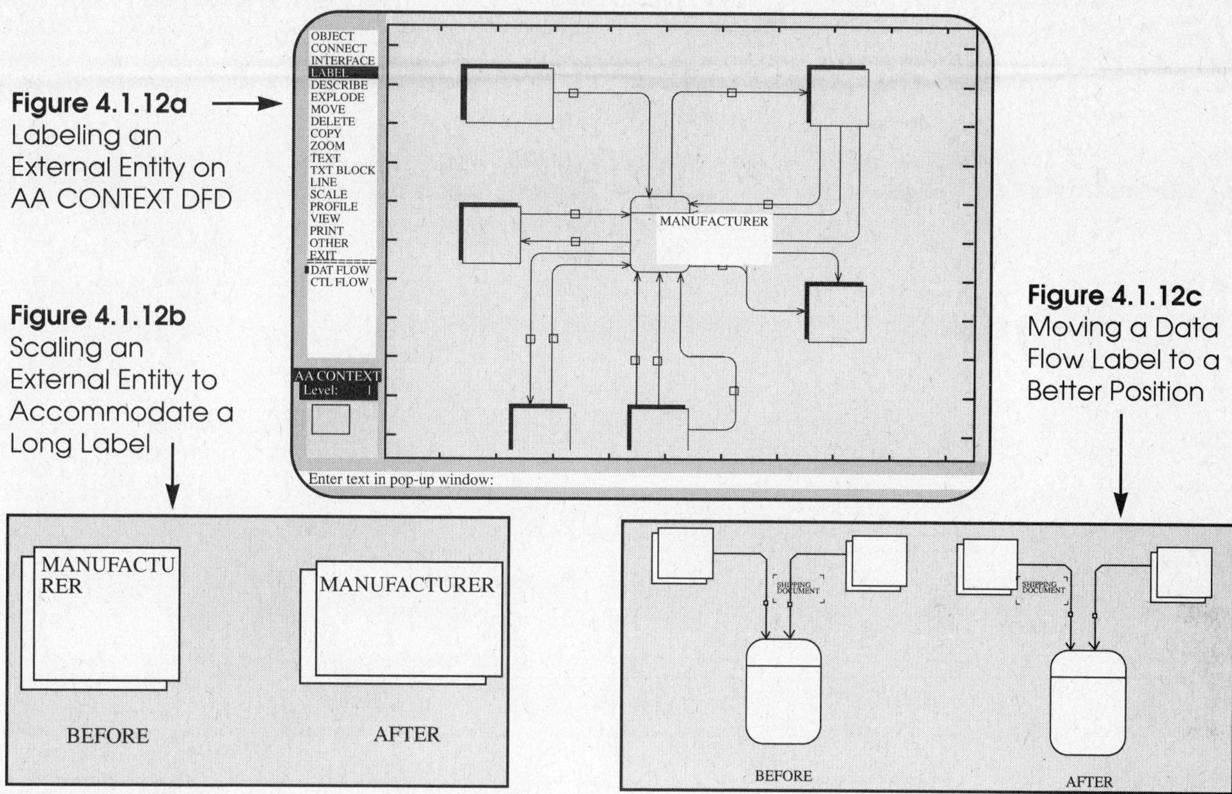

Figure 4.1.12a Labeling an External Entity on AA CONTEXT DFD

Figure 4.1.12b Scaling an External Entity to Accommodate a Long Label

Figure 4.1.12c Moving a Data Flow Label to a Better Position

Figure 4.1.12d AA CONTEXT DFD with Objects and Connections Labeled

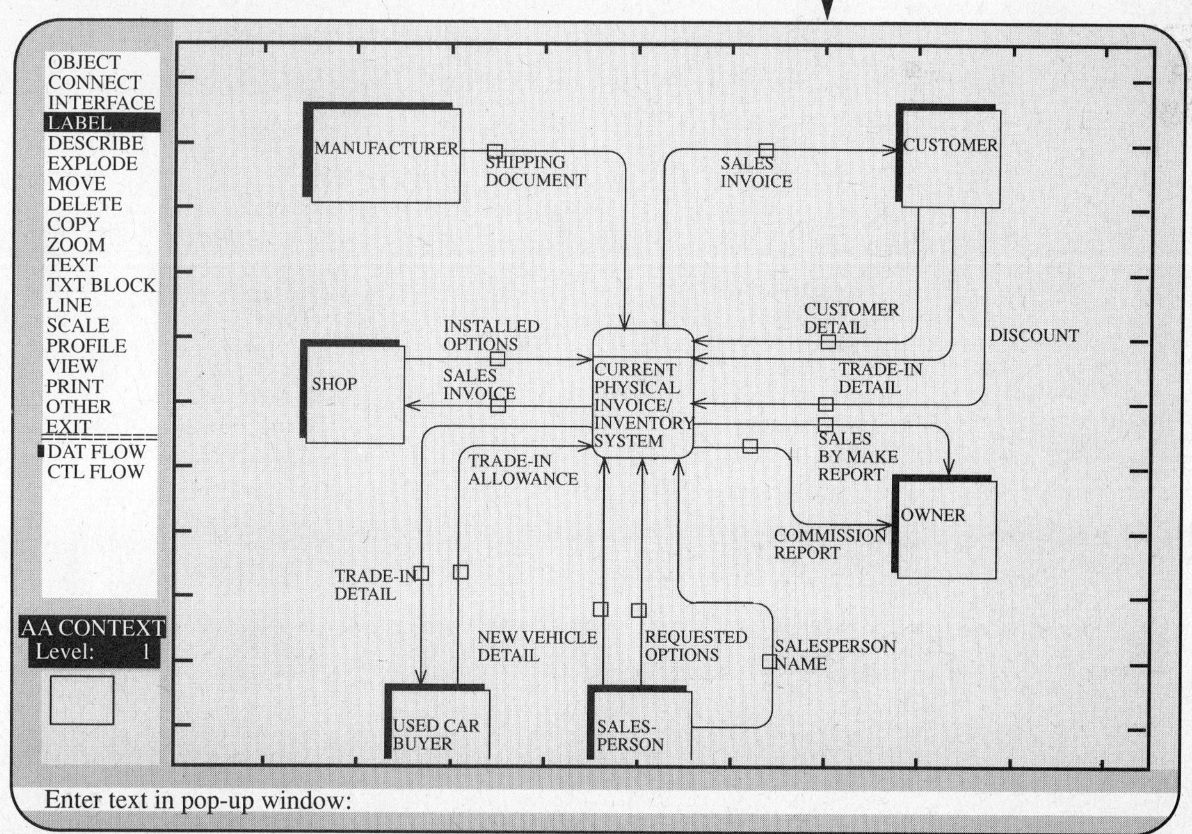

4.1.13 Controlling Label Display

Excelerator provides three label display modes:

- **CLIP** truncates labels by eliminating characters to the right and bottom boundaries of objects being viewed using MEDIUM or LAYOUT ZOOM options. This is the default display mode.
- **WRAP** truncates labels by wrapping characters onto the next line, and then deleting characters near the bottom of the object.
- **COMPLETE** displays and prints the entire label. The label may overwite other graph items.

Three other textual display modes determine whether labels or IDs or both are displayed on graph objects.

- **ALL TXT** (All Text) displays and prints both labels and IDs.
- **LAB ONLY** (Label Only) displays and prints labels only.
- **ID ONLY** displays and prints IDs only. Labels are not displayed.

Examples of these display modes, viewed with LAYOUT and MEDIUM ZOOM options, are shown in Figure 4.1.13a and Figure 4.1.13b. To access label display modes,

- Select **PROFILE** from the Command Menu.
- Select **LABEL MD** from the PROFILE options.

The LABEL MD (Label Mode) options appear in the Command Menu as shown in Figure 4.1.13c. When you have made your selections,

- Press the right mouse button to return to the PROFILE options.

USRLABEL and **SYSLABEL** PROFILE options affect graph connections. SYSLABEL produces a fixed size label which Excelerator positions. USRLABEL gives you control of the size and placement of connection labels. See *Excelerator Facilities and Functions Reference Guide* Pages 3-52 and 3-53.

- Press the right button on the mouse again to return to the Command Menu.

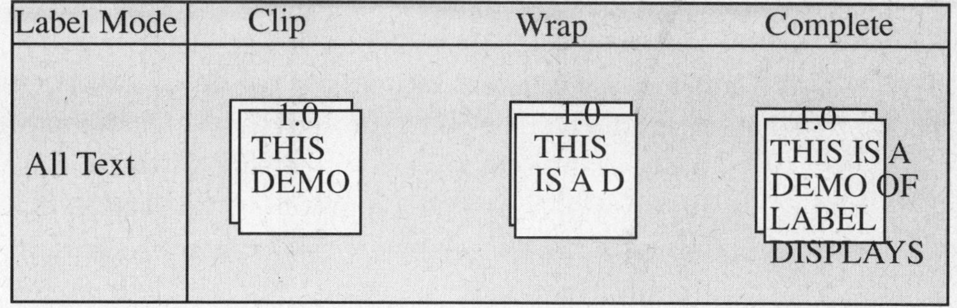

Figure 4.1.13a Label Display Modes Viewed with MEDIUM ZOOM

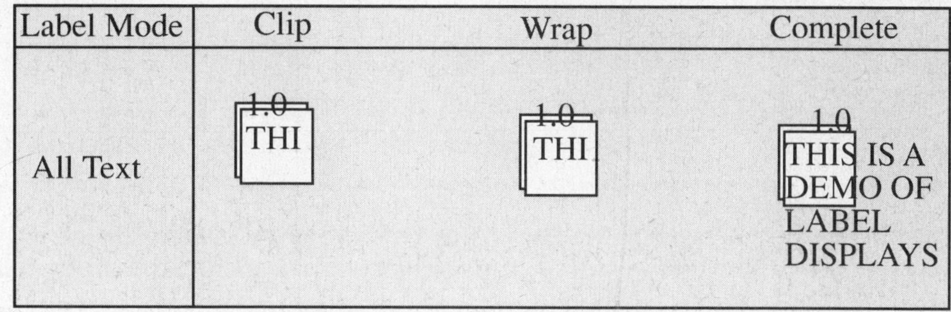

Figure 4.1.13b Label Display Modes Viewed with LAYOUT ZOOM

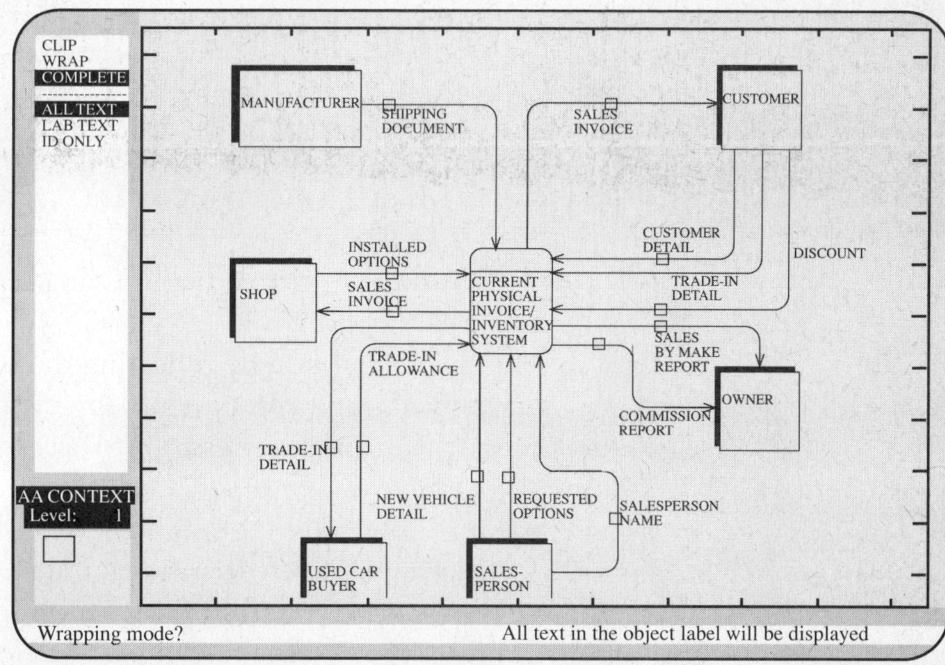

Figure 4.1.13c LABEL MD Options

4.1.14 Initiating Graph Component Descriptions

There are two ways to initiate the description of graph components, from the DFD itself or through the XLDictionary. The first method is best because it allows you to create a description and tie the description to a graph component, label and all, in one process.

To initiate an External Entity description from the DFD itself, access your AA CONTEXT DFD. (Refer to **4.1.1 Initiating Drawings**, substituting **Modify** for **Add** from the Graphics Action Keypad.)

- Select DESCRIBE from the Command Menu.
- Position your mouse cursor over the External Entity labeled MANUFACTURER.
- Select the object by pressing the left mouse button. (When describing connections, select the connection **handle** located on the connection.)

In the status line at the bottom of the screen, Excelerator prompts you: *Enter ID.* The ID is the name by which the object is identified in the XLDictionary. Abbreviations of labels are convenient IDs for External Entities. Short for MANUFACTURER,

- Type **MAN** in the Status Line as shown in Figure 4.1.14a.
- Press ↵.

As shown in Figure 4.1.14b, the first External Entity description screen appears.

- Press F3 to save and return to the drawing screen.

You can modify the description by repeating the same steps. When you select a described graph component, however, the ID appears in the Status Line and you simply press ↵ to access the description.

To initiate the same description through the XLDictionary, follow the steps in **4.2.1 Initiating DFD Descriptions**, but select **Process** from the XLDictionary Menu, select **External Entity** from the Process Menu, and select **Add** from the External Entity Action Keypad.

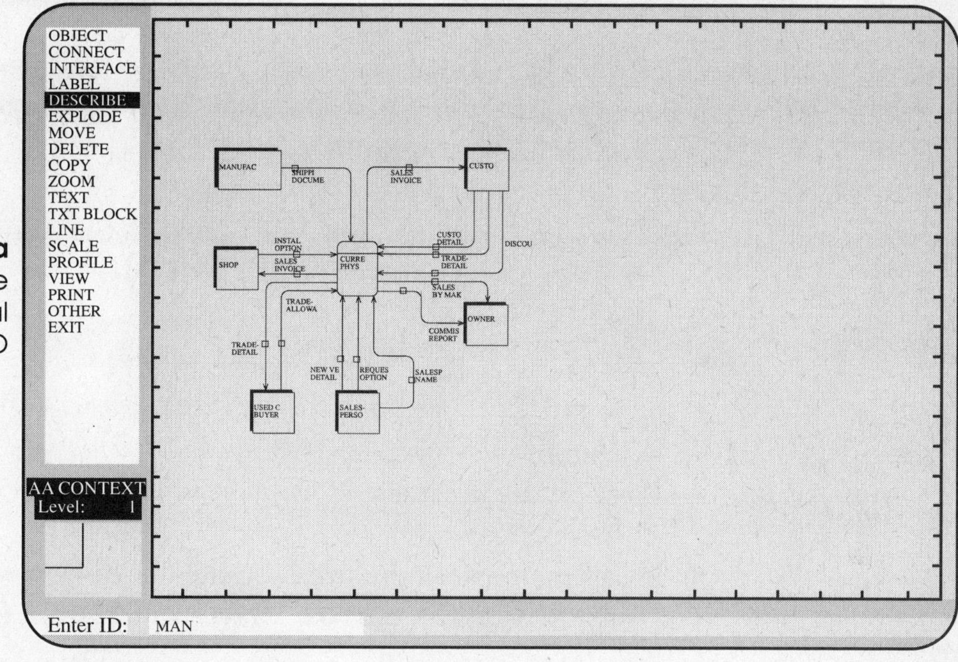

Figure 4.1.14a
Status Line Message Requesting External Entity ID

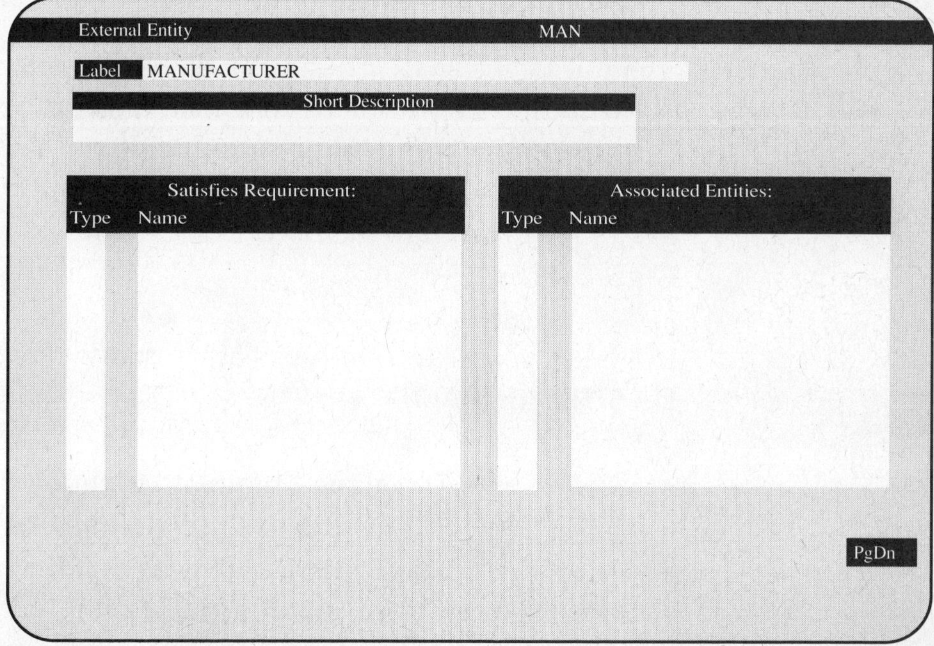

Figure 4.1.14b
First External Entity Description Screen with Label and ID

4.1.15 Using TEXT, LINE, and TXT BLOCK

TEXT and **TXT BLK** (Text Block) are commands used to enhance the appearance of graphs. These tools also allow you to place additional information on your graphs.

TEXT lets you enter a single line of text in the drawing area, using one of three type size options: **SMALL**, **MEDIUM**, and **LARGE**.

- Select [TEXT] from the Command Menu.
- Select [MEDIUM] from the type size options which appear at the bottom of the Command Menu.
- Position the mouse cursor near the upper left corner of the drawing area.
- Select the position by pressing the left button on the mouse.
- Type **`ANONYMOUS AUTOS CONTEXT DFD`** in the status line at the bottom of the screen.
- Press ↵.

The text line appears near the top of the drawing area as shown in Figure 4.1.15a. Text is deleted or moved just like objects.

TXT BLK (Text Block) is used for entering multiple lines of text. Excelerator provides you with a box for entering your data which is bigger than the space actually available in your Text Block, resulting in frustrating truncation of your text. This problem can be addressed by editing your text to fit or by reducing the size of your font. The latter is addressed in **4.1.16 Using PRINT Options**. Avoid TXT BLK or read more about it in the *Excelerator Facilities and Functions Guide* on Pages 3-58 and 3-59.

LINE lets you draw two types of lines anywhere on a graph: **DASHED** or **SOLID**.

- Select [LINE] from the Command Menu.
- Select [DASHED] from the LINE options which appear.
- Select the location where the line is to begin with the mouse.
- Select second, third, and fourth locations with the left mouse button to draw a frame for your graph as shown in Figure 4.1.15b.

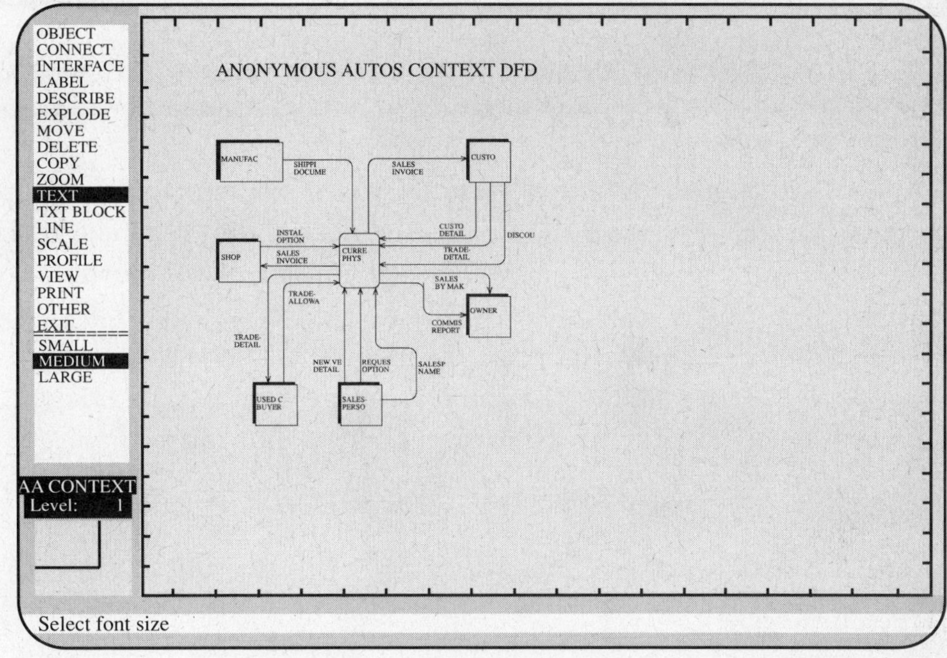

Figure 4.1.15a
TEXT Placed on the AA CONTEXT DFD

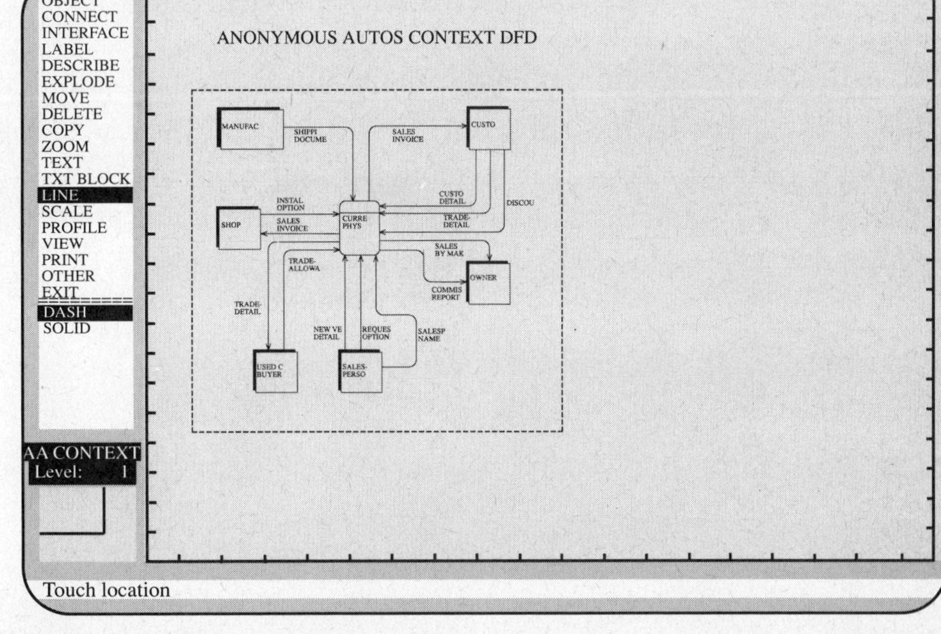

Figure 4.1.15b
DASHED LINE Drawn on the AA CONTEXT DFD

4.1.16 Using PRINT Options

As shown in Figure 4.1.16a, **PRINT** provides three output options allowing you to determine how much of the graph is printed.

- **FULL GPH** (Full Graph) prints the entire graph. When FULL GPH is selected, page delineation lines appear in the drawing area.
- **WINDOW** allows you to print any portion of the graph by selecting the upper left and lower right corner of the area to be printed. A window appears on the screen as shown in Figure 4.1.16b.
- **DRAFT** prints the entire graph on one page regardless of its actual size. DRAFT is a good tool for printing large graphs quickly for preliminary review.

With the AA CONTEXT DFD on your screen,

- Select **PRINT** from the Command Menu.
- Select **FULL GPH** from the PRINT options.
- Select **YES** when asked if you want to print.
- Select **PRINTER**.

Your screen will go black, and while the AA CONTEXT DFD is printing, strange designs parade across your screen. The Drawing Screen re-appears when printing is complete.

SETUP is the last PRINT option displayed on the Command Menu when PRINT is selected. SETUP is used for selecting object and font sizes for each of your graphs. If you want to change the size of your font or objects, it is best to do so before you begin drawing.

- Select **SETUP** from the PRINT options.

The Setup Screen appears as shown in Figure 4.1.16c. Experiment with the Setup Screen, or read about its functions in the *Excelerator Facilities and Functions Reference Guide* on Pages 3-48 thru 3-50.

- Press the right mouse button to exit the Setup Screen.

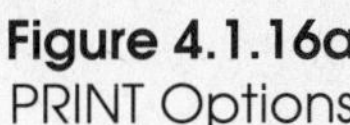

Figure 4.1.16a
PRINT Options

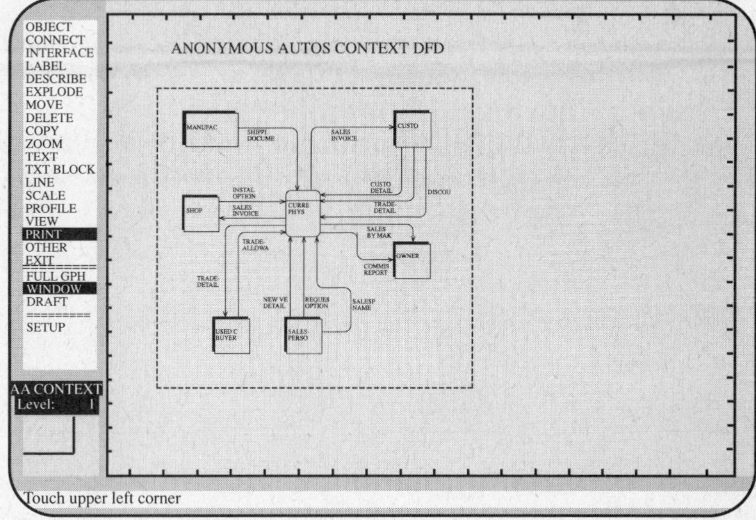

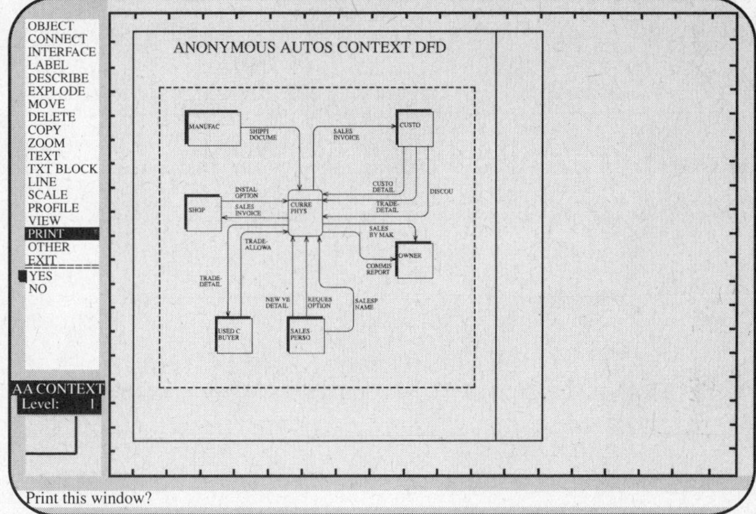

Figure 4.1.16b
PRINT WINDOW
Appearing on the
AA CONTEXT DFD

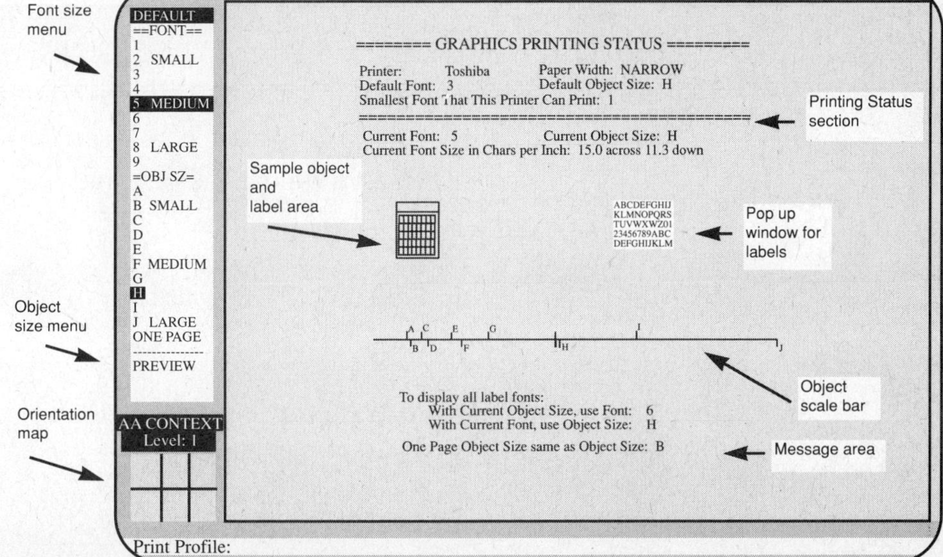

Figure 4.1.16c
Setup Screen

4.1.17 Using OTHER and EXIT Commands

OTHER, on the Command Menu, offers seven useful commands with which you should become familiar.

- Select OTHER from the drawing screen Command Menu.
- Select + to navigate through the list of OTHER options shown in Figure 4.1.17a.

- **SAVE** stores a copy of your graph so you can retrieve it for future use. We strongly recommend that you use SAVE often when drawing. There's nothing worse than losing your work.
- **RETURN** is used for moving up through explosion levels, one level at a time. Graph explosion is discussed in **4.6 Creating Lower Level Data Flow Diagrams (DFDs)**.
- **RETRNTOP** (Return to Top) is used for going directly to the top graph explosion level from any lower level graph.
- **REFRESH** re-draws your graph. This command only affects the screen display; it does not save or delete information. REFRESH simply makes your graph look nicer on the screen.
- **CENTER**, according to the Excelerator manuals, re-orients the entire graph to the center of the page. In our experience, the graph is moved to the top of the page, not the center.
- **CLEAR ID** disassociates a graph component from its XLDictionary description. The label, however, is retained.
- **TITLE** adds a title block to a graph. When a graph is first created, Excelerator provides an on-screen title block as shown in Figure 4.1.17b. An expanded version appears on the printed graph as shown in Figure 4.1.17c. This title block can be moved or deleted just like an object. If you delete the original title block, it is re-created by selecting the TITLE command.

The **EXIT** command is used to terminate a work session and return to the Graphics Action Keypad.

- Select EXIT from the Command Menu.
- Select SAVE from the EXIT options.

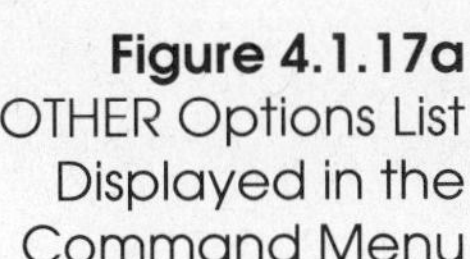

Figure 4.1.17a
OTHER Options List Displayed in the Command Menu

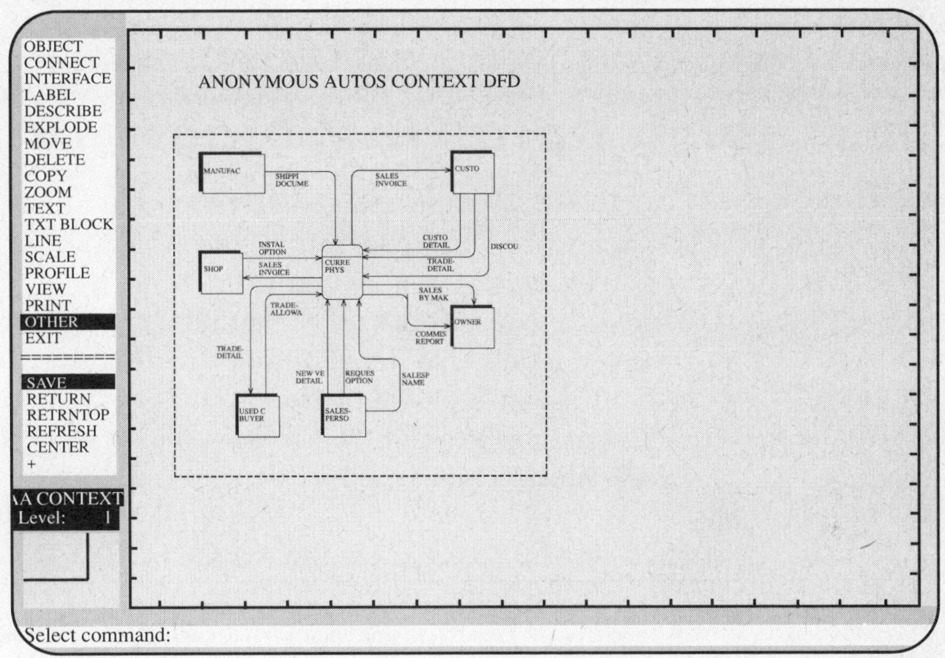

Figure 4.1.17b
On-Screen Title Block Provided By Excelerator for the AA CONTEXT DFD

AA CONTEXT DFD
Created by: ANALYST
Revised by: ANALYST

Figure 4.1.17c
Printed Title Block for AA CONTEXT DFD

AA CONTEXT DFD
ANONYMOUS AUTO CONTEXT DFD
Created by: ANALYST
Revised by: ANALYST
Date Changed: 27-AUG-91

4.2

Describing Data Flow Diagrams (DFDs)

Data Flow Diagrams may be given textual descriptions using XLDictionary DFD description screens as shown by Figure 4.2.

The written description of a graph is a crucial component of the process model. This description provides information about the scope and functions depicted by the graph. The description may also list requirements satisfied by activities shown on the graph, or other Excelerator entities which are associated with the graph.

High-level DFDs, such as the AA CONTEXT DFD for the Anonymous Autos project, are described in general terms. Such graphs give a basic overview of External Entities and data flowing between those External Entities and the system. Therefore, the textual description of a context level DFD should concentrate on the External Entities and their involvement with the system.

System-level DFDs show all of the primary system processes, providing a more detailed view of system functions. Because the system-level DFD is more detailed than the context-level DFD, the textual description should provide more specific information about the system including brief descriptions of each Process and Data Store.

Lower-level DFDs provide detailed views of specific activities within the system. The textual description of lower-level DFDs should be structured and specific, addressing the movement and processing of data structures.

In this section, you will use the XLDictionary DFD description screens to describe the AA CONTEXT DFD for the Anonymous Autos system.

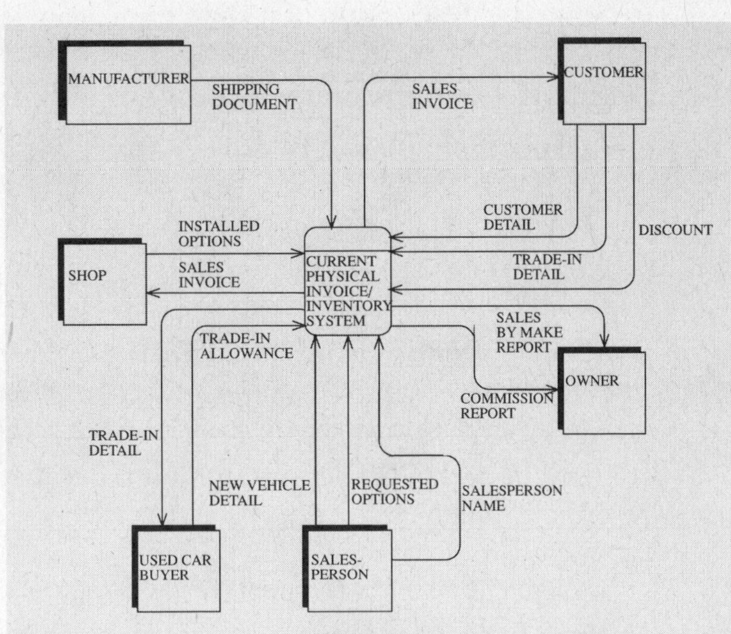

Figure 4.2
Data Flow Diagram is Described on XLDictionary DFD Description Screens

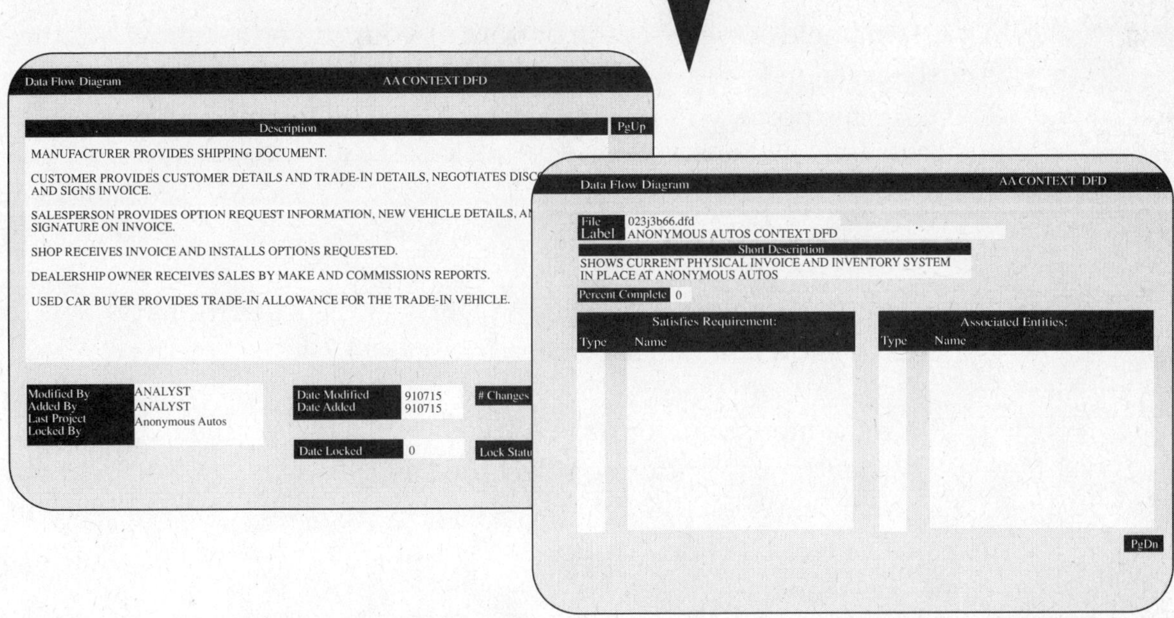

4.2.1 Initiating DFD Descriptions

To begin the description of a Data Flow Diagram (DFD),

- Select **X XLDICTIONARY** from Excelerator's Main Menu as in the first screen in Figure 4.2.1.

The XLDictionary Menu appears as shown in the second screen in Figure 4.2.1.

- Select **GRAPHS** from the XLDictionary Menu.

As shown in the third screen in Figure 4.2.1, the **Graph Menu** appears to the right of the XLDictionary Menu. Because you are going to describe a DFD,

- Select **F Data Flow Diagram** from this menu, and the **DFD Action Keypad** appears.

- Select **Modify** from the DFD Action Keypad.

The **Name** field appears at the bottom of your screen, as shown in the fourth screen in Figure 4.2.1. Excelerator is requesting the name of the DFD. At this point, you may either type the DFD name and press ↵ to access the DFD description screens, or take a short-cut and simply

- Press ↵.

If you used the short-cut, a list of all DFDs in the XLDictionary appears as shown in the last screen in Figure 4.2.1.

- Place the mouse cursor on AA CONTEXT DFD on the list.
- Press left mouse button to select the DFD.

The first of two DFD description screens appears showing the graph name near the top.

The next section, **4.2.2 Completing DFD Description Screens**, explains how to complete the DFD description screens for the AA CONTEXT DFD.

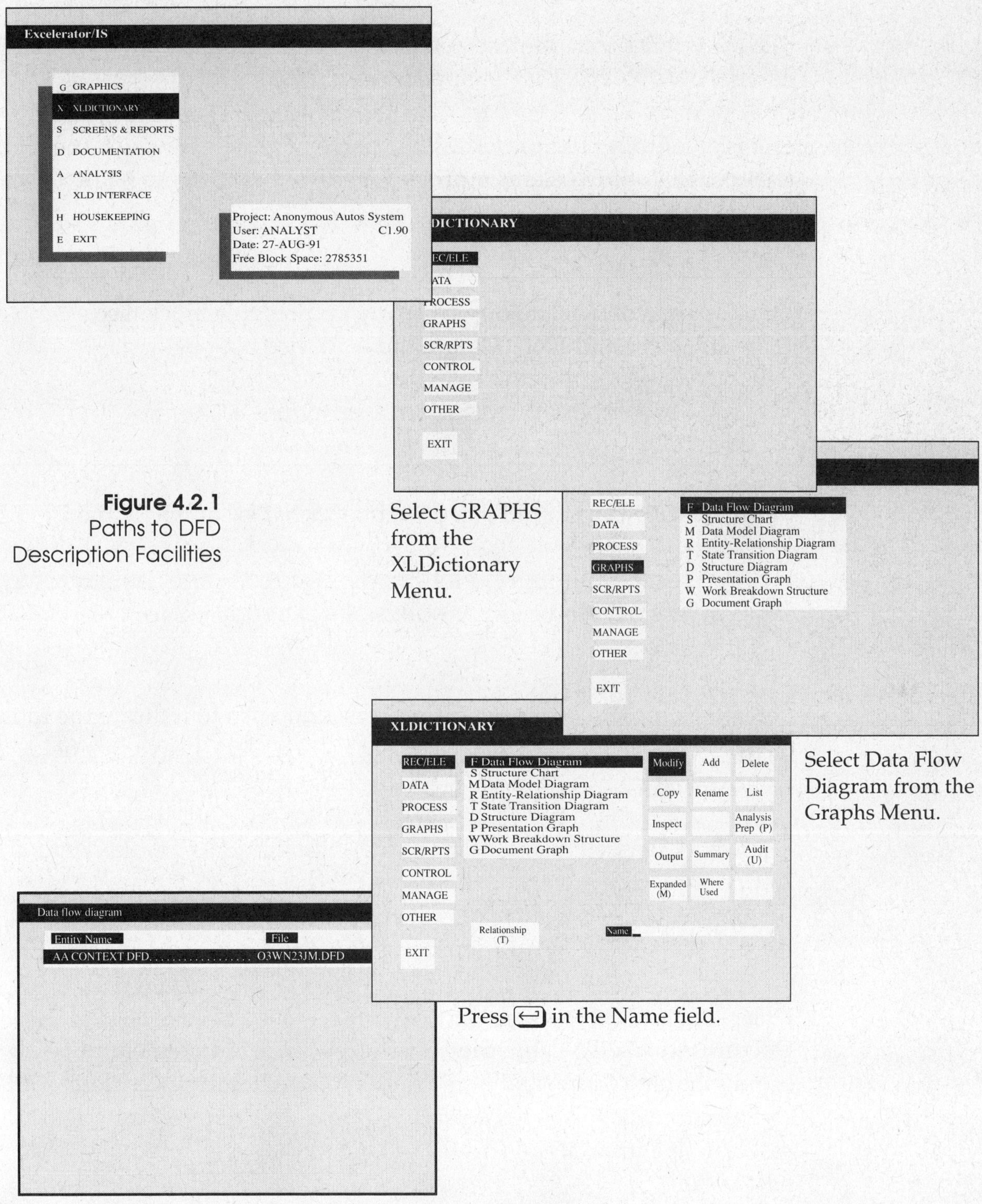

Figure 4.2.1
Paths to DFD Description Facilities

4.2.2 Completing DFD Description Screens

The first DFD description screen is shown in Figure 4.2.2a. The graph name, AA CONTEXT DFD, appears at the top.

File is an output field providing the name of the file in which the DFD is stored in your Excelerator project subdirectory. The file name displayed on your screen will not exactly match the one shown in Figure 4.2.2a.

Label is text you wish to appear in the graph's title block (see **4.1.17 Using OTHER and EXIT Commands**). In the Label field,

- Type **`ANONYMOUS AUTOS CONTEXT DFD`**.
- Press Tab.

Short Description should briefly explain what is shown by the DFD.

- Type **`SHOWS CURRENT PHYSICAL INVOICE AND INVENTORY SYSTEM IN PLACE AT ANONYMOUS AUTOS`** in Short Description.

Percent Complete is provided for users who wish to indicate the ratio of work completed to work remaining on this DFD. Leave this field alone unless you want to track progress on this DFD.

DFDs may satisfy User or Engineering Requirements. See *Excelerator Data & Reports Reference Guide* Pages 2-210 and 2-86. Although such requirements are not developed in this tutorial, they are useful tools. Leave the **Satisfies Requirement** fields blank.

DFDs may be tied to associated Excelerator entities (Notes, Reference Documents, Issues, Categories, Tests, Changes, and Element Lists) by typing the entity type and name in the **Associated Entities** fields. See *Excelerator Data & Reports Reference Guide* . We will not be associating entities in this tutorial, so leave the **Associated Entities** fields blank.

- Press Pg Dn.

The second DFD description screen appears.

Use the second DFD description screen shown in Figure 4.2.2b as a guide, and complete the **Description** of the AA CONTEXT DFD.

When you have finished,

- Press F3 to save and return to the DFD Action Keypad.

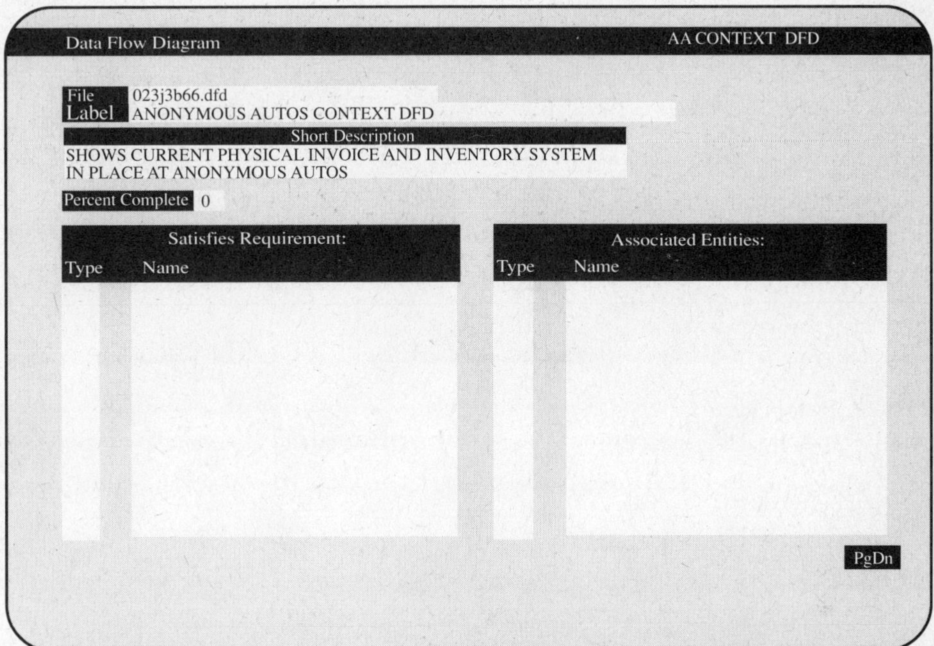

Figure 4.2.2a First DFD Description Screen Completed for AA CONTEXT DFD

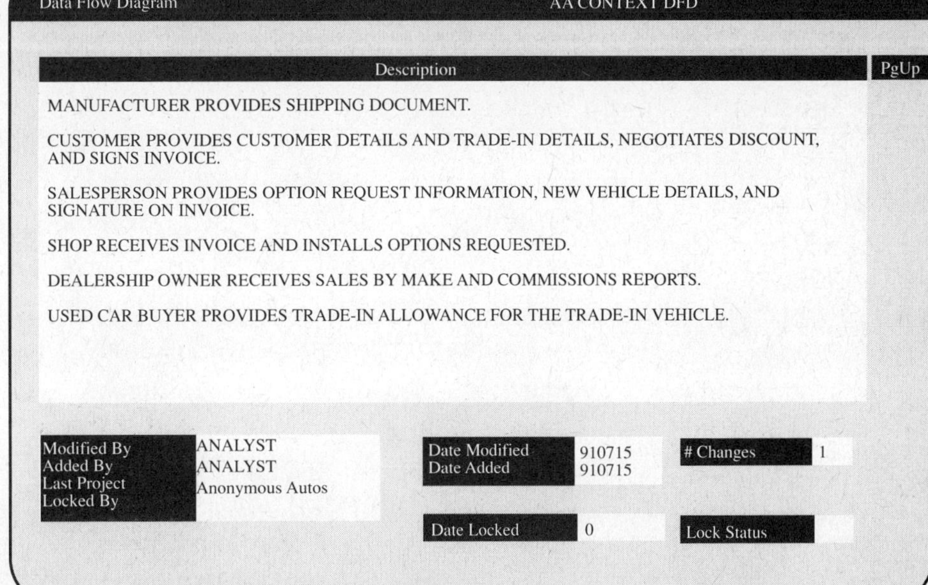

Figure 4.2.2b Second DFD Description Screen Completed for AA CONTEXT DFD

4.2.3 Printing DFD Descriptions

When you've completed a DFD description, you may send it to an output device for printing.

- Select **X XLDICTIONARY** from Excelerator's Main Menu.
- Select **GRAPHS** from the XLDictionary Menu which appears.
- Select **F Data Flow Diagram** from the Graphs Menu.
- Select **Output** from the DFD Action Keypad.

As shown in Figure 4.2.3a, a prompt appears near the bottom of the screen asking for the **Name Range** of DFD(s) you wish to print. If the exact name of the desired DFD is not known,

- Press ↵, and the XLDictionary list of DFDs appears, as shown in Figure 4.2.3b.
- Select the AA CONTEXT DFD with the mouse.

Excelerator asks if you would like output fields to be underlined. Underlining makes the report easier to read.

- Type **Y**.

Next, Excelerator asks where to send the report, providing choices at the bottom of the screen.

- Select **Printer** with the mouse, and the DFD description begins printing.

A specific **range** of DFD descriptions may be printed rather than just one description at a time. This is accomplished by using **wild cards** to define a range. Asterisks (*) are Excelerator's wild card. If you wanted to print all DFD descriptions beginning with the letter **A**, you could type **A*** in the **Name Range** field. Similarly, ***A** would indicate all DFD descriptions ending with the letter **A**.

It is also possible to print all DFD descriptions in the XLDictionary by selecting **All Entities on Selector List**, and then proceeding as you would if you had selected just one name.

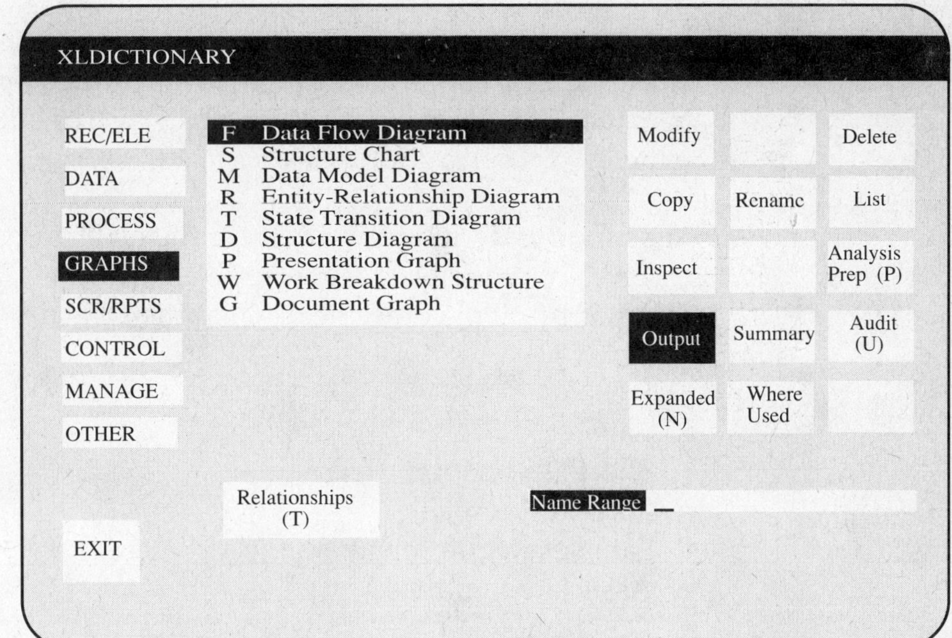

Figure 4.2.3a
Output Selection on XLDictionary DFD Action Keypad

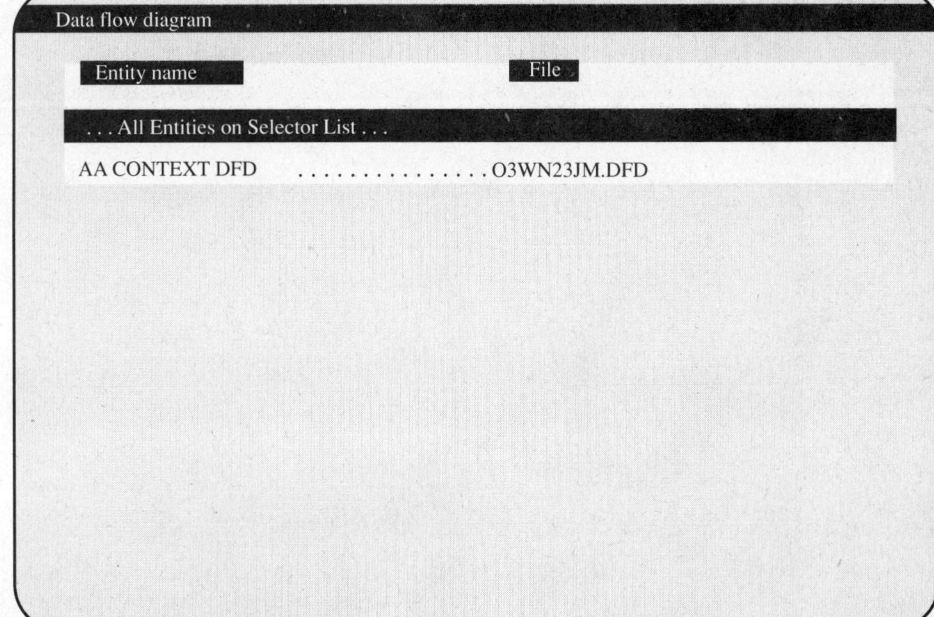

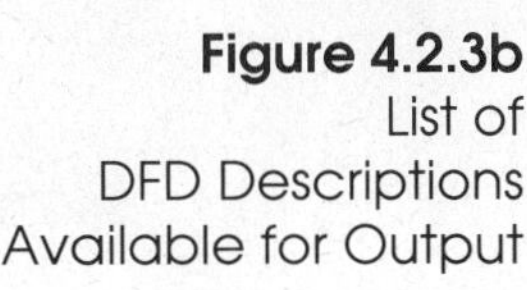
Figure 4.2.3b
List of DFD Descriptions Available for Output

4.2.4 Interpreting Printed DFD Descriptions

Figure 4.2.4 shows the printed DFD description for AA CONTEXT DFD. The date and time the report was printed appear at the top of the page, along with the page number, type of output, and graph name.

This report is designed to resemble the DFD description screens closely. Notice the DFD name appears near the top of the page followed by all the other fields from the DFD description screens:

- File
- Label
- Short Description
- Percent Complete
- Satisfies Requirement
- Associated Entities
- Description
- Audit fields from the bottom of the second DFD description screen.

The lines on the page are the result of responding affirmatively to Excelerator's question, *Do you want output fields underlined?* during the printing process.

Figure 4.2.4 Printed DFD Description with Output Fields Underlined

DATE: 25-AUG-91 DATA FLOW DIAGRAM - OUTPUT PAGE 1
TIME: 18:52 NAME: AA CONTEXT DFD Excelerator / IS

TYPE DATA FLOW DIAGRAM NAME AA CONTEXT DFD

File o3b2w4n.dfd
Label ANONYMOUS AUTOS CONTEXT DFD

Short Description

SHOWS CURRENT PHYSICAL INVOICE AND INVENTORY SYSTEM IN PLACE AT ANONYMOUS AUTOS

Percent Complete 0

Satisfies Requirement: Associated Entities
Type Name Type Name

Description

MANUFACTURER PROVIDES SHIPPING DOCUMENT.

CUSTOMER PROVIDES CUSTOMER DETAILS AND TRADE-IN DETAILS, NEGOTIATES DISCOUNT, AND SIGNS INVOICE.

SALESPERSON PROVIDES OPTION REQUEST INFORMATION, NEW VEHICLE DETAILS, AND SIGNATURE ON INVOICE.

SHOP RECEIVES INVOICE AND INSTALLS OPTIONS REQUESTED.

DEALERSHIP OWNER RECEIVES SALES BY MAKE AND COMMISSIONS REPORTS.

USED CAR BUYER PROVIDES TRADE-IN ALLOWANCE FOR THE TRADE-IN VEHICLE.

Modified By ANALYST
Added By ANALYST
Last Project Anonymous Autos
Locked By

Date Modified 910825
Date Added 910823
Date Locked 0

Changes 13
Lock Status

4.2.5 Using Action Keypad Functions

The Action Keypad is similar for all Excelerator entities. For Data Flow Diagrams, it consists of the options shown in Figure 4.2.5. In this tutorial, we will be discussing only the most commonly used of the Action Keypad functions. The remaining functions are mostly output oriented. They are more useful to advanced users. (See *Excelerator Data & Reports Reference Guide* for further information on functions not discussed here.)

- **Add** is used for creating new data structure descriptions. It is not visible for XLDictionary graphs, because Excelerator will not allow a graph to be described prior to initiating the drawing.
- **Analysis Prep** is selected when Excelerator indicates that an action may not be performed until Analysis Prep has been run. This function establishes and updates links between entities in the XLDictionary.
- **Copy** is used to create an exact duplicate of an existing entity. After selecting Copy, type the name of the entity to be copied and then the name of the new entity you wish to create.
- **Delete** is used for removing unwanted entities from the XLDictionary. The exact name of the entity being deleted must be typed in the field provided. For graphs, this command will delete both the drawing and description.
- **List** is a screen report of the names, alternate names, and short descriptions of all entities of the selected type which exist in the XLDictionary.
- **Modify** is used to locate and facilitate changes to existing entities. After selecting this command, type the name of the desired entity in the provided Name field. If the name is not known, select Modify, then press ⏎ in the Name field.
- **Output** is for sending entity descriptions to a file, the screen, or a printer. Printing DFD descriptions is explained in detail in **4.2.3 Printing DFD Descriptions**.
- **Rename** is used for changing the name of existing records. You type the name of the record you want to rename and then the new name in the provided fields.
- **Summary** initiates the generation of an output report listing all names, alternate names, and short descriptions of selected entities in the XLDictionary.

Figure 4.2.5
Data Flow Diagram
Action Keypad

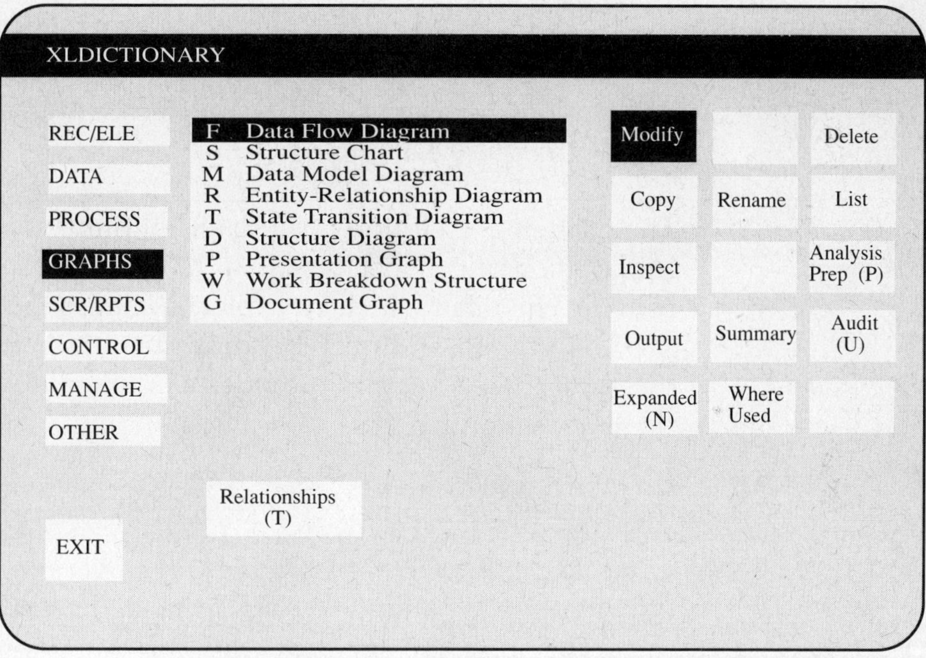

4.3

Describing External Entities (EXTs)

In Data Flow Diagrams, External Entities define the boundaries of a system. They represent anything which provides data required by the system or which receives data from the system. External Entities can represent people, organizations, departments, or other information systems.

External Entities, represented by boxes on DFDs, may be given textual descriptions using XLDictionary External Entity description screens as shown in Figure 4.3.

The written description of an External Entity should include an explanation of the specific data it requires or supplies. Excelerator provides fields in which an explosion data structure (Record, Data Model Diagram, or Entity-Relationship Diagram) may be named. The explosion data structure provides a detailed view of data provided by the External Entity.

The External Entity description may list satisfied system requirements and associated Excelerator entities.

In this section, you will describe the External Entities appearing on the AA CONTEXT DFD for the Anonymous Autos system.

Figure 4.3
External Entity is Described on XLDictionary External Entity Description Screens

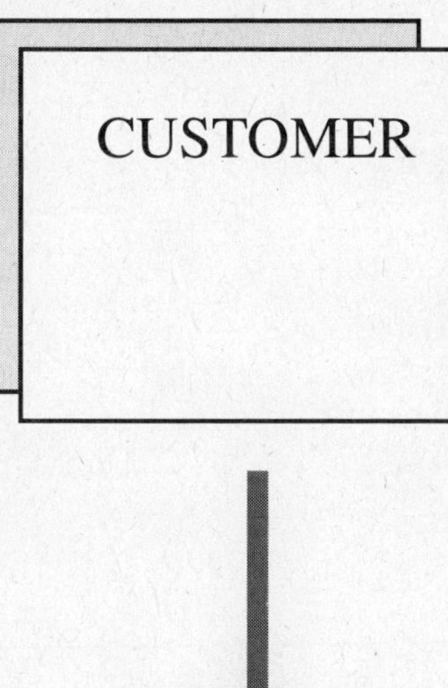

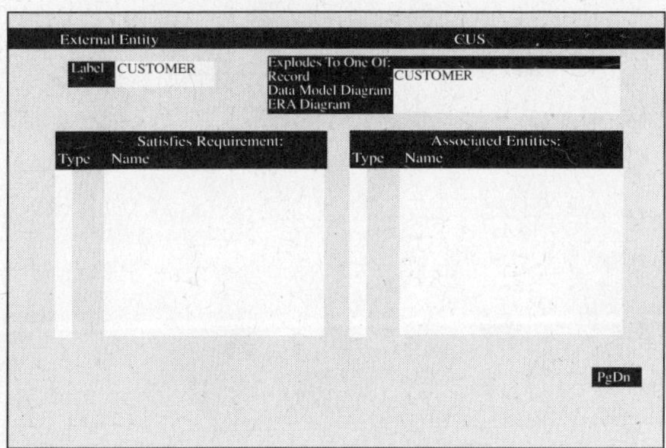

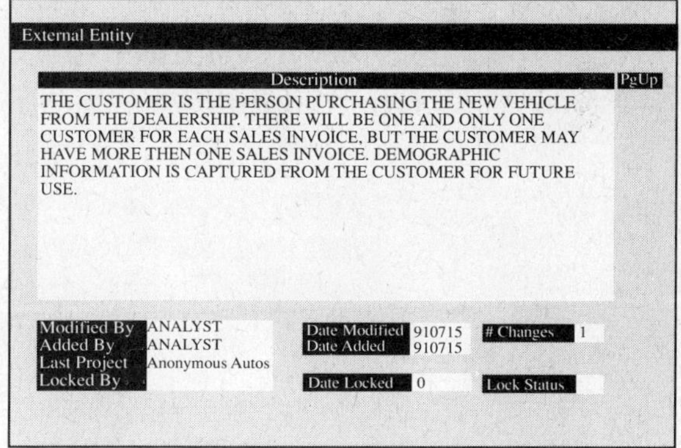

4.3.1 Completing External Entity Description Screens

If it is not already on your screen, retrieve the AA CONTEXT DFD. Refer to **4.1.1 Initiating Drawings**, if necessary, substituting **Modify** for **Add** on the Graphics Action Keypad.

- Select **DESCRIBE** from the drawing screen Command Menu.
- Place the mouse cursor on the External Entity labeled MANUFACTURER on your graph.
- Press the left button on the mouse to select the External Entity.

The object's ID appears in the status line at the bottom of the screen.

- Press ↵.

The first description screen for MANUFACTURER is displayed as shown in Figure 4.3.1a. The ID, MAN, appears at the top, and the label you created on the graph itself appears in the **Label** field.

- Press Tab.

Short Description, is a brief explanation of the role played by the External Entity in the system.

- Type **`VEHICLE MANUFACTURER PROVIDES NEW VEHICLE AND SHIPPING DOCUMENT`** in Short Description.

As with DFDs, External Entities may satisfy user or engineering requirements. External Entities may also be associated with other Excelerator entities. As stated in **4.2.2 Completing DFD Description Screens**, none of these topics are discussed in this tutorial.

- Press Pg Dn.

The second External Entity Description screen appears.
Use the second External Entity Description screen shown in Figure 4.3.1b as a guide, and complete the long **Description** of MANUFACTURER. When you have finished

- Press F3 to save and return to the drawing screen.

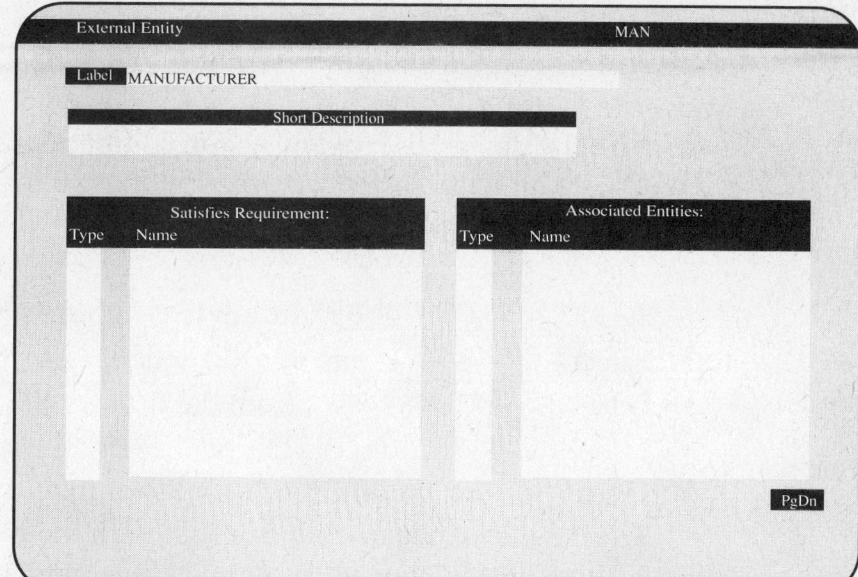
External Entity MAN

Label MANUFACTURER

Short Description

Satisfies Requirement:

Type Name

Associated Entities:

Type Name

PgDn

Figure 4.3.1a First External Entity Description Screen Completed for MANUFACTURER

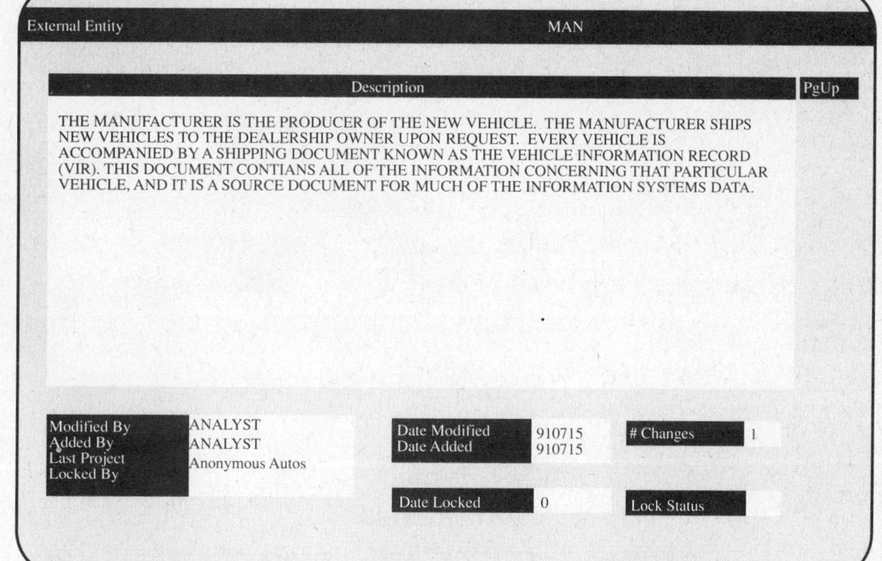
External Entity MAN

Description PgUp

THE MANUFACTURER IS THE PRODUCER OF THE NEW VEHICLE. THE MANUFACTURER SHIPS NEW VEHICLES TO THE DEALERSHIP OWNER UPON REQUEST. EVERY VEHICLE IS ACCOMPANIED BY A SHIPPING DOCUMENT KNOWN AS THE VEHICLE INFORMATION RECORD (VIR). THIS DOCUMENT CONTIANS ALL OF THE INFORMATION CONCERNING THAT PARTICULAR VEHICLE, AND IT IS A SOURCE DOCUMENT FOR MUCH OF THE INFORMATION SYSTEMS DATA.

Modified By ANALYST
Added By ANALYST
Last Project Anonymous Autos
Locked By

Date Modified 910715
Date Added 910715

Changes 1

Date Locked 0

Lock Status

Figure 4.3.1b Second External Entity Description Screen Completed for MANUFACTURER

Exercise 4.3.1

Describe the remaining four External Entities on your AA CONTEXT DFD. It may be helpful to refer back to **3. The Anonymous Autos Project** for a refresher. In your descriptions of these External Entities, specify what information each gives and gets. Another example of an External Entity description is shown in Figure 4.3 on Page 81.

4.3.2 Printing External Entity Descriptions

As with the description of any graph component, when you've completed an External Entity description, you may send it to an output device for printing.

- Select **X XLDICTIONARY** from Excelerator's Main Menu.
- Select **PROCESS** from the XLDictionary Menu which appears.
- Select **E External Entity** from the Process Menu.
- Select **Output** from the External Entity Action Keypad.
- Press ⏎, and the XLDictionary list of External Entities appears.
- Select **All Entities on Selector List** with the mouse.
- Type `Y` when asked if input fields should be underlined.
- Select **Printer** as the output device, and the External Entity descriptions begin printing.

Graph component descriptions can be printed one at a time, within specified ranges, or all together. See **4.2.3 Printing DFD Descriptions** .

The report Excelerator generates for each External Entity resembles the External Entity description screens. Figure 4.3.2 shows the printed description of MANUFACTURER. Notice the type of entity and the entity name appear near the top of the page followed other fields from the description screens:

- Label
- Short Description
- Satisfies Requirement
- Associated Entities
- Description
- Audit fields from the bottom of the second External Entity description screen.

The lines on the report are the result of responding affirmatively to Excelerator's question, *Do you want output fields underlined?* during the printing process.

Figure 4.3.2
Printed External Entity Description with Output Fields Underlined

DATE: 25-AUG-91 EXTERNAL ENTITY - OUTPUT PAGE 1
TIME: 18:52 NAME: * Excelerator / IS

TYPE External Entity NAME MAN

Label MANUFACTURER

Short Description

VEHICLE MANUFACTURER PROVIDES NEW VEHICLE AND SHIPPING DOCUMENT TO THE DEALERSHIP OWNER

Satisfies Requirement:		Associated Entities	
Type	Name	Type	Name

Description

THE MANUFACTURER IS THE PRODUCER OF THE NEW VEHICLE. THE MANUFACTURER SHIPS NEW VEHICLES TO THE DEALERSHIP OWNER UPON REQUEST. EVERY VEHICLE IS ACCOMPANIED BY A SHIPPING DOCUMENT KNOWN AS THE VEHICLE INFORMATION RECORD (VIR). THIS DOCUMENT CONTIANS ALL OF THE INFORMATION CONCERNING THAT PARTICULAR VEHICLE, AND IT IS A SOURCE DOCUMENT FOR MUCH OF THE INFORMATION SYSTEMS DATA.

Modified By	ANALYST	Date Modified	910825	# Changes	13
Added By	ANALYST	Date Added	910823		
Last Project	Anonymous Autos				
Locked By		Date Locked	0	Lock Status	

4.4

Describing Processes (PRCs)

A Process may represent a single activity or a complex network of activities. A Process transforms data into information for use in another Process, or for transmission to a Data Store or External Entity.

Typical low-level Processes calculate, summarize, compare, or perform file or database operations. Such Processes are given labels which include a strong verb (i.e., generate, create, record, calculate, read, delete, modify, compile) and a noun to be acted upon: For example, Record Purchase Data.

The labels of high-level Processes, such as 1.0 INVENTORY SUB-SYSTEM shown in Figure 4.4, are often the names of DFDs they represent rather than activity descriptions.

XLDictionary Process description screens facilitate complete textual description of Processes. The description should include an explanation of the activities performed by the Process. Excelerator provides fields in which an explosion data structure (Data Flow Diagram, Structure Chart, Structure Diagram, Primitive Process Specification, or Presentation Graph) may be named. The explosion data structure provides a representation of activities performed by the Process.

Excelerator provides fields for listing system requirements satisfied by the Process and other Excelerator entities with which it is associated.

In this section, you will completely describe the Process appearing on the AA CONTEXT DFD for the Anonymous Autos system.

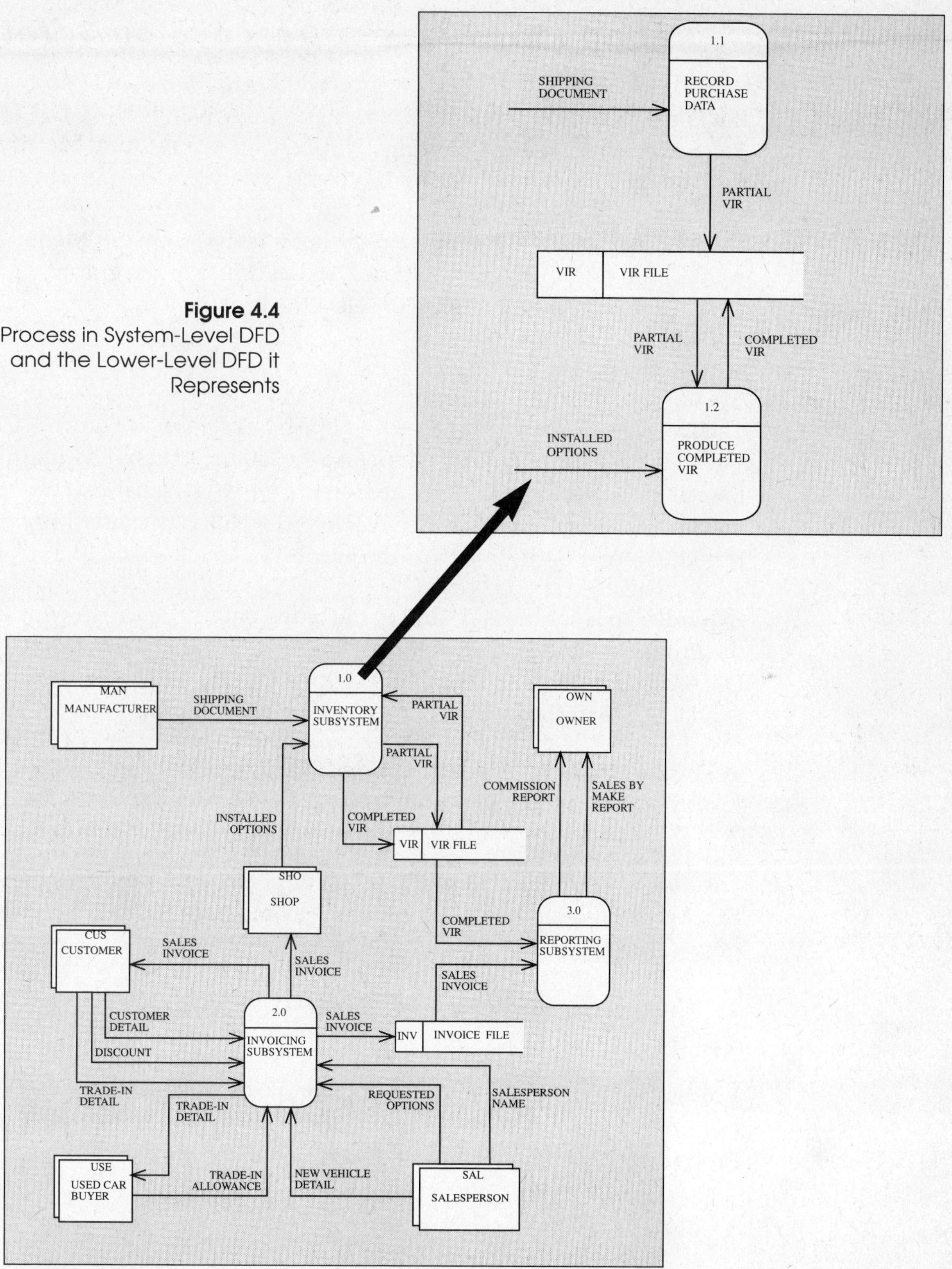

Figure 4.4
Process in System-Level DFD and the Lower-Level DFD it Represents

4.4.1 Completing First Process Description Screen

If it is not already on your screen, retrieve the AA CONTEXT DFD. Refer to **4.1.1 Initiating Drawings**, if necessary, substituting **Modify** for **Add** on the Graphics Action Keypad.

- Select **DESCRIBE** from the drawing screen Command Menu.
- Position the cursor on the Process in the center of the graph.
- Press the left mouse button to select the Process.
- Type `0.0` in the status line.
- Press [↵].

The first Process description screen appears as shown in Figure 4.4.1. The Process ID appears at the top, and the label you assigned it in Exercise 4.1.12 appears in the **Label** field (Note: The label may be displayed with extra spaces between words. This is because the text is formatted to fit in the object on the graph.)

Explodes To is for the type and name of the data structure to which the Process explodes. One of the explosion data structure options is a DFD. Because this is the context-level process, it should be exploded to a DFD which shows the entire Anonymous Autos system.

- Type **`DFD`** in the **Type** field under Explodes To.
- Type **`AA SYSTEM DFD`** in the **Name** field under Explodes To.
- Press [Tab].

Location is for the department, group, or person that performs the Process being described. This Process encompasses the entire current physical system.

- Type **`INVOICE/INVENTORY SYSTEM`** in Location.
- Press [Tab].

Process Category is for the type of process being performed: For example, batch and on-line. Since this field is geared for lower-level Processes, leave it blank for the context-level Process.

- Press [Tab].

Duration Value is the number of times the Process occurs for each unit of time in **Duration Type**. Again, since these fields are geared for lower-level Processes describing more specific events, leave them blank for the context-level Process.

- Press [Tab] two times.

Manual or Computer requires a value of **M** (manual) or **C** (computer) Because Anonymous Autos system is currently manual,

- Type **M** in Manual or Computer.
- Press [Pg Dn], and the second Process description screen appears.

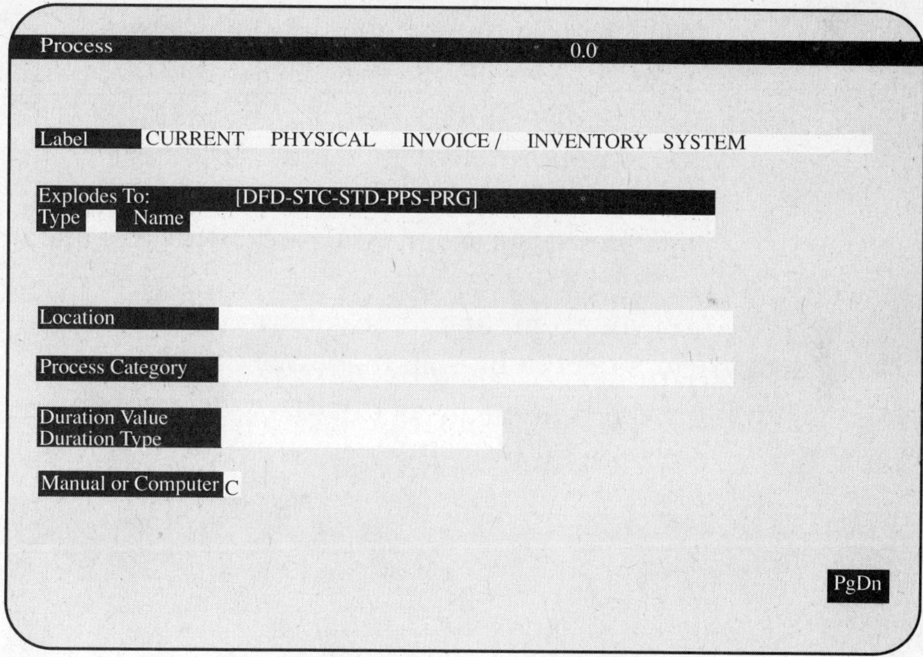

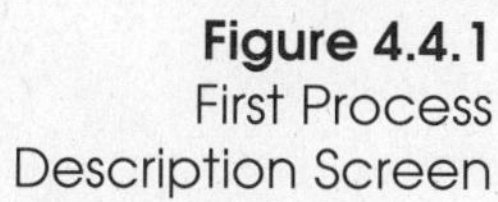
Figure 4.4.1 First Process Description Screen

4.4.2 Completing Last Process Description Screens

The second Process description screen is shown in Figure 4.4.2a.

As explained in **4.2.2 Completing DFD Description Screens, Satisfies Requirements** and **Associated Entities** will not be addressed in this tutorial. Leave these fields blank unless you have developed User and Engineering Requirements on your own.

- Press [Pg Dn].

The third Process description screen appears.

The **Description** field on this last screen is for a detailed, free-form description of the Process. This is your opportunity to give a textual rather than graphical explanation of Process activities. Complete the Description field using Figure 4.4.2b as a guide.

- Press [F3] when you are done to save and return to your graph.

If your computer has a color monitor, the Process will now appear in a different color from the rest of the graph components. This is because you identified the entity to which the Process explodes on the first description screen.

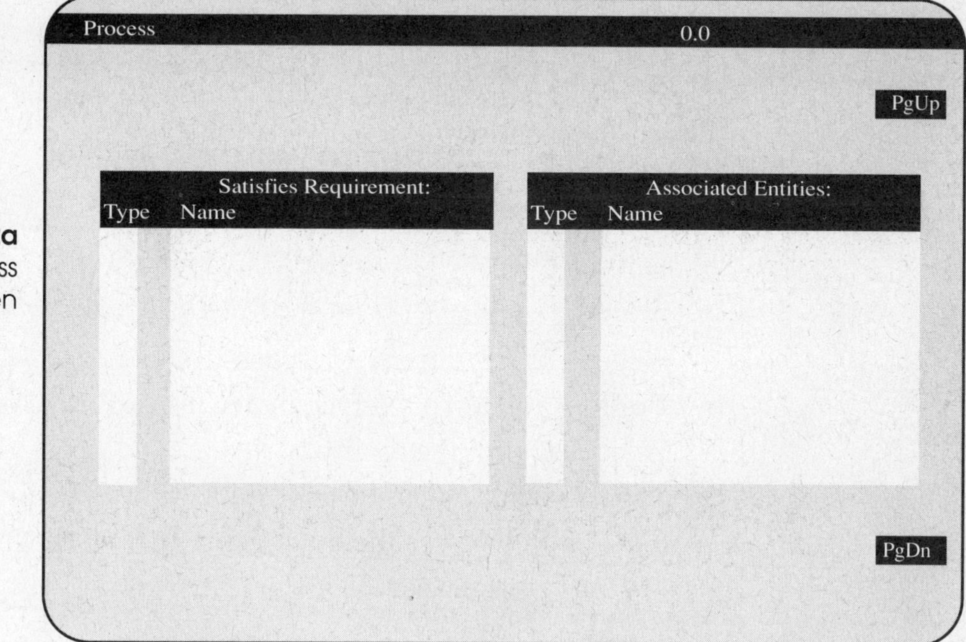

Figure 4.4.2a
Second Process Description Screen

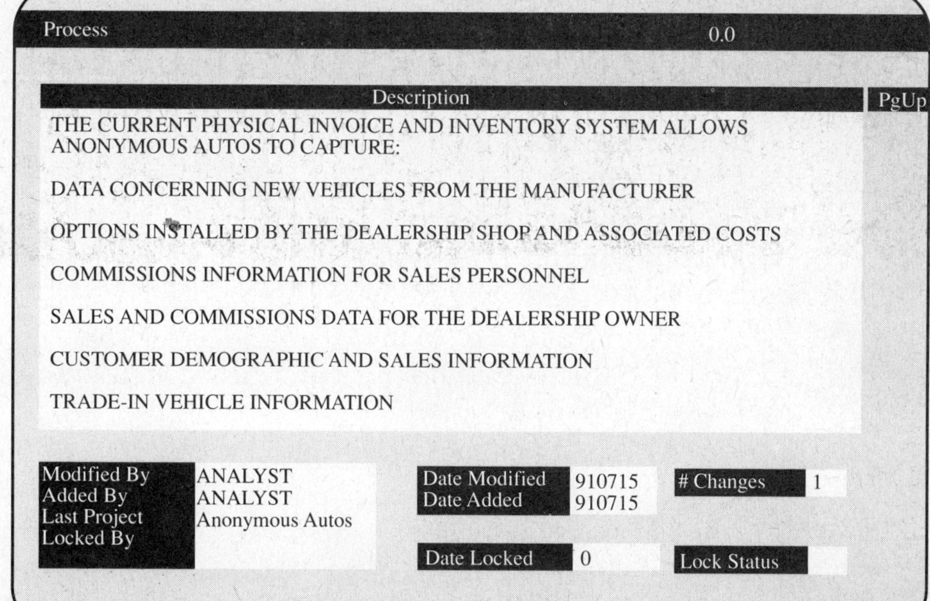

Figure 4.4.2b
Third Process Description Screen

4.4.3 Printing Process Descriptions

As with the description of any graph component, when you've completed an Process description, you may send it to an output device for printing.

- Select **X XLDICTIONARY** from Excelerator's Main Menu.
- Select **Process** from the XLDictionary Menu which appears.
- Select **P Process** from the Process Menu.
- Select **Output** from the Process Action Keypad.
- Press ⏎, and the XLDictionary list of Processes appears.
- Select **0.0** with the mouse.
- Type **Y** when asked if input fields should be underlined.
- Select **Printer** as the output device, and the Process description begins printing.

Graph component descriptions can be printed one at a time, within specified ranges, or all together. See **4.2.3 Printing DFD Descriptions**.

The report Excelerator generates for a Process closely resembles the Process description screens. Figure 4.4.3 shows the printed description of context Process 0.0. The entity type and Process name appear near the top of the page followed by other fields from the description screens:

- Label
- Explodes To
- Location
- Process Category
- Duration Value
- Duration Type
- Computer or Manual
- Satisfies Requirement and Associated Entities
- Description
- Audit fields from the third Process Description screen.

The lines on the report are the result of responding affirmatively to Excelerator's question, *Do you want output fields underlined?* during the printing process.

Figure 4.4.3
Printed Process Description with Output Fields Underlined

DATE: 25-AUG-91
TIME: 18:52

PROCESS - OUTPUT
NAME: 0.0

PAGE 1
Excelerator / IS

TYPE PROCESS

NAME 0.0

Label CURRENT PHYSICAL INVOICE / INVENTORY SYSTEM

Explodes To: [DFD-STC-STD-PPS-PRG]
Type DFD Name AA SYSTEM DFD

Location INVOICE/INVENTORY SYSTEM

Process Category

Duration Value
Duration Type

Manual or Computer M

Satisfies Requirement:
Type Name

Associated Entities
Type Name

Description

THE CURRENT PHYSICAL INVOICE AND INVENTORY SYSTEM ALLOWS ANONYMOUS AUTOS TO CAPTURE:

DATA CONCERNING NEW VEHICLES FROM THE MANUFACTURER

OPTIONS INSTALLED BY THE DEALERSHIP SHOP AND ASSOCIATED COSTS

COMMISSIONS INFORMATION FOR SALES PERSONNEL

SALES AND COMMISSIONS DATA FOR THE DEALERSHIP OWNER

CUSTOMER DEMOGRAPHIC AND SALES INFORMATION

TRADE-IN VEHICLE INFORMATION

Modified By ANALYST
Added By ANALYST
Last Project Anonymous Autos
Locked By

Date Modified 910825
Date Added 910823
Date Locked 0

Changes 13
Lock Status

4.5

Describing Data Flows (DAFs)

A Data Flow describes data which flows to or from a Process.

In a physical Data Flow Diagram, a Data Flow can represent a document, form, report, memo, screen, or a computer to computer transmission. This often means that some of the data transmitted is not used at the destination of the data flow. Labels for physical Data Flows are often names of physical packets of data like Sales Invoice, Vehicle Inventory Record, and Shipping Document.

In a logical DFD, a Data Flow contains only the data required at the destination for further processing, storage, or use by an External Entity. This means the labels for logical Data Flows are usually names of the specific data structures to which they explode.

XLDictionary Data Flow description screens facilitate textual description of Data Flows. The description should include an explanation of the data transmitted by the Data Flow. Excelerator provides fields in which an explosion data structure may be named. The explosion data structure provides a detailed view of data transmitted by the Data Flow. Explosion data structure options for Data Flows are shown in Figure 4.5.

In this section, you will completely describe the Data Flows appearing on the AA CONTEXT DFD for the Anonymous Autos system.

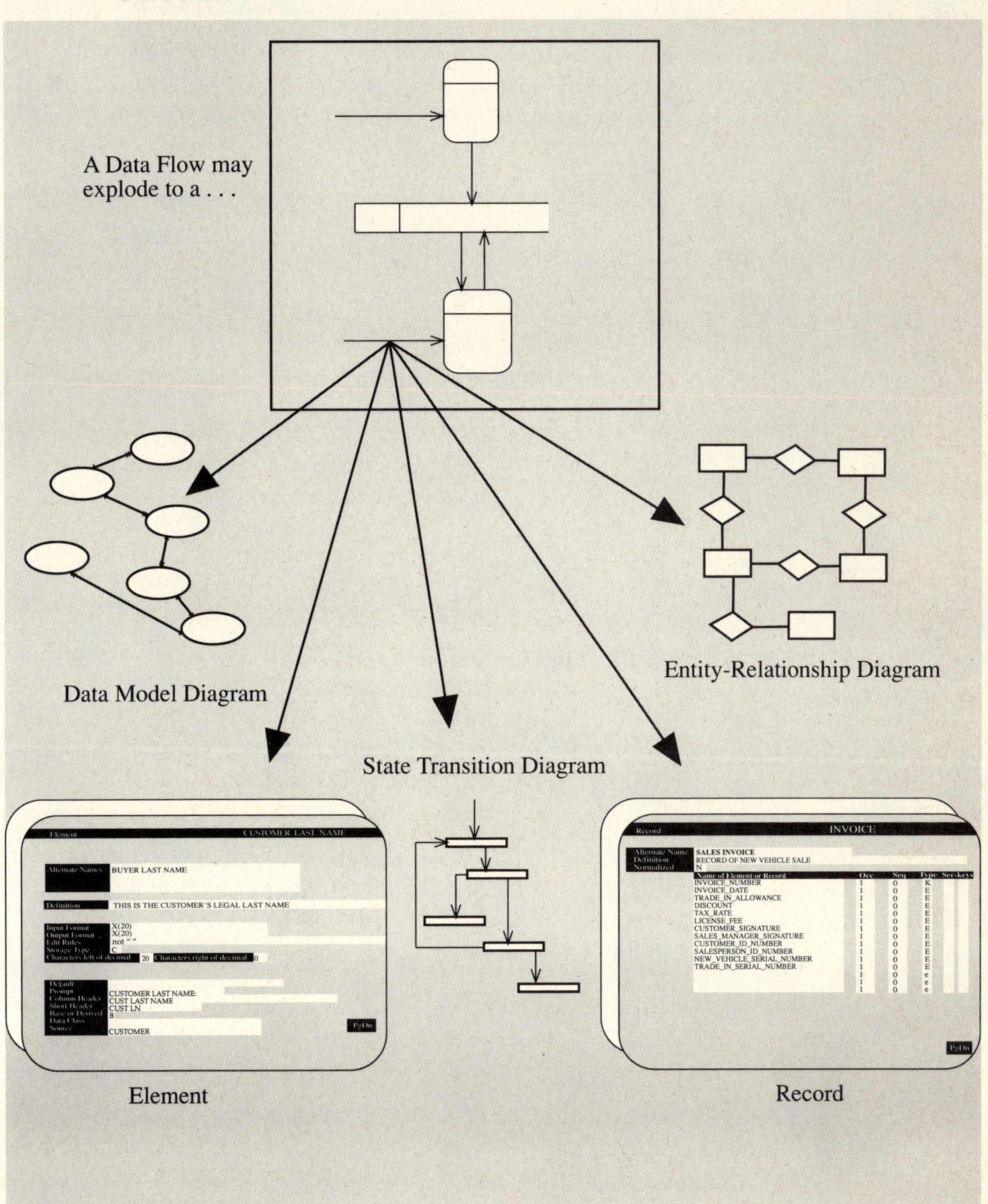

Figure 4.5
Explosion Options for Data Flows

4.5.1 Completing Data Flow Description Screens

If it is not already on your screen, retrieve the AA CONTEXT DFD. Refer to **4.1.1 Initiating Drawings**, if necessary, substituting **Modify** for **Add** on the Graphics Action Keypad.

- Select **DESCRIBE** from the drawing screen Command Menu.
- Position the cursor on the handle of the Data Flow labeled SHIPPING DOCUMENT.
- Press the left mouse button to select the Data Flow.
- Replace the ID in the status line with the letters **SD**.
- Press ⏎.

The first Data Flow description screen appears as shown in Figure 4.5.1a. The Data Flow ID appears at the top, and the label appears in the **Label** field.

Data Flow explosion is explained in **5.3.2 Exploding Data Flows**. Leave the **Explodes To** fields blank for now.

- Press Tab three times moving the insertion point to Duration Value.

Duration Value is the maximum expected number of times the flow of data occurs for each unit of time in **Duration Type**. For example, Anonymous Autos may receive a maximum of 100 new vehicles each month. If a Shipping Document accompanies each new vehicle, then the Duration Value is 100, and the Duration Type is Month.

- Type **100** in Duration Value.
- Press Tab.
- Type **MONTH** in Duration Type.
- Press Tab.

Access Type describes the function of the Data Flow: **A** (add), **U** (update), **R** (read), or **D** (delete). The data received from the Shipping Document is used to create a Vehicle Inventory Record. Therefore, it adds information to the system.

- Type **A** in Access Type.

Leave the **Satisfies Requirements** and **Associated Entities** fields blank.

- Press [Pg Dn], and the second Data Flow description screen appears.

Description on this last screen is for a detailed, free-form description of the Data Flow. Complete this screen using Figure 4.5.1b as a guide.

- Press [F3] when you're done to save and return to your graph.

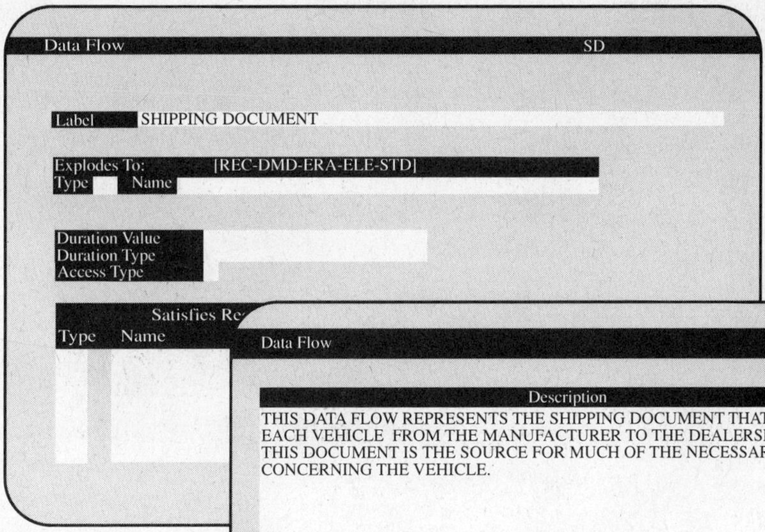

Data Flow SD

Label SHIPPING DOCUMENT

Explodes To: [REC-DMD-ERA-ELE-STD]
Type Name

Duration Value
Duration Type
Access Type

Satisfies Re
Type Name

Figure 4.5.1a
First Data Flow Description Screen

Data Flow SD

Description PgUp

THIS DATA FLOW REPRESENTS THE SHIPPING DOCUMENT THAT IS SENT WITH EACH VEHICLE FROM THE MANUFACTURER TO THE DEALERSHIP OWNER. THIS DOCUMENT IS THE SOURCE FOR MUCH OF THE NECESSARY DATA CONCERNING THE VEHICLE.

Modified By ANALYST
Added By ANALYST
Last Project Anonymous Autos
Locked By

Date Modified 910715
Date Added 910715
Changes 1
Date Locked 0
Lock Status

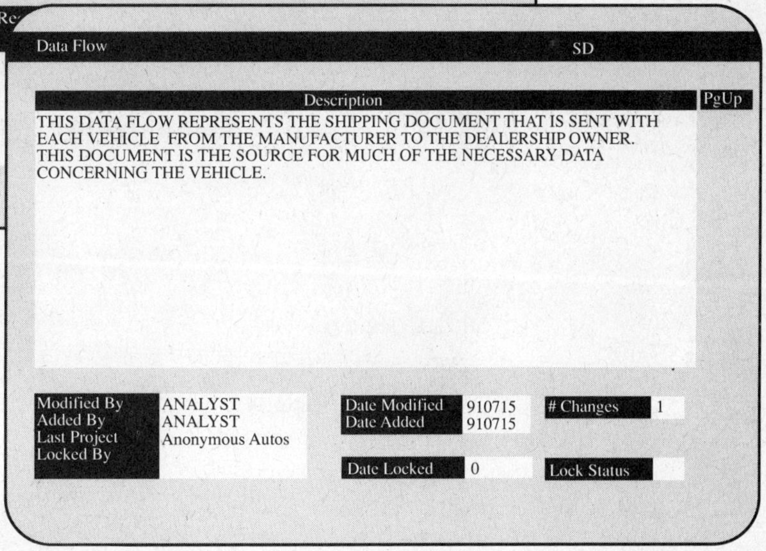

Figure 4.5.1b
Second Data Flow Description Screen

Exercise 4.5.1

Describe the remaining Data Flows on the AA CONTEXT DFD. When assigning IDs, try to make them meaningful. Using acronyms from Data Flow labels often works well for creating IDs.

4.5.2 Printing Data Flow Descriptions

As with the description of any graph component, when you've completed an Process description, you may send it to an output device for printing.

- Select **X XLDICTIONARY** from Excelerator's Main Menu.
- Select **DATA** from the XLDictionary Menu which appears.
- Select **F Data Flow** from the Data Menu.
- Select **Output** from the Data Flow Action Keypad.
- Press ↵, and the XLDictionary list of Data Flows appears.
- Select **All Entities on Selector List** with the mouse.
- Type `Y` when asked if input fields should be underlined.
- Select **Printer** as the output device, and the Data Flow descriptions begin printing.

The reports Excelerator generates for your Data Flows closely resemble the Data Flow Description screens. Figure 4.5.2 shows the printed description of the SHIPPING DOCUMENT Data Flow. Notice the entity type and Data Flow ID (in the Name field) appear near the top of the page followed by other fields from the description screens:

- Label
- Explodes To
- Duration Value
- Duration Type
- Access Type
- Satisfies Requirement
- Associated Entities
- Description
- Audit fields from the bottom of the second Data Flow description screen.

The lines on the report are the result of responding affirmatively to Excelerator's question, *Do you want output fields underlined?* during the printing process.

DATE: 25-AUG-91 DATA FLOW - OUTPUT PAGE 1
TIME: 18:52 NAME: * Excelerator / IS

TYPE Data Flow NAME SHIPPING DOCUMENT

Label SHIPPING DOCUMENT

Explodes To: [REC-DMD-ERA-ELE-STD]
Type ___ Name

Duration Value 100
Duration Type MONTH
Access Type A

Satisfies Requirement:
Type Name

Associated Entities:
Type Name

Description

THIS DATA FLOW REPRESENTS THE SHIPPING DOCUMENT THAT IS SENT WITH EACH VEHICLE FROM THE MANUFACTURER TO THE DEALERSHIP OWNER. THIS DOCUMENT IS THE SOURCE FOR MUCH OF THE NECESSARY DATA CONCERNING THE VEHICLE.

Modified By ANALYST
Added By ANALYST
Last Project Anonymous Autos
Locked By

Date Modified 910825
Date Added 910823
Date Locked 0

Changes 13
Lock Status

Figure 4.5.2 Printed Data Flow Description for SHIPPING DOCUMENT (SD) with Output Fields Underlined

Exercise 4.5.2

The AA CONTEXT DFD is now complete. It has been drawn and described, and all of its components have been described. Refer, if necessary, to **4.1.16 Using PRINT Options**, and print the completed Data Flow Diagram, AA CONTEXT DFD.

4.6

Creating Lower Level Data Flow Diagrams (DFDs)

The context-level DFD for the Anonymous Autos system is now complete. It has been drawn and described. All of its components have been described. The explosion data structure for the context-level Process has been identified: AA SYSTEM DFD.

With all of this done, you are now ready to develop the lower-level physical DFDs for the current Anonymous Autos system. The first of these is the system-level DFD, called AA SYSTEM DFD, which gives an overview of the system's primary activities.

The three primary activities or subsystems within the Anonymous Autos system are represented by Processes on the AA SYSTEM DFD. These subsystems are Inventory, Invoicing, and Reporting. Each of the three system-level Processes explodes to a low-level DFD providing a more detailed view of subsystem activities.

The final result is a physical process model composed of three DFD explosion levels, as shown in Figure 4.6, and a total of five DFDs (context, system, and three low-level DFDs).

In the Anonymous Autos physical process model, the Data Flow labels are identical from one explosion level to another. This is a common practice used to promote a consistent net flow of data between a Process and the DFD to which it explodes, a concept called **level-balancing**.

In this section, you will complete the physical process model for the existing Anonymous Autos system.

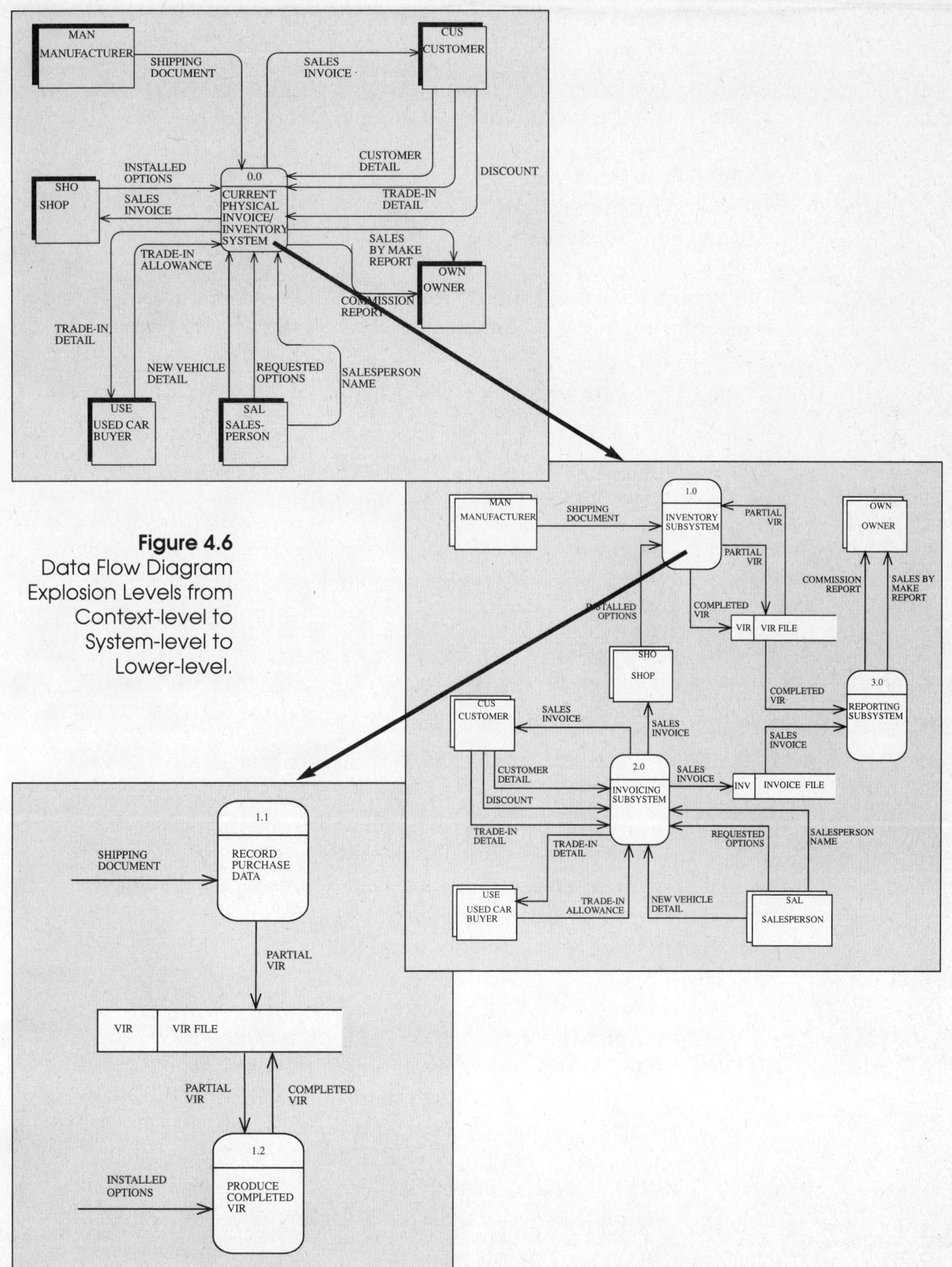

Figure 4.6
Data Flow Diagram Explosion Levels from Context-level to System-level to Lower-level.

4.6.1 Drawing the System DFD

The Anonymous Autos system is made up of three subsystems, each of which will appear on the system-level DFD as a Process:

- Inventory Subsystem
- Reporting Subsystem
- Invoicing Subsystem

The system level DFD should also show all External Entities (from the context level DFD) and the files in which system data is stored.

- Select **G GRAPHICS** from Excelerator's Main Menu.
- Select **F Data Flow Diagram** from the Graphics Menu.
- Select **Add** from the DFD Action Keypad.
- Type **AA SYSTEM DFD** in the Name field.
- Press ↵.

A blank drawing screen appears on which you may draw your system level DFD.

Exercise 4.6.1

Using the methods presented in this chapter, draw the AA SYSTEM DFD as shown in Figure 4.6.1. Don't worry about making your DFD look identical to the one in Figure 4.6.1. Make sure yours is functionally the same. (Note: The oblong open-ended boxes are Data Stores. You will describe them in **4.7 Describing Data Stores (DASs)**.) After you have drawn and labeled your graph,

- Complete the DFD description screens.
- Complete description screens for the three Processes using the IDs shown at the top of the Processes in Figure 4.6.1. (In the Explodes To fields for each, identify DFDs with names matching each Process: 1.0 INVENTORY SUBSYSTEM, 2.0 INVOICING SUBSYSTEM, and 3.0 REPORTING SUBSYSTEM.)
- Complete description screens for any new Data Flows.

Continued on Next Page

- Using the DESCRIBE command, identify the External Entities and any previously described Data Flows with the same IDs as on the context-level DFD. This allows the XLDictionary to tie existing descriptions to these new graph components.

Skip any fields on descriptions screens with which you are not comfortable or which you feel are inapplicable.

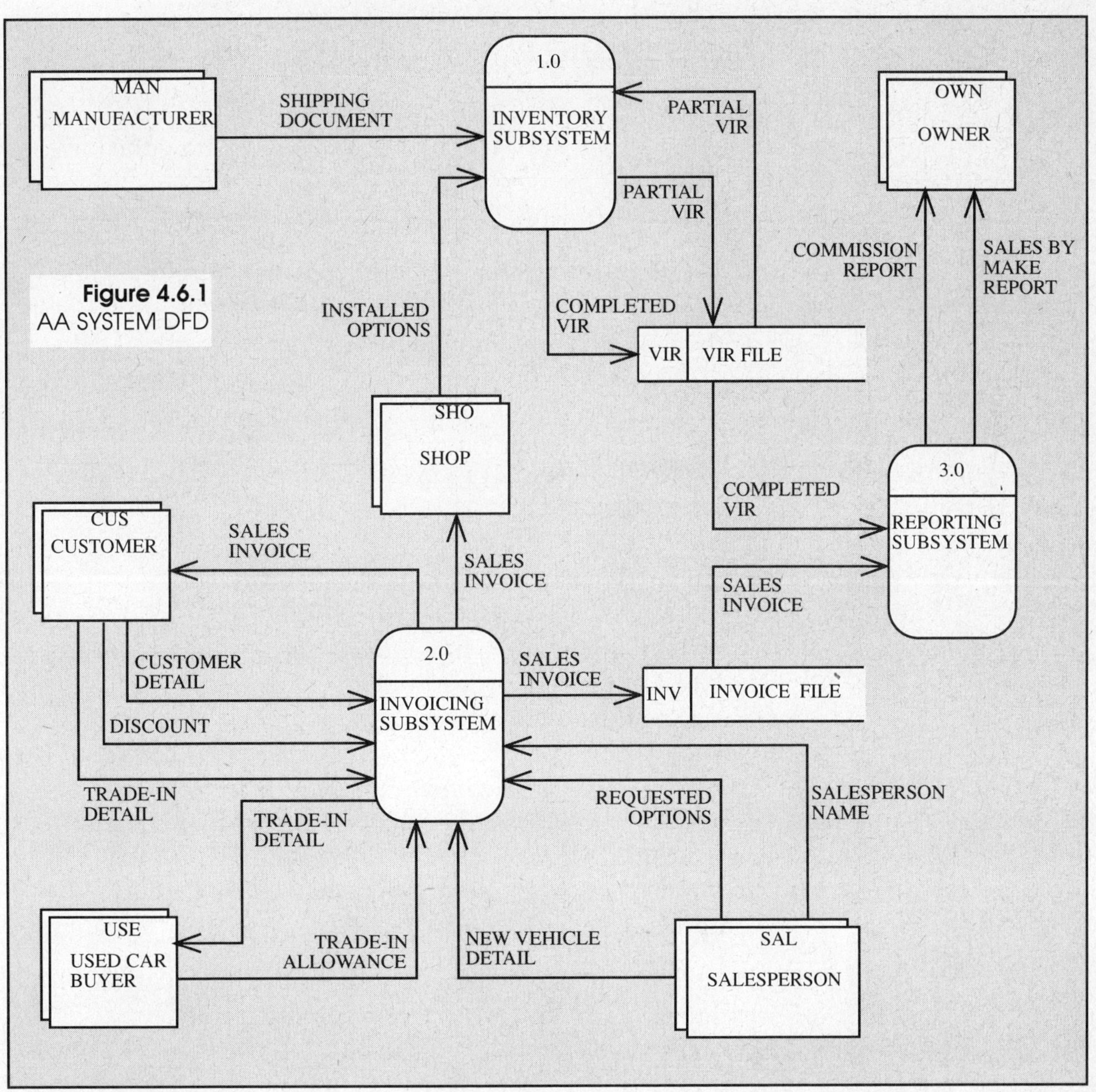

Figure 4.6.1
AA SYSTEM DFD

4.6.2 Drawing Low-Level DFDs

There are three low-level DFDs remaining to be drawn in order to complete the Process Model of the current physical system at Anonymous Autos: **1.0 INVENTORY SUBSYSTEM, 2.0 INVOICING SUBSYSTEM**, and **3.0 REPORTING SUBSYSTEM**.

- Select **G GRAPHICS** from Excelerator's Main Menu.
- Select **F Data Flow Diagram** from the Graphics Menu.
- Select **Add** from the DFD Action Keypad.
- Type **1.0 INVENTORY SUBSYSTEM** in the Name field.
- Press ⏎.

A blank drawing screen appears on which you may draw the low-

Exercise 4.6.2

Using the methods presented in this chapter, draw the 1.0 INVENTORY SUBSYSTEM Data Flow Diagram shown in Figure 4.6.2. (Use the INTRFACE command and INPUT option to create the Data Flows labeled SHIPPING DOCUMENT and INSTALLED OPTIONS.) After you have drawn and labeled your graph,

- Complete the DFD description screens.
- Complete description screens for the two Processes using IDs shown at the top of the Processes in Figure 4.6.2. (Leave the Explodes To fields blank.)
- Complete the description screens for any new Data Flows.
- Using the DESCRIBE command, give previously described Data Flows and Data Stores the same IDs as on the context-level DFD. This allows the XLDictionary to tie existing descriptions to these new graph components.

Skip any fields on descriptions screens with which you are not comfortable or which you feel are inapplicable.

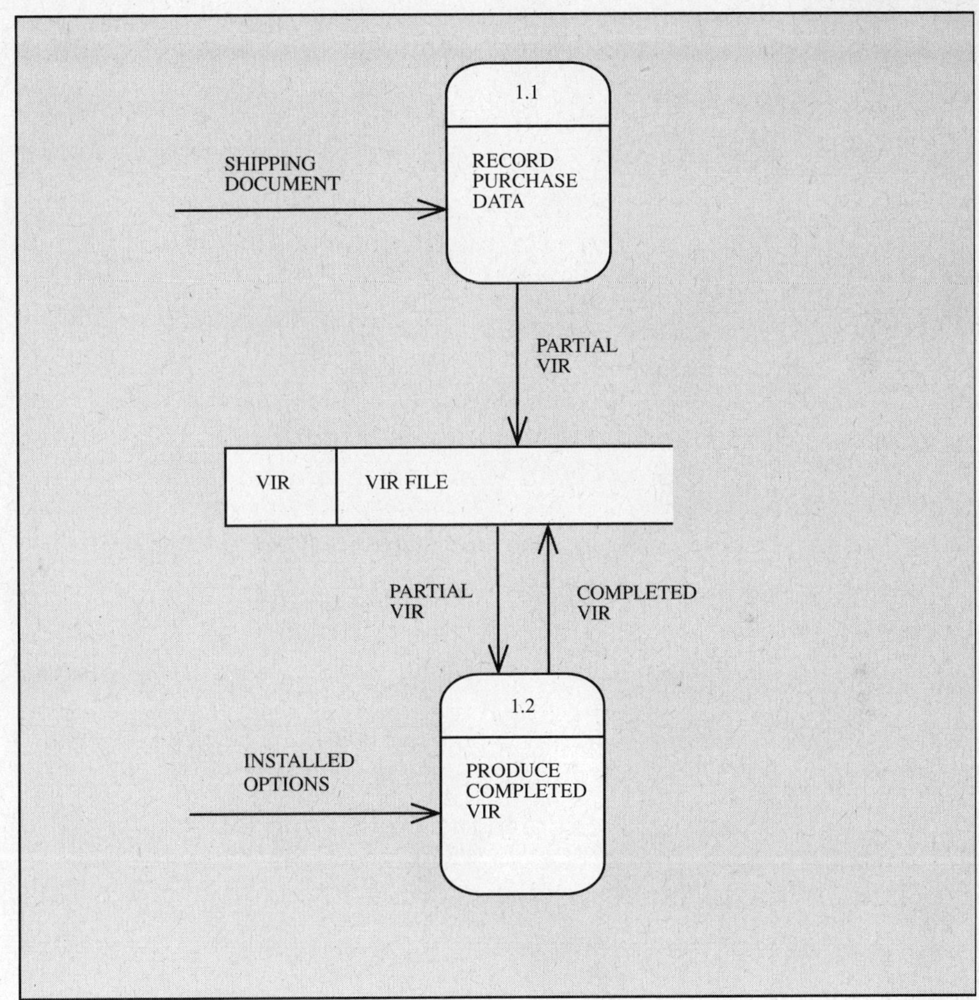

Figure 4.6.2
1.0 INVENTORY SUBSYSTEM

4.7

Describing Data Stores (DASs)

A Data Store represents the storage of data within a system. The storage period of data may be short-term, as in computer memory, or long-term, as in a filing cabinet full of forms.

XLDictionary Data Store description screens facilitate textual description of Data Stores. The description should include an explanation of the data stored.

Excelerator provides fields in which an explosion data structure may be named. The explosion data structure provides a detailed view of data stored. As shown in Figure 4.7, a Data Store may explode to a Record, a Data Model Diagram, or an Entity-Relationship Diagram.

A Data Store which explodes to Record usually represents either a physical or computerized file system, or a short term memory storage area. A Data Store which explodes to a Data Model Diagram or an Entity-Relationship Diagram represents a database. When a Data Store represents a database, it is often the only Data Store in the process model, storing all data required by the system. When a Data Store represents a Record, however, there is almost always more than one Data Store in the process model.

In this section, you will completely describe the Data Stores in the Anonymous Autos physical process model.

Figure 4.7
Explosion Options for Data Stores

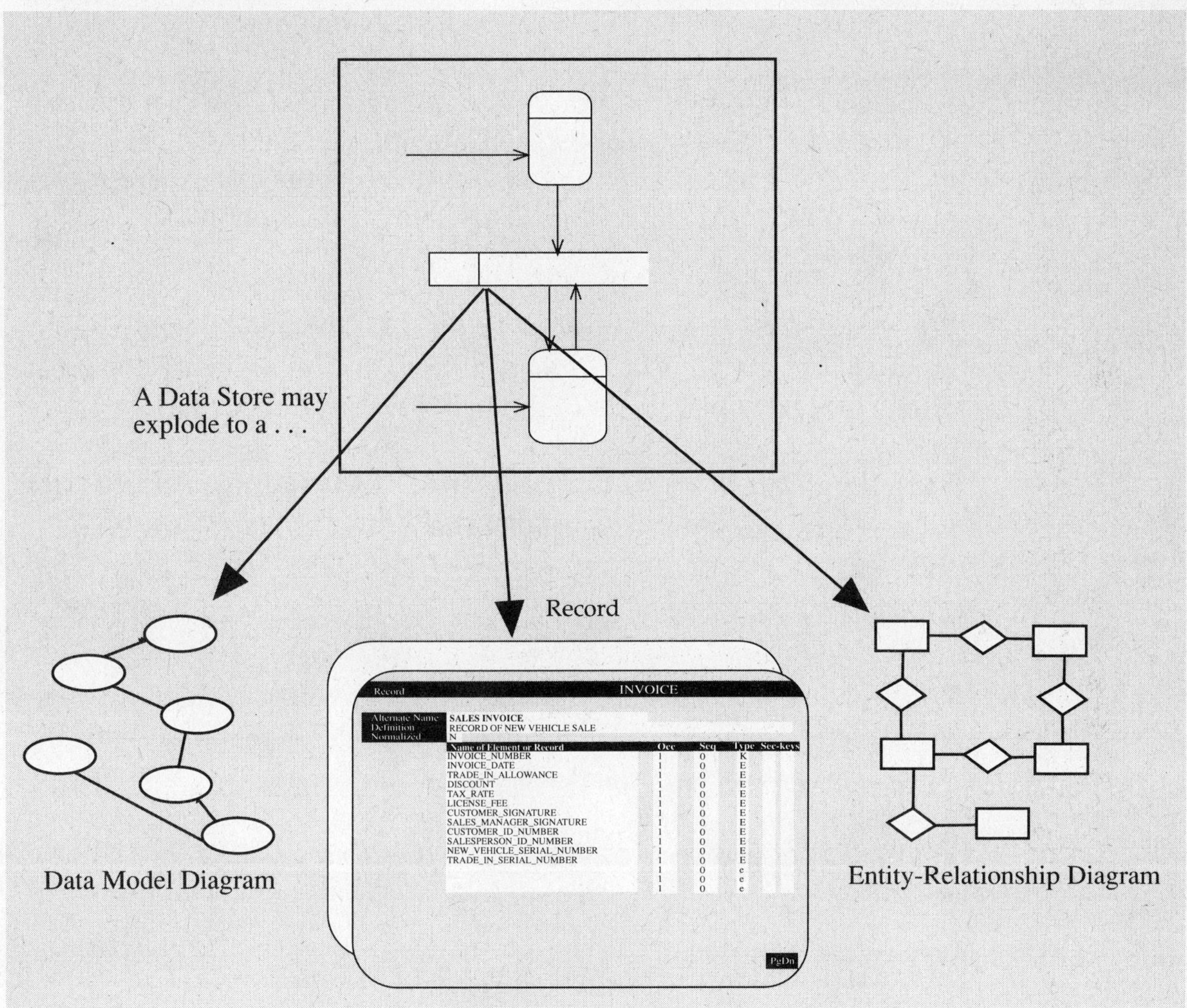

4.7.1 Completing Data Store Description Screens

Retrieve the AA SYSTEM DFD. Refer to **4.1.1 Initiating Drawings**, if necessary, substituting **Modify** for **Add** on the Graphics Action Keypad, and typing AA SYSTEM DFD in the Name field.

- Select DESCRIBE from the drawing screen Command Menu.
- Place the mouse cursor on the Data Store labeled VIR FILE.
- Press the left button on the mouse to select the Data Store.
- Type **VIR** in the status line. (This is the Data Store ID.)
- Press ↵.

The first description screen for VIR FILE is displayed as shown in Figure 4.7.1. The ID, VIR, appears at the top, and the label you created on the graph itself appears in the **Label** field.

Exploding Data Stores is discussed in **5.3.1 Exploding and Indexing Data Stores**. For now, leave the **Explodes To One Of** fields blank.

- Press Tab until the insertion point is in the Location field.

Location is the physical place where the Data Store resides. Since it is the accounting department at Anonymous Autos that maintains the Vehicle Inventory Records (VIRs),

- Type **ACCOUNTING DEPARTMENT** in Location.
- Press Tab.

Manual or Computer requires a value of **M** (manual) or **C** (computer). Because the Anonymous Autos system is currently manual,

- Type **M** in Manual or Computer.

Total Number of Records is for the maximum number of Vehicle Inventory Records in the VIR FILE. **Average Number of Records** is for the typical number of VIRs in the file at any one time.

- Type **500** in Total Number of Records.
- Press Tab.

- Type **200** in Average Number of Records.
- Press Tab

Index Elements are discussed in **5.3.1 Exploding and Indexing Data Stores**. Leave these fields blank for now.

- Press Pg Dn, and the second Data Store description screen appears.

Satisfies Requirements and **Associated Entities** are not addressed in this tutorial. Leave these fields blank.

- Press Pg Dn, and the third Data Store description screen appears.

The **Description** field on this last screen is for a free-form description of the data contained in this Data Store. Describe the Vehicle Inventory Record File in your own words, or use our description shown in Figure 4.7.2.

- Press F3 when you are done to save and return to your graph.

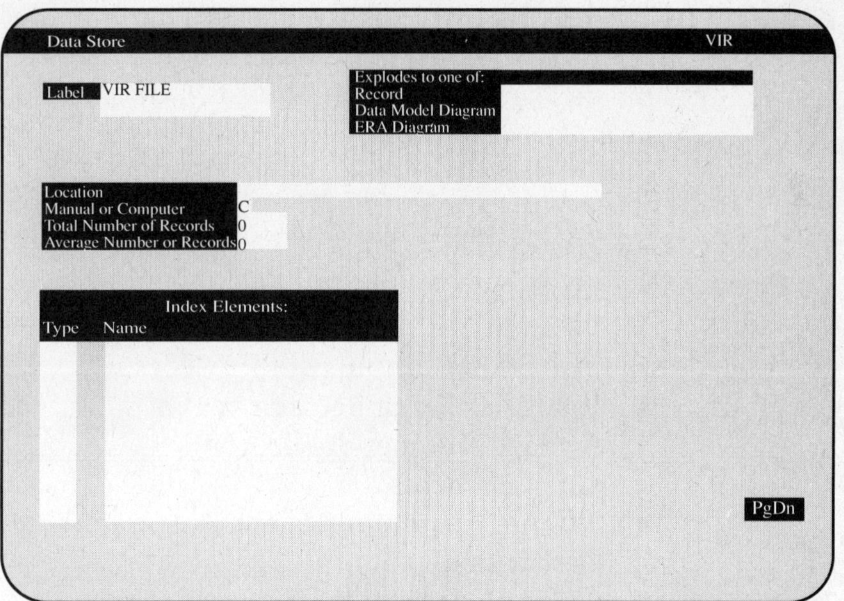

Figure 4.7.1
First Data Store Description Screen

Exercise 4.7.1

Describe the Data Store labeled INVOICE FILE on your AA SYSTEM DFD. Describe the Data Store on 1.0 INVENTORY SUBSYSTEM with the ID **VIR**, so Excelerator will be able to tie to it the existing Data Store description with that ID.

4.7.2 Printing Data Store Descriptions

As with the description of any graph component, when you've completed a Data Store description, you may send it to an output device for printing.

- Select **X XLDICTIONARY** from Excelerator's Main Menu.
- Select **DATA** from the XLDictionary Menu which appears.
- Select **S Data Store** from the Data Menu.
- Select **Output** from the Data Store Action Keypad.
- Press ↵ and the XLDictionary list of Data Stores appears.
- Select **All Entities on Selector List** with the mouse.
- Type Y when asked if input fields should be underlined.
- Select **Printer** as the output device, and the Data Store descriptions begin printing.

The reports Excelerator generates for your Data Stores closely resemble the Data Store description screens. Figure 4.7.2 shows the printed description of VIR FILE. Notice the Data Store ID appears near the top of the page followed by all the other fields from the description screens:

- Label
- Explodes To
- Location
- Manual or Computer
- Total Number of Records
- Average Number of Records
- Index Elements
- Satisfies Requirements and Associated Entities
- Description
- Audit fields from the bottom of the second Data Store description screen.

The lines on the report are the result of responding affirmatively to Excelerator's question, *Do you want output fields underlined?* during the printing process.

Figure 4.7.2
Printed Data Store Description for VIR FILE with Output Fields Underlined

DATE: 25-AUG-91 DATA STORE - OUTPUT PAGE 1
TIME: 18:52 NAME: * Excelerator / IS

TYPE Data Store NAME VIR FILE

Label VIR FILE

Explodes To One Of:
Record
Data Model Diagram
ERA Diagram

Location ACCOUNTING DEPARTMENT
Manual or Computer M
Total Number of Records 500
Average Number of Records 200

Index Elements:

Satisfies Requirement:
Type Name

Associated Entities
Type Name

Description

THE VIR DATA STORE CONTAINS THE RECORD PURCHASE DATA AND INSTALLED OPTIONS DATA NEEDED TO COMPLETE THE VIR FORM.

Modified By ANALYST
Added By ANALYST
Last Project Anonymous Autos
Locked By

Date Modified 910825
Date Added 910823
Date Locked 0

Changes 13
Lock Status

Excelerating Your Skills ... in Process Modeling

In working your way through this chapter, you have successfully completed the context, system, and one low-level Data Flow Diagram showing Rich Royce's existing information system at Anonymous Autos. You are now ready to develop the remaining two low-level DFDs on your own:

- 2.0 INVOICING SUBSYSTEM
- 3.0 REPORTING SUBSYSTEM

This is a good time to go back and re-read **3. The Anonymous Autos Project**. As you read, think about the processes taking place. The AA SYSTEM DFD, shown again on the opposite page, is also a valuable resource.

Develop and draw the two remaining low-level DFDs, then describe them and describe all previously undescribed components.

Leave the lowest level processes unexploded. You will get a chance to explode them to Structure Charts in ***Excelerating Your Skills in Structure Design*** on Page 274. For now, provide detailed process specifications in the Description field on the last Process description screen.

When you've finished, print out all the graphs, their descriptions, and their components' descriptions.

There is no right solution to this exercise. Everyone has different ideas about how best to model systems with Data Flow Diagrams.

5

IDENTIFYING DATA

There are two basic methods for developing the data requirements of an information system: bottom-up and top-down.

In the bottom-up method the analyst determines all of the Data Elements required for the system under development. These Data Elements are then aggregated into Records describing real-world entities and entity relationships.

The top-down method uses a data modeling technique, such as Entity-Relationship Diagramming, to examine relationships among entities described in the system. The entities are then examined for relevant attributes (Data Elements) and organized into physical Records.

In this chapter, the bottom-up method is used to develop the data requirements of a new information system for Anonymous Autos.

Records and Data Elements are identified and described. Relationships among Records are determined, and those relationships are expressed using Excelerator Record description screens.

5.1

Creating Records (RECs)

A **Record**, often referred to as a **table** in systems development, is a collection of attributes (known in Excelerator as Data Elements) describing a common **entity**. Records allow system designers to organize associated data into groups that can serve many different purposes. Records can be used in DFDs to represent Data Flows or Data Stores, in Entity-Relationship Diagrams to represent Data Entities or Data N-ary Relationships, in Structure Charts to represent Structure Graph Connections, and in Primitive Process Specifications.

Records are identified by examining the data requirements of a system. The Sales Invoice in Figure 5.1 shows much of the data required by the Anonymous Autos system.

The Sales Invoice itself is an entity about which information is captured. Every piece of data captured on the Sales Invoice relates to or describes the sale. Therefore, the Sales Invoice will become a Record in the Anonymous Autos system.

Records can be **nested** within one another. Look at the Sales Invoice again. There are several entities about which data is captured nested within the Sales Invoice.

The customer name, address, and telephone number are captured. This data comprises a Record because the customer name, customer address, and customer telephone number all describe and relate to a common entity: the customer.

There are other Records nested in the Sales Invoice. The new car, the trade-in, and the options are all entities comprising Records because data describing and relating to each is captured.

Another potential Record is the salesperson. Although only the salesperson's name is captured on the Sales Invoice, it would be useful to the accounting department to capture additional data like the salesperson's address, telephone number, and social security number.

Figure 5.1
Sales Invoice and Nested Entities Comprising Records

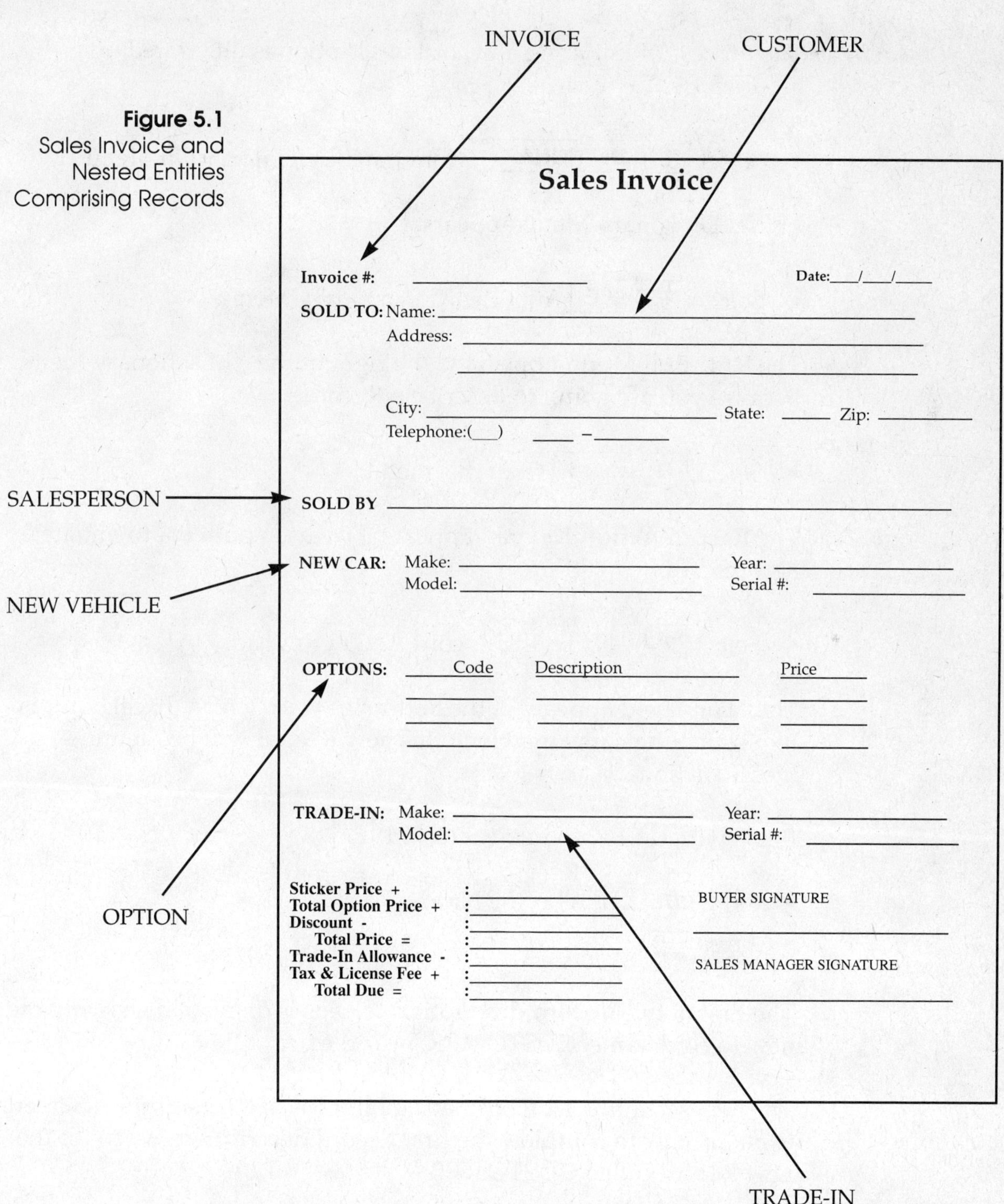
Sales Invoice

Invoice #: ______ Date: __/__/__

SOLD TO: Name: ______

Address: ______

City: ______ State: ____ Zip: ______

Telephone:( ) ____ – ______

SOLD BY ______

NEW CAR: Make: ______ Year: ______

Model: ______ Serial #: ______

OPTIONS:

Code	Description	Price

TRADE-IN: Make: ______ Year: ______

Model: ______ Serial #: ______

Sticker Price + : ______
Total Option Price + : ______
Discount - : ______
Total Price = : ______
Trade-In Allowance - : ______
Tax & License Fee + : ______
Total Due = : ______

BUYER SIGNATURE ______

SALES MANAGER SIGNATURE ______

5.1.1 Initiating Record description

The process of initiating a Record description is illustrated by Figure 5.1.1. To begin,

- Select **X XLDICTIONARY** from the Excelerator Main Menu.

The XLDictionary Menu appears.

- Select **REC/ELE** from the XLDictionary Menu.

The **REC/ELE Menu** appears to the right of the XLDictionary Menu. Because you are going to describe a Record,

- Select **R Record** from this menu.

The **Record Action Keypad** appears. Because you want to initiate a new Record description,

- Select **Add** from the Record Action Keypad.

The **Name** field appears at the bottom of your screen. Excelerator is requesting the name by which this new Record will be identified in the XLDictionary.

Begin with the Sales Invoice Record.

- Type **CUSTOMER** in the **Name** field.
- Press ⏎.

The first of two Record description screens is displayed showing the new Record name, CUSTOMER, near the top.

The next section, **5.1.2 Completing First Record Description Screen,** explains how to complete the first Record description screen for the new Record called CUSTOMER.

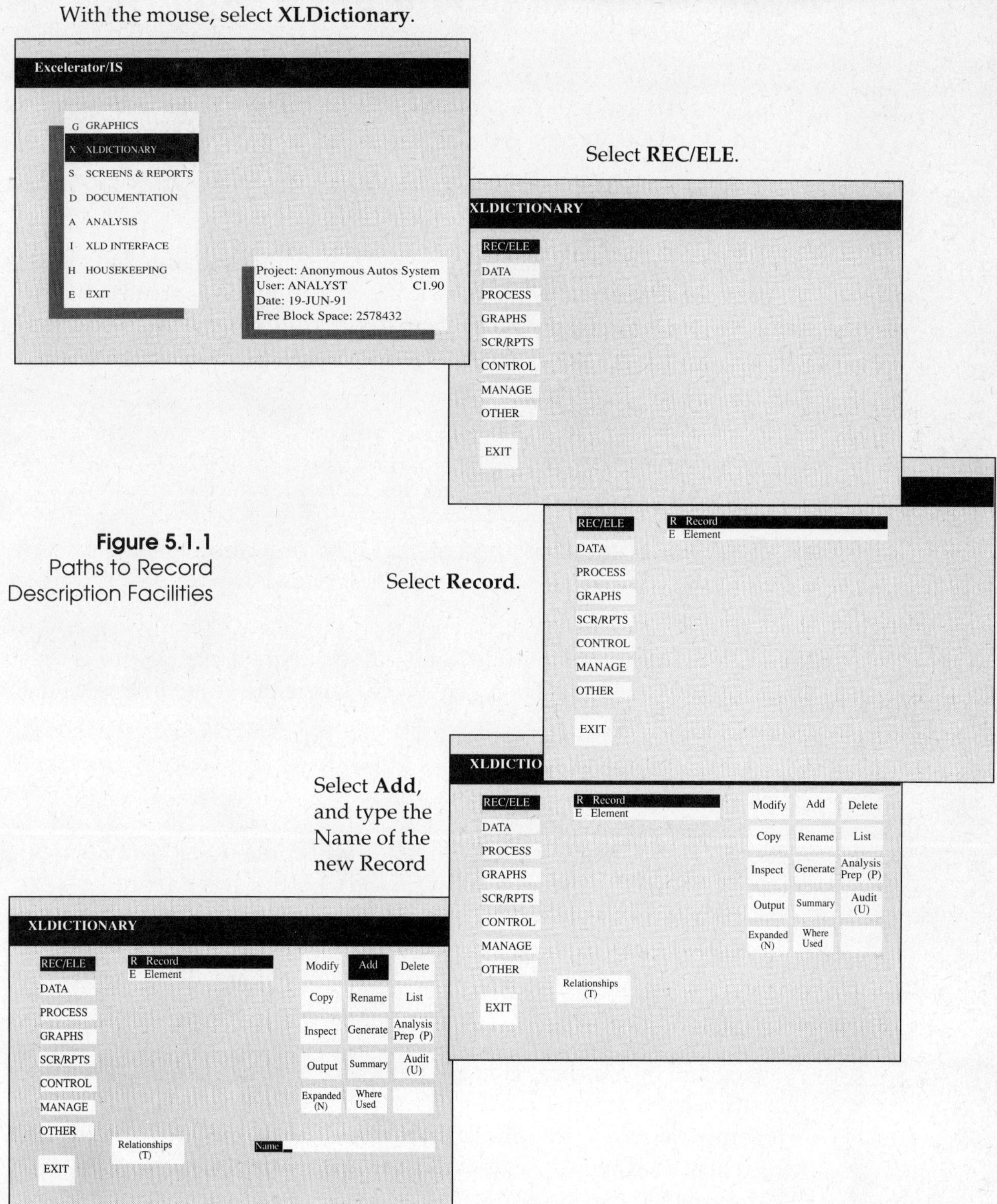

Figure 5.1.1
Paths to Record Description Facilities

5.1.2 Completing First Record Description Screen

If it is not on your screen, retrieve the description of CUSTOMER. Refer, if necessary, to **5.1.1 Initiating Record Description** and select **Modify** from the Record Action Keypad instead of **Add**.

The first Record description screen is shown in Figure 5.1.2.

The **Alternate Name** is an **alias** for the Record. It is a name by which users may sometimes refer to the data. At Anonymous Autos, customers are not commonly referred to by any other term. For this reason, leave the Alternate Name field blank.

- Press [Tab].

The **Definition** field is for a short description of the Record.

- Type `PURCHASER OF VEHICLE` in the Definition field.
- Press [Tab].

The **Normalized** field has a default value of **N**; when a Record is first created, it has not yet been normalized. Leave the value in this field alone for now.

- Press [Tab].

The **Name of Element or Record** fields will contain the Data Element and Record names contained within the CUSTOMER Record.

The Sales Invoice form in Figure 5.1 on Page 117 indicates that the customer name, address, and telephone number are all captured. This data should, therefore, be included in the CUSTOMER Record.

To facilitate flexible access to the database, people's names should be captured as two or three Data Elements: customer first name, customer middle name, and customer last name. Similarly, addresses are actually a group of several Data Elements: street address, city, state, zip code, and country (if applicable). Telephone numbers may also be broken up into two Data Elements: area code and telephone number.

Use Figure 5.1.2 as a guide, and enter the names of the Data Elements included in the CUSTOMER Record. Use Tab to move from field to field.

The field labeled **Occ** is used to indicate how many times each Data Element (E) or Record (R) **occurs** within the Record. This field should contain a value of **1** for each Data Element or Record contained in this Record.

The **Seq** fields may be used indicate the **sequence** in which Data Elements are to appear within the Record. The contents are sorted into a designated sequence after the Record is saved and retrieved. Unless you want to change the sequence of Data Elements in this Record, leave default values in the **Seq** column at **0**.

The **Sec-Keys** fields are used to designate secondary keys. (See **5.1.4 Identifying Key Data Elements**.) Leave these fields blank for now.

When you have finished entering the Data Elements in Figure 5.1.2,

- Press Pg Dn to go on to the second Record description screen, or
- Press F3 to save and exit the Record description.

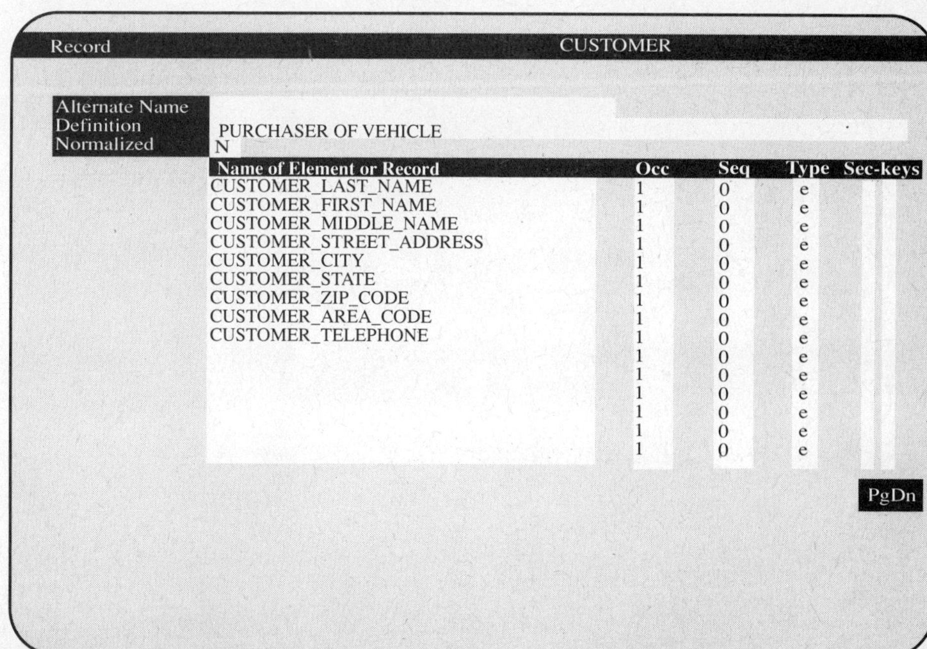

Figure 5.1.2 First Record Description Screen Completed for CUSTOMER

5.1.3 Completing Second Record Description Screen

If it is not already on your screen, retrieve your description of CUSTOMER. Refer, if necessary, to **5.1.1 Initiating Record Description** and select **Modify** from the Record Action Keypad instead of **Add**. When the first CUSTOMER Record description screen is displayed,

- Press Pg Dn .

The second description screen for CUSTOMER appears as shown in Figure 5.1.3.

Excelerator fills the **Record Length** field automatically once the Data Elements contained in the Record have been described. Leave the default value of **0** in the Record Length field.

As with many other Excelerator data structures, Records may satisfy User or Engineering Requirements. Records may also be associated with other Excelerator entities. As stated in **4.2.2 Completing DFD Description Screens**, these topics are not discussed in this tutorial.

- Press F3 to save and exit the Record description.

Exercise 5.1.3

You have just completed the CUSTOMER Record. Now create the OPTION, NEW VEHICLE, TRADE-IN, and SALESPERSON Records. Our versions of these Records appear in Figure 5.1.4.

Notice that all data captured by the Sales Invoice shown on Page 117 in Figure 5.1 is identified in the Records you create.

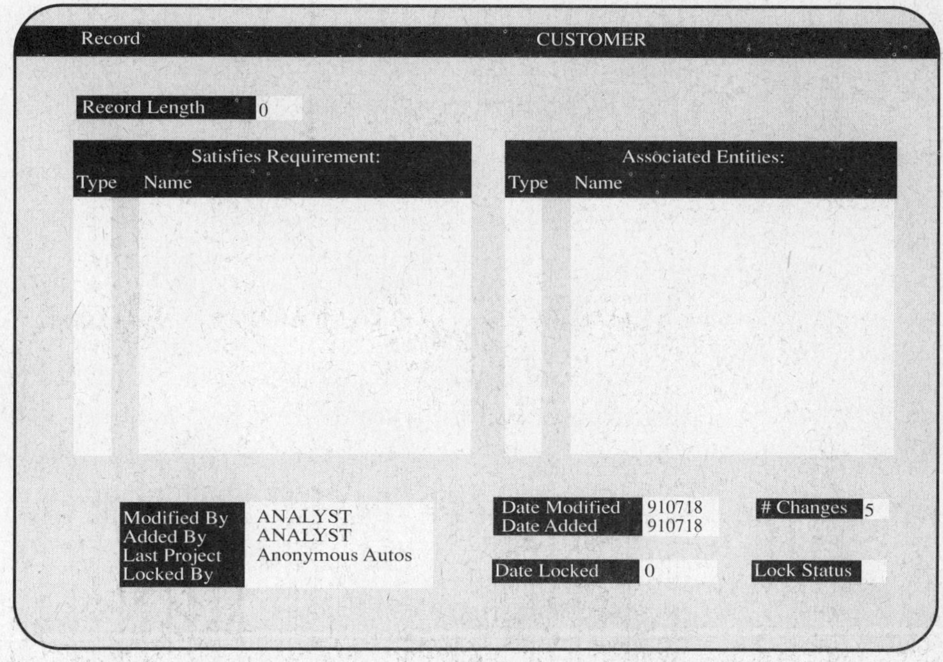

Figure 5.1.3 Second Record Description Screen for CUSTOMER

5.1.4 Identifying Key Data Elements

For a Record to be identifiable within the database, it must contain a Data Element value (or group of values) unique to that particular Record. Any Data Element value (or group of Data Element values) which uniquely identifies a Record is called a candidate key. Records may contain one or more candidate keys.

Once a candidate key has been designated as the primary identifier of the Record, it becomes the primary key. The primary key may be just one Data Element such as a serial number or invoice number. The primary key may be composed of several Data Elements comprising a unique identifier when combined. Keys composed of more than one Data Element are called concatenated keys.

Records may also have one or more secondary keys. These are alternative Data Elements used for accessing Records. Secondary keys are not necessarily unique. They may be used for accessing data when the primary key is not known or for Record sorting.

Think about candidate keys for the Records you have just created. The Records should look something like the ones shown in Figure 5.1.4.

OPTION has OPTION_CODE which uniquely identifies each option from all others in the database. NEW VEHICLE has NEW_VEHICLE_SERIAL_NUMBER which uniquely identifies the vehicle from all others. Similarly, TRADE-IN has TRADE-IN_SERIAL_NUMBER. SALESPERSON has SALESPERSON_LAST_NAME, SALESPERSON_FIRST_NAME, and SALESPERSON_MIDDLE_NAME, which together, will probably provide unique Record identification. SOCIAL_SECURITY_NUMBER is another SALESPERSON candidate key.

In the next section, **5.1.5 Designating Key Data Elements**, you will learn how to designate primary keys in Excelerator.

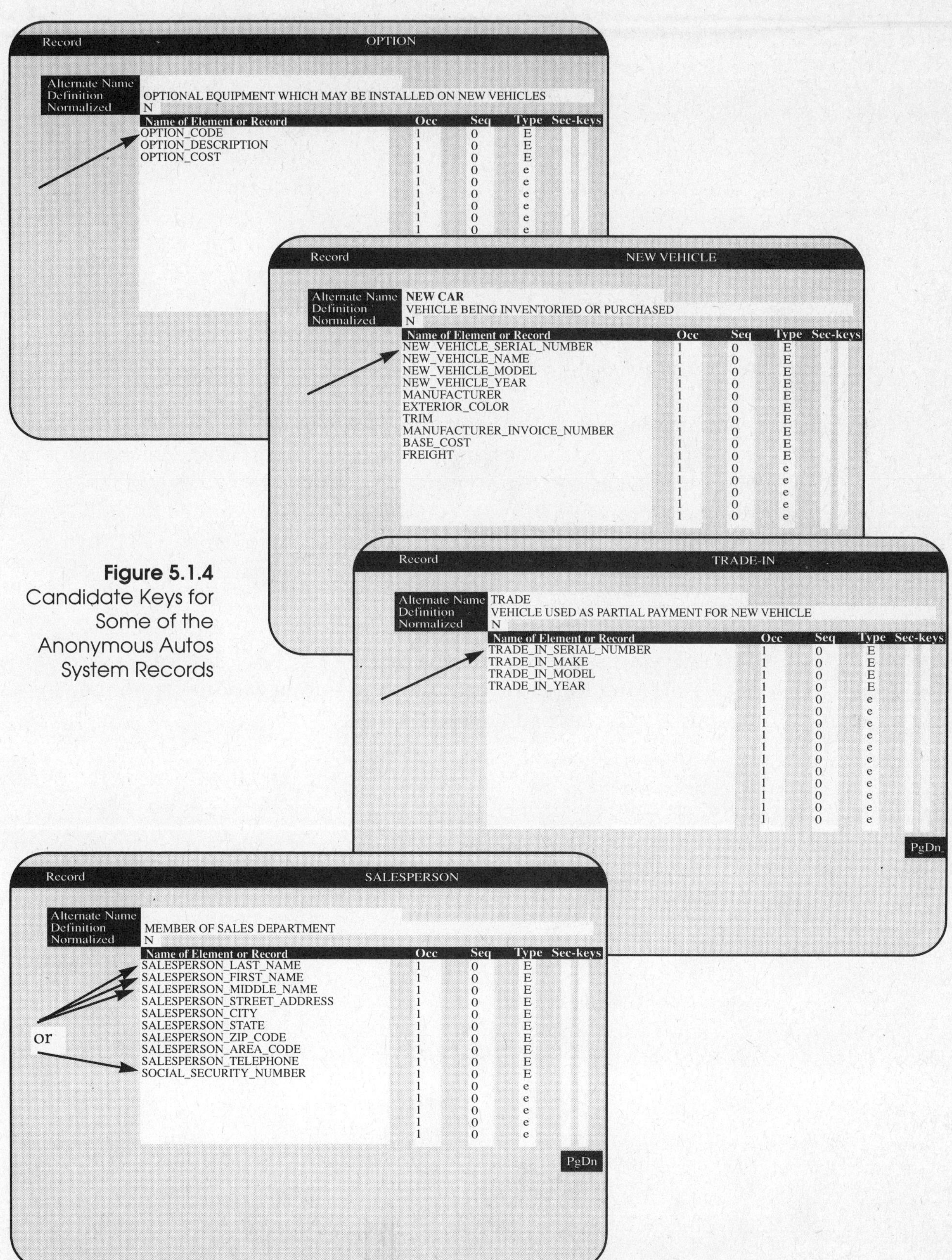

Figure 5.1.4 Candidate Keys for Some of the Anonymous Autos System Records

5.1.5 Designating Key Data Elements

Once key Data Elements have been identified, as with OPTION, NEW VEHICLE, and TRADE-IN, it is easy to designate them in Excelerator. On the first Record description screen, the letter **K** is placed in the **Type** field corresponding to the key Data Element.

For concatenated primary keys, the number **1** is placed in the Type field corresponding to the first member of the key, a **2** is placed in the Type field corresponding to the second member, etc. Excelerator allows concatenated keys with up to nine members, but that many are not recommended.

For secondary keys, the letter **S** is placed in the first **Sec-Keys** field corresponding to the designated Data Element. Secondary keys may be concatenated by identifying each member of the key with the numbers **1** through **9**. Two Sec-Keys fields are provided to accommodate the possibility that a single Data Element is both a secondary key by itself and a member of a concatenated secondary key.

Retrieve your description of the Record OPTION. If necessary, refer to **5.1.1 Initiating Record Description**, selecting **Modify** from the Record Action Keypad instead of **Add.**

Use the mouse or keyboard to position the insertion point in the Type field opposite OPTION_CODE,

- Press [Delete] to remove the E.
- Type **K** .

OPTION_CODE is now the designated primary key of OPTION as shown by the top screen in Figure 5.1.5.

Exercise 5.1.5

As shown in Figure 5.1.5, designate the primary keys of the NEW VEHICLE and TRADE-IN Records.

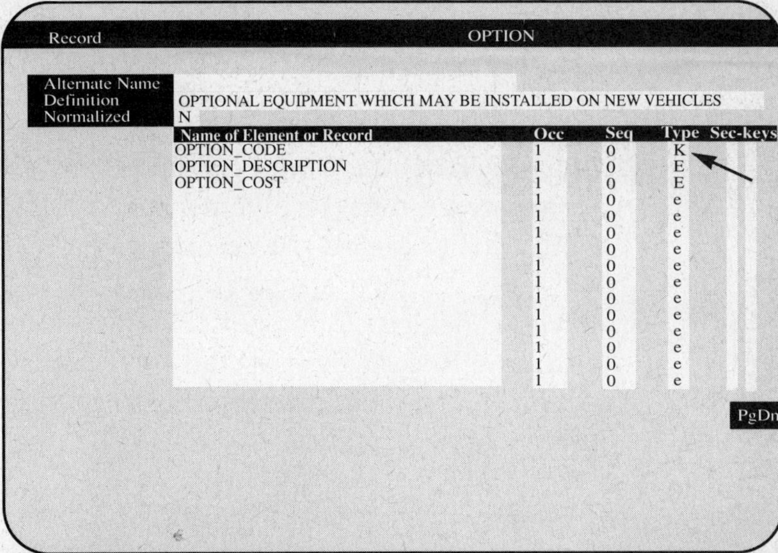

Record OPTION

Alternate Name
Definition OPTIONAL EQUIPMENT WHICH MAY BE INSTALLED ON NEW VEHICLES
Normalized N

Name of Element or Record	Occ	Seq	Type	Sec-keys
OPTION_CODE	1	0	K	
OPTION_DESCRIPTION	1	0	E	
OPTION_COST	1	0	E	
	1	0	e	
	1	0	e	
	1	0	e	
	1	0	e	
	1	0	e	
	1	0	e	
	1	0	e	
	1	0	e	
	1	0	e	
	1	0	e	
	1	0	e	
	1	0	e	

PgDn

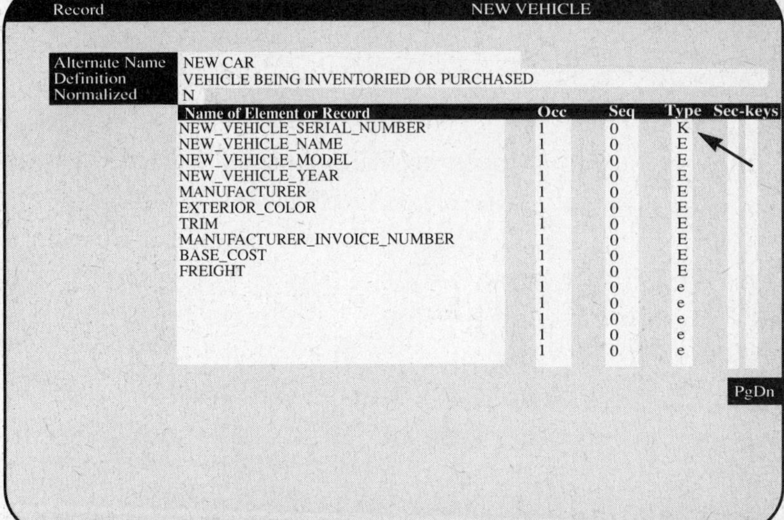

Record NEW VEHICLE

Alternate Name NEW CAR
Definition VEHICLE BEING INVENTORIED OR PURCHASED
Normalized N

Name of Element or Record	Occ	Seq	Type	Sec-keys
NEW_VEHICLE_SERIAL_NUMBER	1	0	K	
NEW_VEHICLE_NAME	1	0	E	
NEW_VEHICLE_MODEL	1	0	E	
NEW_VEHICLE_YEAR	1	0	E	
MANUFACTURER	1	0	E	
EXTERIOR_COLOR	1	0	E	
TRIM	1	0	E	
MANUFACTURER_INVOICE_NUMBER	1	0	E	
BASE_COST	1	0	E	
FREIGHT	1	0	E	
	1	0	e	
	1	0	e	
	1	0	e	
	1	0	e	
	1	0	e	

PgDn

Figure 5.1.5 Designated Primary Keys for Some of Anonymous Autos System Records

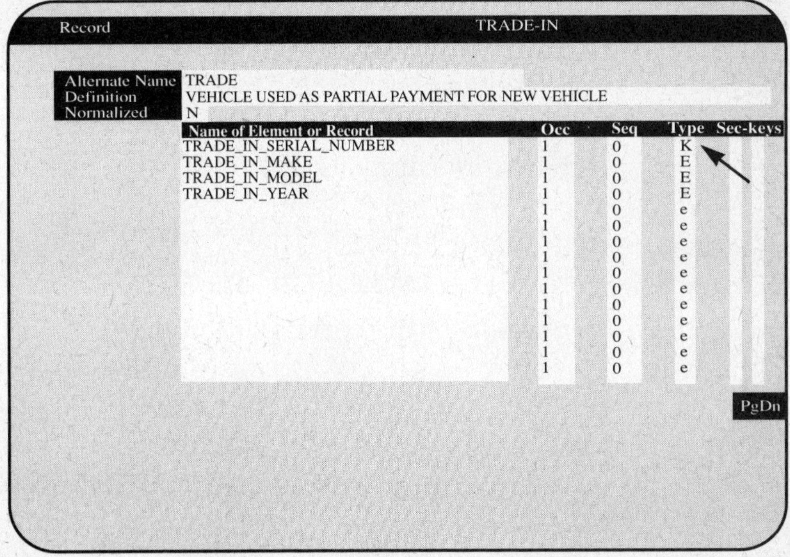

Record TRADE-IN

Alternate Name TRADE
Definition VEHICLE USED AS PARTIAL PAYMENT FOR NEW VEHICLE
Normalized N

Name of Element or Record	Occ	Seq	Type	Sec-keys
TRADE_IN_SERIAL_NUMBER	1	0	K	
TRADE_IN_MAKE	1	0	E	
TRADE_IN_MODEL	1	0	E	
TRADE_IN_YEAR	1	0	E	
	1	0	e	
	1	0	e	
	1	0	e	
	1	0	e	
	1	0	e	
	1	0	e	
	1	0	e	
	1	0	e	
	1	0	e	
	1	0	e	
	1	0	e	

PgDn

5.1.6 Inventing Key Data Elements

Not all Records contain candidate keys. When this happens, a new Data Element must be invented to identify the Record. The CUSTOMER Record is an example of a Record with no candidate key.

Retrieve the description of CUSTOMER. If necessary, refer to **5.1.1 Initiating Record Description** and select **Modify** from the Record Action Keypad instead of **Add**. It should resemble the screen shown in Figure 5.1.6a.

Examine the Data Elements listed on the Record. Do any of them uniquely identify the Record? CUSTOMER_LAST_NAME is a tempting key, but is it possible for more than one customer to have the same last name? Of course. In fact, it's likely. This means that CUSTOMER_LAST_NAME is not a unique identifier.

How about creating a concatenated primary key composed of the CUSTOMER_LAST_NAME, CUSTOMER_FIRST_NAME, and CUSTOMER_MIDDLE_NAME? Although it is unlikely, it is possible for Anonymous Autos to have more than one customer with the same first, middle and last names. This concatenated key might not uniquely identify the Record either. Because address and telephone are subject to change, they are too unstable to be used as key Data Elements. Since nothing is left, it is necessary to invent a candidate key.

- Place the insertion point on the C in CUSTOMER_ LAST_NAME.
- Press and hold F1.
- Press Ins.

A blank line appears above CUSTOMER_LAST_NAME.

- Release F1.
- Type **CUSTOMER_ID_NUMBER** on the new line.
- Type **K** in the corresponding **Type** field.

As shown in Figure 5.1.6b, CUSTOMER_ID_NUMBER is now the primary key for CUSTOMER. Creating identification numbers is a standard method for keying Records with no natural candidate keys.

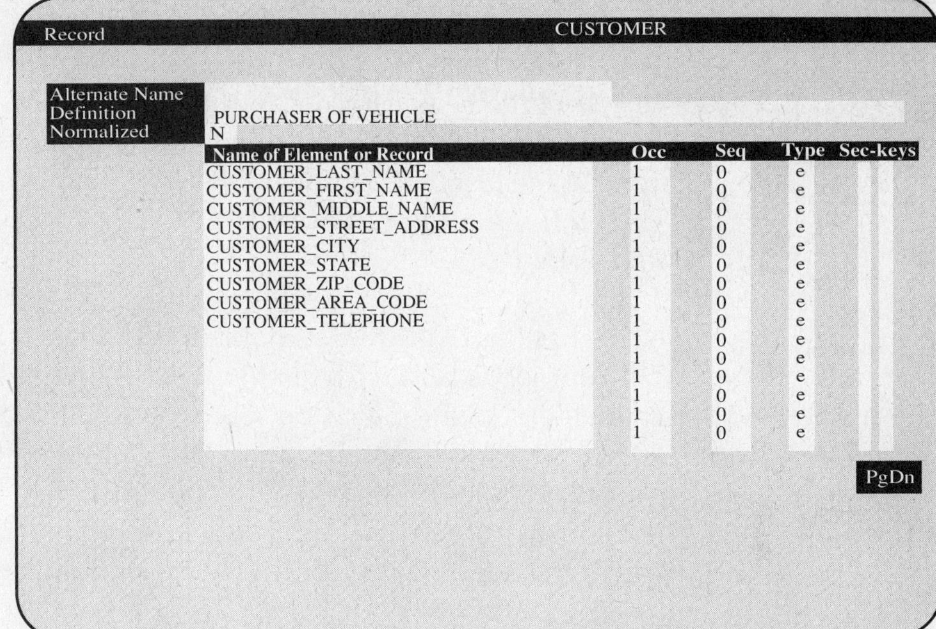

Figure 5.1.6a
CUSTOMER Record Description with No Candidate Key

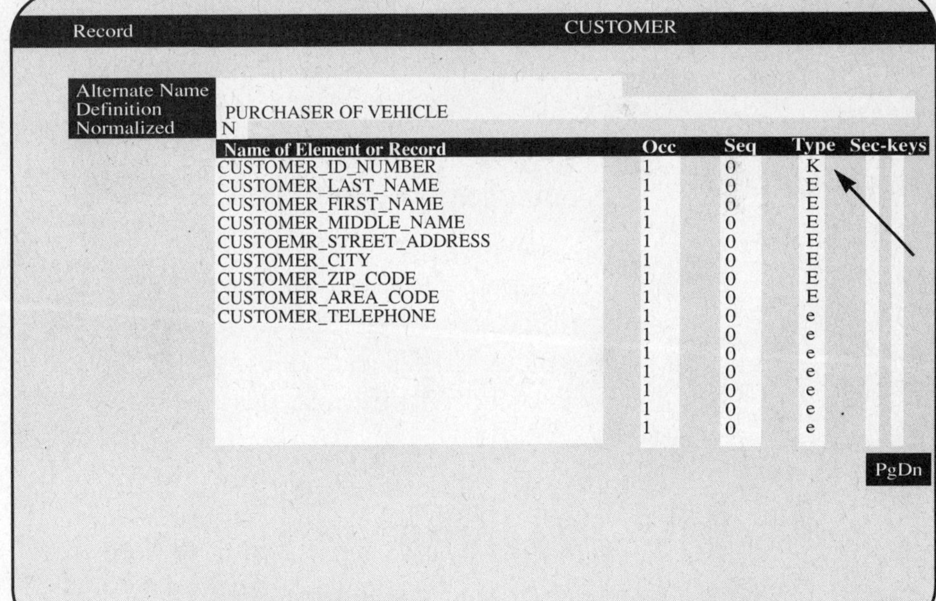

Figure 5.1.6b
CUSTOMER Record Description with a Designated Primary Key

Exercise 5.1.6

Invent and designate a primary key for the Record SALESPERSON.

5.1.7 Introducing Record Relationships

The Sales Invoice is a Record in the Anonymous Autos system. This Record contains other Records nested within it as shown in Figure 5.1.7a. In the last few sections, you have defined these nested Records: CUSTOMER, SALESPERSON, NEW VEHICLE, OPTION, and TRADE-IN.

The nested Records are clearly related to the Sales Invoice in some way. Your job is two-fold. First you must understand the nature of the relationship or cardinality between Records. In other words, you need to figure out how many instances of one Record there are for each instance of another. (For example, how many NEW VEHICLES are there for each Sales Invoice? There is only one.) Secondly, you must express the relationship using foreign keys.

In order to begin the process of defining the relationship between Records, the Sales Invoice Record must be created. Refer to **5.1.1 Initiating Record Description**, and initiate the description of a Record called INVOICE.

- Type `SALES INVOICE` in the Alternate **Name** field.
- Type `RECORD OF NEW VEHICLE SALE` in the **Definition** field.

Enter the element names displayed under Name of Element or Record on the first Record description screen as shown in Figure 5.1.7b. None of these Elements are calculated values, nor are they members of Records nested within the Sales Invoice.

The next section, **5.1.8 Determining Cardinality Between Records**, explains the first step involved in relating other Records to INVOICE, and relating INVOICE to other Records.

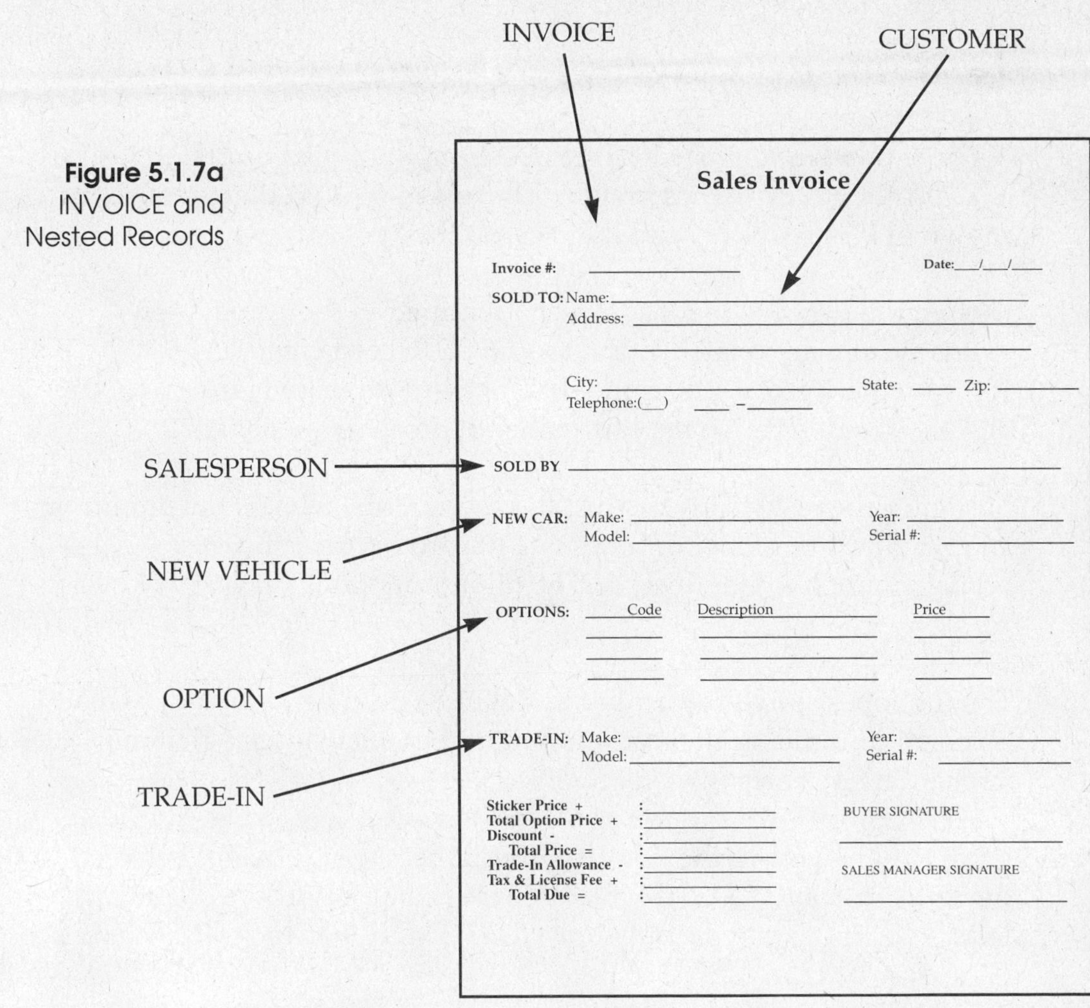

Sales Invoice

Invoice #: ________ **Date:** ___/___/___

SOLD TO: Name: ________
Address: ________
____
City: ________ State: ____ Zip: ________
Telephone:(___) ___ – ____

SOLD BY ________

NEW CAR: Make: ________ Year: ________
Model: ________ Serial #: ________

OPTIONS: Code Description Price

TRADE-IN: Make: ________ Year: ________
Model: ________ Serial #: ________

Sticker Price + : ________
Total Option Price + : ________
Discount - : ________
Total Price = : ________
Trade-In Allowance - : ________
Tax & License Fee + : ________
Total Due = : ________

BUYER SIGNATURE ________

SALES MANAGER SIGNATURE ________

Figure 5.1.7a
INVOICE and Nested Records

Record INVOICE

Alternate Name SALES INVOICE
Definition RECORD OF NEW VEHICLE SALE
Normalized N

Name of Element or Record	Occ	Seq	Type	Sec-keys
INVOICE_NUMBER	1	0	K	
INVOICE_DATE	1	0	E	
TRADE_IN_ALLOWANCE	1	0	E	
DISCOUNT	1	0	E	
TAX_RATE	1	0	E	
LICENSE_FEE	1	0	E	
CUSTOMER_SIGNATURE	1	0	E	
SALES_MANAGER_SIGNATURE	1	0	E	
	1	0	e	
	1	0	e	
	1	0	e	
	1	0	e	
	1	0	e	
	1	0	e	
	1	0	e	

PgDn

Figure 5.1.7b
First Record Description Screen of INVOICE with Non-relational and Non-Calculated Data Elements

5.1.8 Determining Cardinality Between Records

It's time to ask and answer some questions about Record relationships in the Anonymous Autos system. The questions and their answers are shown in Figure 5.1.8. Read them carefully.

Each of the Records that have been identified in the Anonymous Autos system are related to the INVOICE Record created in **5.1.7 Introducing Record Relationships**. The questions in Figure 5.1.8 are designed to determine the cardinality of those relationships.

Each question asks, How many? In other words, what is the minimum and maximum number of times one Record occurs for each occurrence of another Record? The minimum value may be as low as zero.

The first question in the list in Figure 5.1.8 could be restated as, what is the minimum and the maximum number of customers that may appear on one Sales Invoice?

From the answers to the first two questions, the cardinality between the INVOICE and CUSTOMER Records can be determined: For each INVOICE, there may be only **one** CUSTOMER. For each CUSTOMER, there may be **many** INVOICEs.

Hint
This is an important concept and sometimes difficult to understand at first. Take some extra time with the exercise to become comfortable with cardinality.

Here is another way to state the relationship: There is a **one-to-many** relationship between INVOICE and CUSTOMER. Therefore, we would say that the cardinality of the relationship is one-to-many.

In stating the cardinality between Records, use the maximum number of occurrences possible for each end of the relationship. For example, there can be one and only **one** CUSTOMER for each INVOICE, as stated by the answer to the second question in Figure 5.1.8. Because there may be between one and **many** INVOICEs for each CUSTOMER, the result is a **one-to-many** relationship.

Figure 5.1.8
Determining the Cardinality of Record Relationships

Question	Answer
For each INVOICE, how many CUSTOMERs are there? *Even if two names appear on the Sales Invoice, Anonymous Autos will recognize the two names as one customer.*	One
For each CUSTOMER, how many INVOICEs are there? *A person does not become a customer until he/she buys a car, and a customer may buy more than one car.*	One to Many
For each INVOICE, how many SALESPERSONs are there? *A sales invoice must contain the name of one and only one salesperson.*	One
For each SALESPERSON, how many INVOICEs are there? *A salesperson may not yet have sold any cars, or a salesperson may have sold many cars.*	Zero to Many
For each INVOICE, how many NEW VEHICLEs are there? *One and only one new vehicle is sold per sales invoice.*	One
For each NEW VEHICLE, how many INVOICEs are there? *A new vehicle may be in inventory which has not yet been sold. Once sold, though, a new vehicle will appear on only one sales invoice.*	Zero to One
For each INVOICE, how many OPTIONs are there? *A Sales Invoice may show no options or it may show one or more options.*	Zero to Many
For each OPTION, how many INVOICEs are there? *An option may not be shown on any Sales Invoices or it may be shown on one or more.*	Zero to Many
For each INVOICE, how may TRADE-INs are there? *There may be no more than one trade-in per invoice.*	Zero to One
For each TRADE-IN, how many INVOICEs are there? *A vehicle may be traded in on a new car, then sold to someone else who comes back to Anonymous Autos and trades it in again.*	One to Many

Exercise 5.1.8

Using the technique described in this section, determine the cardinality between the remaining Records in the Anonymous Autos system. On a piece of paper, record each relationship as one-to-one, one-to-many, or many-to-many.

5.1.9 Defining One-to-One & One-to-Many Relationships

Whenever the primary key in a Record occurs as a non-key Element in another Record, it becomes a foreign key in the second Record. Foreign keys are used to define and facilitate the relationships you discovered in **5.1.8 Determining Cardinality Between Records**.

When you add foreign keys to Records, Excelerator is able to identify them by checking each non-key Data Element to see if it is designated as a primary key in another Record. Once Excelerator has identified the foreign keys in a Record, it uses them to determine Record relationships. Figure 5.1.9a illustrates Excelerator's use of foreign keys to define one-to-one and one-to-many relationships between Records.

In Exercise 5.1.8, three one-to-many relationships should have been identified: TRADE-IN to INVOICE, CUSTOMER to INVOICE, and SALESPERSON to INVOICE. The many end of each of these relationships is at INVOICE. According to Figure 5.1.9a, this means that the primary keys of TRADE-IN, CUSTOMER, and SALES-PERSON should appear as non-key Elements or foreign keys in INVOICE.

In Exercise 5.1.8 you should have found a one-to-one relationship between NEW VEHICLE and INVOICE. According to Figure 5.1.9a, this means the primary key of NEW VEHICLE must appear as a non-key Element or foreign key in INVOICE. Similarly, the primary key of INVOICE must appear as a foreign key in NEW VEHICLE.

Exercise 5.1.9

Add the four foreign keys discussed above to INVOICE. The result should look like Figure 5.1.9b. Then retrieve the Record NEW VEHICLE, and add the foreign key discussed in this section to relate NEW VEHICLE to INVOICE.

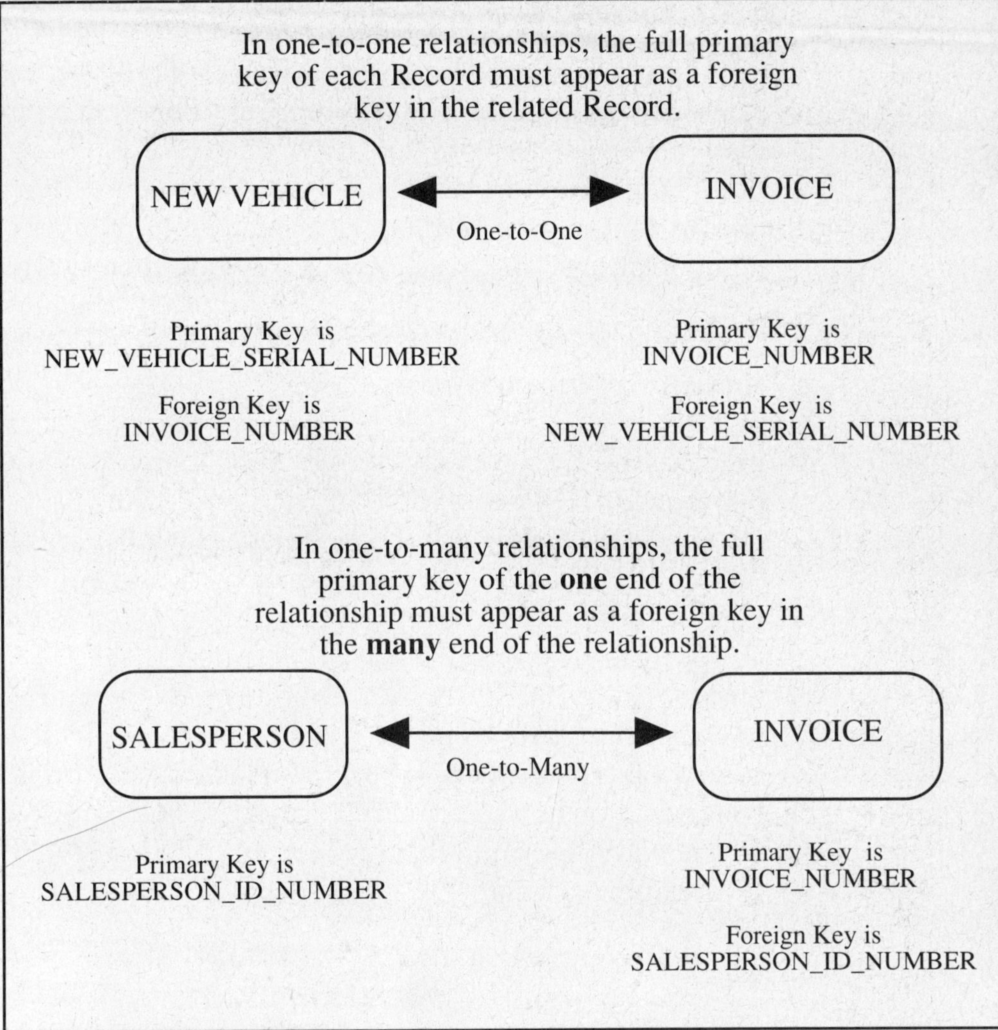

Figure 5.1.9a Using Foreign Keys to Define Record Relationships

Record INVOICE

Alternate Name SALES INVOICE
Definition RECORD OF NEW VEHICLE SALE
Normalized N

Name of Element or Record	Occ	Seq	Type	Sec-keys
INVOICE_NUMBER	1	0	K	
INVOICE_DATE	1	0	E	
TRADE_IN_ALLOWANCE	1	0	E	
DISCOUNT	1	0	E	
TAX_RATE	1	0	E	
LICENSE_FEE	1	0	E	
CUSTOMER_SIGNATURE	1	0	E	
SALES_MANAGER_SIGNATURE	1	0	E	
CUSTOMER_ID_NUMBER	1	0	E	
SALESPERSON_ID_NUMBER	1	0	E	
NEW_VEHICLE_SERIAL_NUMBER	1	0	E	
TRADE_IN_SERIAL_NUMBER	1	0	E	
	1	0	e	
	1	0	e	
	1	0	e	

PgDn

Figure 5.1.9b First Record Description Screen Completed for INVOICE

5.1.10 Defining Many-to-Many Relationships

Many-to-many relationships require a different description technique than one-to-one and one-to-many relationships. Foreign keys are not used. Instead, a new relational Record is created. This relational Record contains the primary keys from each member of the many-to-many relationship. These primary keys are then concatenated to form the primary key of the relational Record. Relational Records may seem mysterious at first, but after you've created one for yourself, the concept will become clearer.

In Exercise 5.1.8, you may have found a many-to-many relationship between OPTION and NEW VEHICLE by asking questions about those two Records similar to the ones shown in Figure 5.1.8. Many NEW VEHICLEs may have the same OPTION, and many OPTIONs may be installed on the same VEHICLE.

Figure 5.1.10a illustrates the creation of a relational Record designed to define the many-to-many relationship between OPTION and NEW VEHICLE. The primary key of the relational Record is the concatenation of the primary keys of OPTION and NEW VEHICLE: OPTION_CODE and NEW_ VEHICLE_SERIAL_NUMBER. We call this relational Record INSTALLED OPTION.

Exercise 5.1.10

Initiate a new Record called INSTALLED OPTION, referring to **5.1.1 Initiating Record Description** if necessary. Use Figure 5.1.10b as a guide to creating this relational Record. It may also be helpful to review **5.1.5 Designating Key Data Elements** for a refresher on designating concatenated keys.

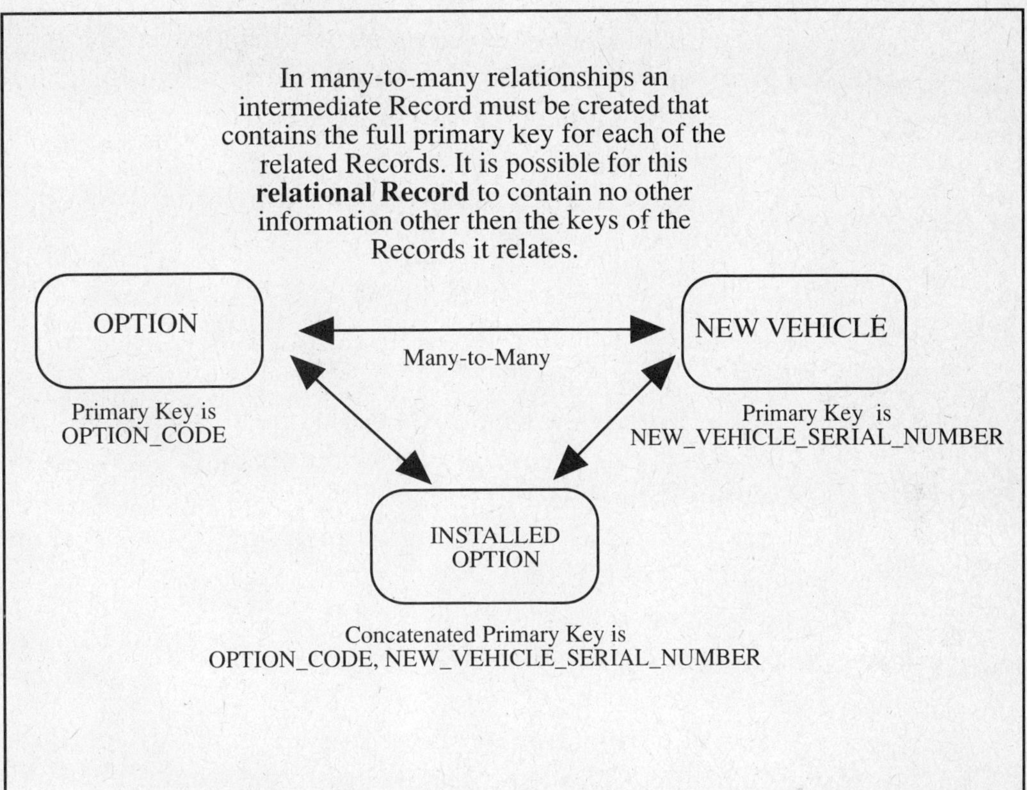

Figure 5.1.10a Using Relational Records to Define Many-to-Many Relationships

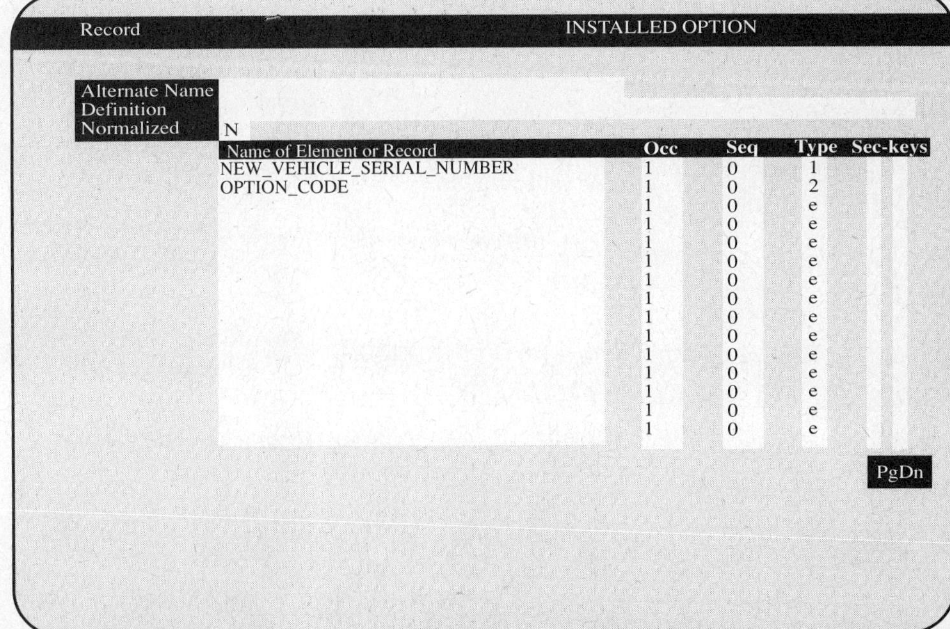

Figure 5.1.10b INSTALLED OPTION Defining the Many-to-Many Relationship Between NEW VEHICLE and OPTION

5.1.11 Printing Record descriptions

As with all Excelerator data structures, Record descriptions may be printed. The procedure closely resembles that for printing other descriptions. As shown in Figure 5.1.11a,

- Select **X XLDICTIONARY** from Excelerator's Main Menu.
- Select **REC/ELE** from the XLDictionary Menu which appears.
- Select **R Record** from the REC/ELE Menu.
- Select **Output** from the Record Action Keypad.

A prompt appears near the bottom of the screen asking for the **Name Range** of the Record(s) you wish to print. A name entered in the Name Range field must exactly match one of the Records defined in the XLDictionary. Defining name ranges is discussed in **4.2.3 Printing DFD Descriptions** .

- Press ↵.

The XLDictionary list of Records appears. A Record description may be printed by selecting a Record name from the list. All of the Records on the list are printed by selecting **All Entities on Selector List**.

- Select **CUSTOMER** with the mouse.

Excelerator asks where you want the output sent, as shown in Figure 5.1.11b. (Excelerator's Record description report is wide, so be sure to select condensed print if you are using a dot matrix printer. Laser printers need no special adjustment to print the report correctly.)

- Select **Printer** with the mouse, and the Record description is printed.

The printed Record description for CUSTOMER is shown in Figure 5.1.11c. The information in this report can be used to examine the structure of Records in the XLDictionary.

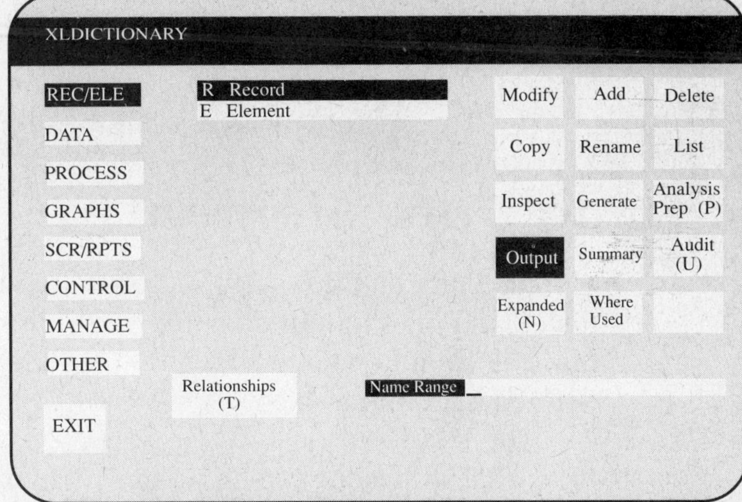

Figure 5.1.11a
Output Selection on XLDictionary Record Action Keypad

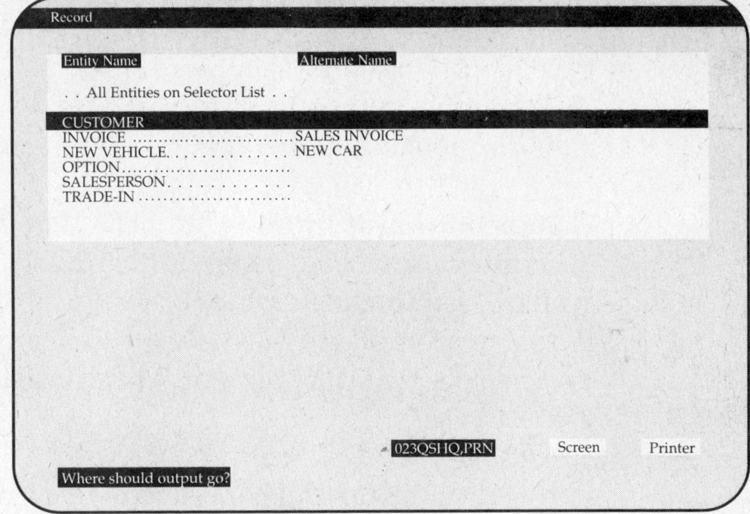

Figure 5.1.11b
List of Records Available for Output with CUSTOMER Selected

Figure 5.1.11c
Printed Record Output for CUSTOMER (Condensed Print Selected)

DATE: 25-JUL-91
TIME: 08: 33

RECORD - EXPLOSION
NAME: CUSTOMER

PAGE 1
Exceleratpr/IS

NAME: CUSTOMER
ALIAS:

DEFINITION:
PURCHASER OF VEHICLE N

ELEMENT/RECOR	OFF	OCC	TYPE	LEN	DEFINITION
CUSTOMER_ID_NUMBER	000	001	K		
CUSTOMER_LAST_NAME	000	001	E		
CUSTOMER_FIRST_NAME	000	001	E		
CUSTOMER_MIDDLE_NAME	000	001	E		
CUSTOMER_STREET_ADDRESS	000	001	E		
CUSTOMER_CITY	000	001	E		
CUSTOMER_STATE	000	001	E		
CUSTOMER_ZIP_CODE	000	001	E		
CUSTOMER_AREA_CODE	000	001	E		
CUSTOMER_TELEPHONE	000	001	E		

5.2

Describing Data Elements (ELEs)

A Data Element, often referred to as an attribute or field in systems development, is a defined value. It is one piece of data such as a serial number. Data Elements allow system designers to capture specifically defined data required by the system.

Figure 5.2 shows the screen sequence involved in accessing Excelerator's Data Element description facilities.

Excelerator's Data Element description facilities are comprehensive, including the definition of format, storage type, edit rules, length, and an indication of whether the Data Element is base or derived.

Completion of the prompt and header portions of the Data Element description can increase the standardization of display in the new system. Defining prompts and headers allows the programmer to use the same prompt and header each time a report or screen is designed using a specific Data Element. This consistency makes the system easier to use.

In this section you will complete the description of Data Elements named in the Records created in the previous section, thereby completing the definition of physical data requirements for the new Anonymous Autos system.

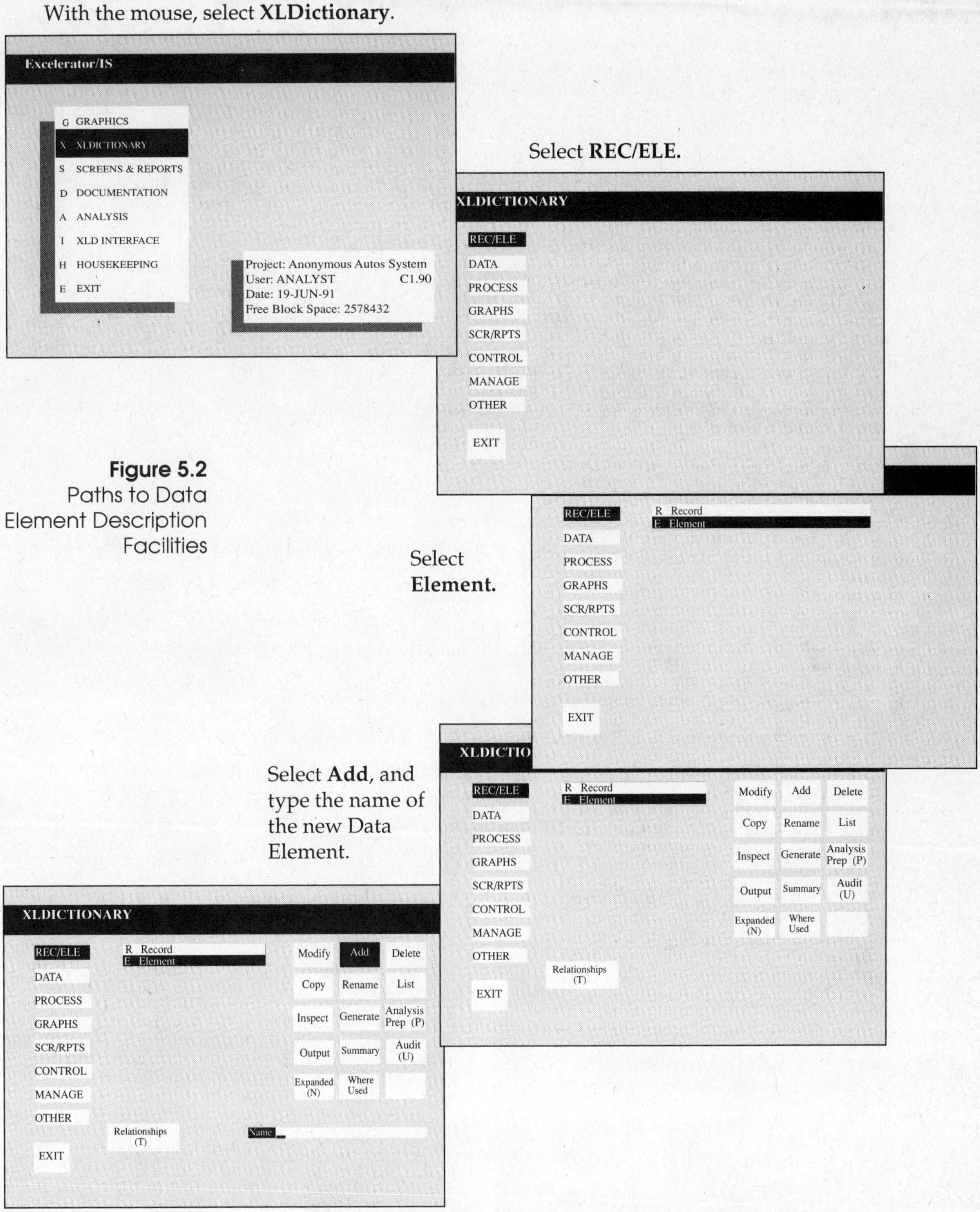

With the mouse, select **XLDictionary**.

Select **REC/ELE.**

Select **Element.**

Select **Add**, and type the name of the new Data Element.

Figure 5.2
Paths to Data Element Description Facilities

5.2.1 Initiating Data Element Description

As shown in Figure 5.2.1a, to begin the Data Element description process,

- Select **X XLDICTIONARY** from Excelerator's Main Menu.

The XLDictionary Menu is displayed.

- Select **REC/ELE** from the XLDictionary Menu.

The REC/ELE Menu appears to the right of the XLDictionary Menu. Because you want to describe a Data Element,

- Select **E Element** from this menu.

The **Element Action Keypad** appears. Because we want to begin a new Element,

- Select **Add** from the Element Action Keypad, as shown in Figure 5.2.1b.

The **Name** field is displayed at the bottom of your screen. Excelerator is requesting the name by which this new Data Element will be identified in the XLDictionary. Begin with CUSTOMER_LAST_NAME.

- Type **CUSTOMER_LAST_NAME** in the **Name** field.
- Press ↵.

The first of three Data Element description screens appears showing the new Data Element name, CUSTOMER_LAST_NAME, near the top as shown in Figure 5.2.1c.

In the next section, **5.2.2 Defining Data Element Attributes**, you will complete the Alternate Name and Definition of CUSTOMER_LAST_NAME.

Figure 5.2.1a
Main Menu

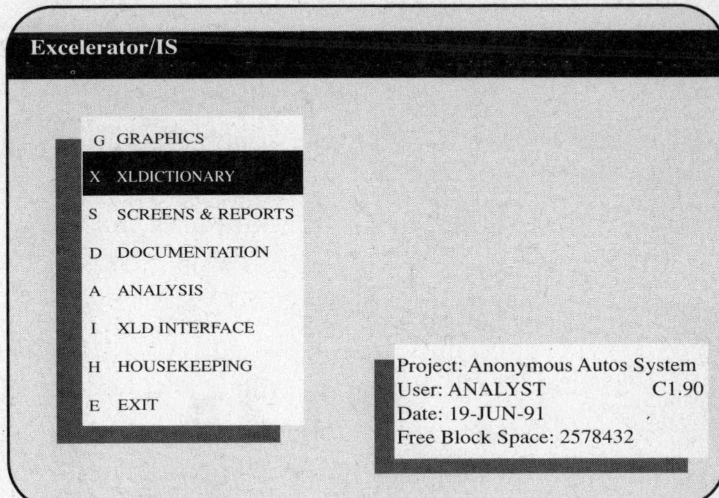

Figure 5.2.1b
XLDictionary Menu and Element Action Keypad

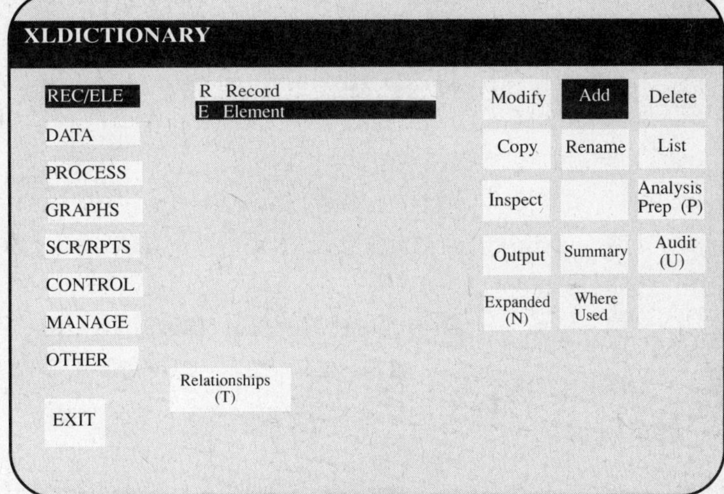

Figure 5.2.1c
First Data Element Description Screen

Element CUSTOMER LAST NAME

Alternate Names

Definition

Input Format
Output Format
Edit Rules
Storage Type C
Characters left of decimal 0 Characters right of decimal 0

Default
Prompt
Column Header
Short Header
Base or Derived B
Data Class
Source

PgDn

5.2.2 Defining Data Element Attributes

Figure 5.2.2 explains each Data Element attribute provided by the Excelerator Data Element description screens. Read Figure 5.2.2 carefully; these attributes can make the description of your data very specific.

When defining Data Element attributes, avoid Storage Types other than C (character) unless you want to do some research in the *Excelerator Facilities & Functions Guide* on Page 4-35. Using other storage types will cause you grief if you do not understand how to use them properly. In this tutorial we will be dealing exclusively with the character storage type.

Retrieve your description of CUSTOMER_LAST_NAME. If necessary, refer to **5.2.1 Initiating Data Element Description**, selecting **Modify** instead of **Add** from the Element Action Keypad.

Use [Tab] to move from field to field on the first Data Element description screen for CUSTOMER_LAST_ NAME.

- Type **`BUYER_LAST_NAME`** in the **Alternate Names** field.
- Type **`THIS IS THE CUSTOMER'S LEGAL LAST NAME`** in the **Definition** field.

The next section, **5.2.3 Defining Input and Output Formats**, will guide you through completing the next two fields on the first Data Element description screen.

Figure 5.2.2 Element Description Screen Attributes

Field Name	Size	Description
Alternate Names	32 X 3	User defined aliases for this Element.Three aliases are possible.
Definition	60	Short description of this Element.
Input Format	25	Valid picture clause or edit mask for input value.
Output Format	25	Valid picture clause or edit mask for output value.
Edit Rules	60	Input criteria for filtering input into fields linked to this Element. Edit rules can be for specific or non-specific characters.
Storage Type	1	**C**(character), **B**(binary), **D**(date), **F**(float), **P**(packed), **V**(variable character), **M**(time), **I**(bit), or **R**(picture).
Characters Left of Decimal	3	Digits to the left of the decimal are for packed or picture fields, or this figure indicates the number of characters in the Element.
Character Right of Decimal	2	Digits to the right of the decimal. This is used for packed or decimal picture Elements only.
Default	32	System-generated value displayed for this Element. This value is user-defined. It will display if no other value is indicated for this Element.
Prompt	20	Default prompt and input field header for Element. This is the prompt that should appear on the input screen.
Column Header	47	Default column header for Element in reports and displays.
Short Header	15	Default short column header for Element in reports and displays.
Base or Derived of	1	B(base) Element is primitive or basic; D(derived) Element is result some processing of data.
Data Class	32	User-Assigned data grouping.
Source	32	Internal or external point of origin for this Element.
Satisfies Requirement: Type	3x10	Three-letter code of an Engineering or User Requirement associated with this Element.
Satisfies Requirement: Name	32x10	Identifier of an Engineering or User Requirement associated with with this Element.
Associated Entities: Type	3x10	Three-letter code of an entity associated with this Element.
Associated Entities: Name	32x10	Identifier of an entity associated with this Element.
Description	70x60	Detailed, free-form description of this Element. You may notice that this field has 60 input lines. They are contained in a scroll block.

Derived from *Excelerator Data & Reports Reference Guide* with permission from Intersolv, Inc.

5.2.3 Defining Input and Output Formats

Input and output formats tell the system what type of data to accept and how to display data.

An Element defined with an input format of XXX (alphanumeric) is three characters long. It can contain both letters and numbers. An Element with an input format of 999 (numbers only) is three characters long and must be a numeric value. AAA (alpha only) mandates a three-character alpha value. An attempt to enter a character type not consistent with the input format results in an error message.

Although the input format may consist of a generic string of numbers, it is desirable for the output format to be in a familiar form. For example, dates are usually stored in the computer as a string of six or eight numeric characters such as 010191 or 01011991, the input format being 999999 or 99999999.

If you were to output a date like that, it would be hard to understand and hard to use. It would be much easier to use like this: 01-01-91 or 01-01-1991, since this is an easily recognized standard format. The output format is MM-DD-YY or MM-DD-YYYY.

Excelerator is capable of generating COBOL data structures, and COBOL rules are used to create input and output formats. If you are unfamiliar with these rules a few examples are shown in Figure 5.2.3a.

If not on your screen, retrieve the first CUSTOMER_LAST _NAME Data Element description screen. Use Tab to move from field to field.

- Type `X(20)` in the **Input Format** field.
- Type `X(20)` in the **Output Format** field.
- Type `20` in the **Characters left of decimal** field.

As shown in Figure 5.2.3b, CUSTOMER_LAST_NAME is now defined as being no more than 20 alphanumeric characters long with identical input and output formats.

In the next section, **5.2.4 Defining Edit Rules**, you will be guided through the completion of the next field, **Edit Rules**.

Figure 5.2.3a
Element Input/Output Formats

X	Alphanumeric character (Numbers or Letters)
9	Numeric character (Numbers only)
A	Alpha character (Letters only)
V	Decimal
(6)	Repeat character (Repeat six times as in X(9) for 9 alphanumeric characters)
B	Blank space
S	Positive or negative sign
Y	Year
M	Month
D	Day
,	Comma
.	Period
$	Dollar sign
+	Plus sign
-	Minus sign
Z	Non-zero digit or space

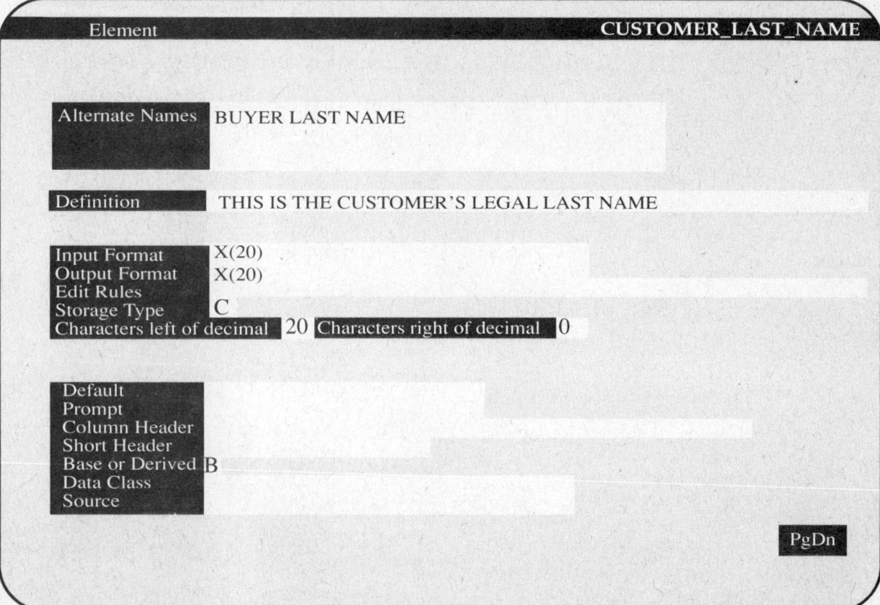

Figure 5.2.3b
First Data Element Description Screen with Input and Output Formats Defined

5.2.4 Defining Edit Rules

Edit rules fall into two categories. Either they test for a specific value or they refer to values in a table of codes. Edit rules help to keep data consistent. They also reduce the frequency errors are made by end-users.

When testing for specific values, non-numeric values must be enclosed by quotation marks. (Numeric values do not require quotation marks.) Figure 5.2.4a shows some examples of valid edit rules.

A table of codes is a user-defined list of values and corresponding meanings. By referencing a table of codes in an edit rule, all Data Element values will be compared to values in the table referenced. If the table does not contain a particular Data Element value, you will receive an error message. This allows you to build error checking features into your system.

If it is not on your screen, retrieve the first Data Element description screen for CUSTOMER_LAST _NAME .

- Type **not " "** in the **Edit Rules** field as shown in Figure 5.2.4b.

This edit rule mandates that CUSTOMER_ LAST_NAME contain no blank spaces.

In the next section, **5.2.5 Completing First Element Description Screen**, you will be guided through the completion of this Data Element description screen.

Figure 5.2.4a Examples of Data Element Edit Rules

Tests for a Specific Value

Edit Rule	Meaning
"Y", "N"	Acceptable values are Y and N.
1,0	Acceptable values are 1 and 0.
"Male", "Female"	Acceptable values are Male and Female.
not " "	Value may not be null.
OPT"A*"	Acceptable values begin with A and the presence of a value is optional (value may be null).
"A*" > "E*"	Acceptable values begin with A, B, C, D, or E.
0 THRU 100	Values between 0 and 100 are acceptable.

Tests for a Table of Codes Value

Edit Rule	Meaning
From "Options Table"	Values must be from the Options Table.
Not From "Parts Table"	Values from the Parts Table are unacceptable.

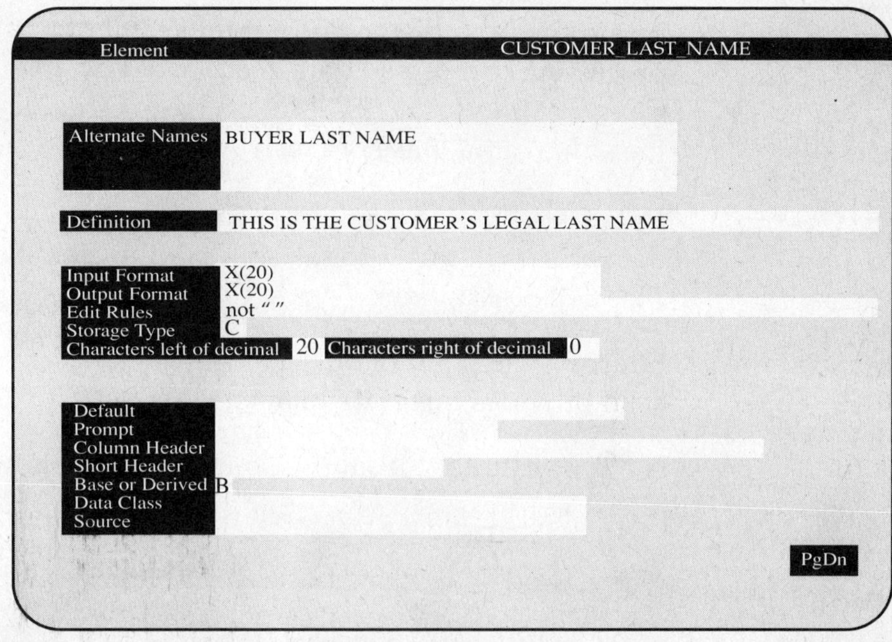

Figure 5.2.4b First Data Element Description Screen with Edit Rules Defined

5.2.5 Completing First Element Description Screen

The fields at the bottom of the first Data Element description screen must now be completed: **Default**, **Prompt**, **Column Header**, **Short Header**, **Base or Derived**, **Data Class**, and **Source**. Each of these fields is described in Figure 5.2.2 .

If it is not already on your screen, retrieve your description of CUSTOMER_LAST_NAME.

Because this Data Element is the name of a person, it should not have a default value. Default values are useful when a Data Element often has the same value. Leave Default blank.

Prompt is for text that should precede the Data Element value on reports and input/output screens. The prompt should be easily recognizable by the user.

- Type **`CUSTOMER LAST NAME:`** in the **Prompt** field.

A Column Header is a default header appearing on reports and displays. Like the prompt, column headers should describe the data.

- Type **`CUST LAST NAME`** in the **Column Header** field.
- Type **`CUST LN`** in the **Short Header** field.

The default value for the **Base or Derived** field is **B** for base. This means the Data Element is not the result of a calculation or of processing (processed data is indicated by a **D** for derived). CUSTOMER_ LAST_NAME is a basic Data Element, so do not change the value in the **Base** or **Derived** field.

Data Class is for a user-assigned data grouping. We will not be using data classes in this tutorial, so leave this field blank on all of your Data Element descriptions.

Source is the point of origin of the data. Because it is the customer who provides this Data Element,

- Type **`CUSTOMER`** in the **Source** field as shown in Figure 5.2.5.
- Press Pg Dn .

The second Data Element description screen appears.

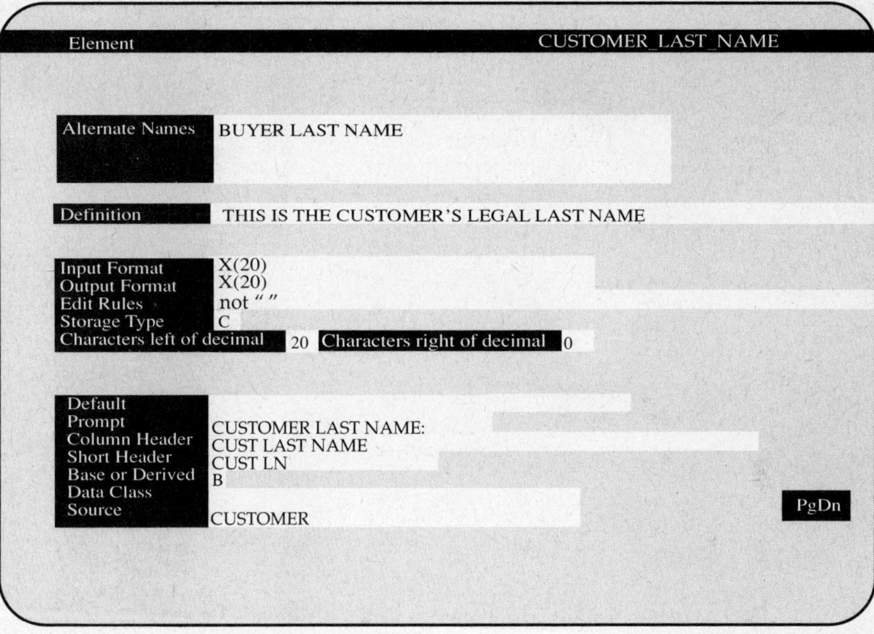

Figure 5.2.5
Completed First Element Description Screen for CUSTOMER_LAST_ NAME

5.2.6 Completing Last Element Description Screens

Data Elements may satisfy User or Engineering Requirements. They may also be associated with other Excelerator entities. As stated in **4.2.2 Completing DFD Description Screens**, none of these topics is discussed in this tutorial. Leave the **Satisfies Requirement** and **Associated Entities** fields blank.

- Press [Pg Dn] to go to the next screen.

The third Data Element description screen is shown in Figure 5.2.6b. This is the final Data Element description screen. It contains only one input field: **Description**. This field is for the textual description of the Data Element.

- Type **`THIS IS THE LEGAL LAST NAME OF THE PERSON PURCHASING A NEW CAR.`**

CUSTOMER_LAST_NAME is now completely described.

- Press [F3] to save and exit the Data Element description screens.

Exercise 5.2.6

Describe the remaining Data Elements contained in the Records you created in Exercise 5.1.3. You may find it convenient to initiate the description of Data Elements from within the Record in which they are contained. This is done by placing the insertion point on a Data Element name on the first Record description screen and then pressing [F4]. The Data Element's first description screen will appear. Once the description is complete, pressing [F3] will return you to the parent Record description. The next Data Element name is then selected. Repeat the process until all Data Elements in each Record have been described.

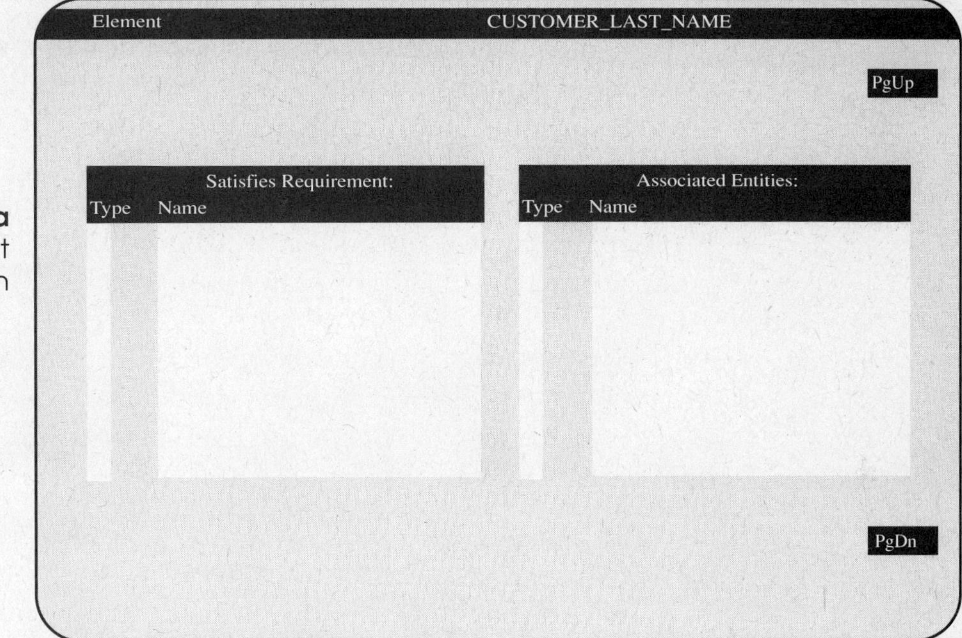

Figure 5.2.6a
Second Element Description Screen

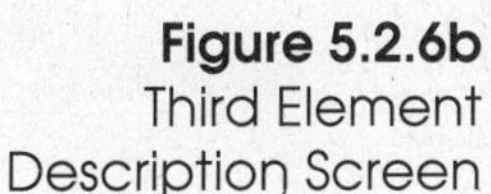

Figure 5.2.6b
Third Element Description Screen

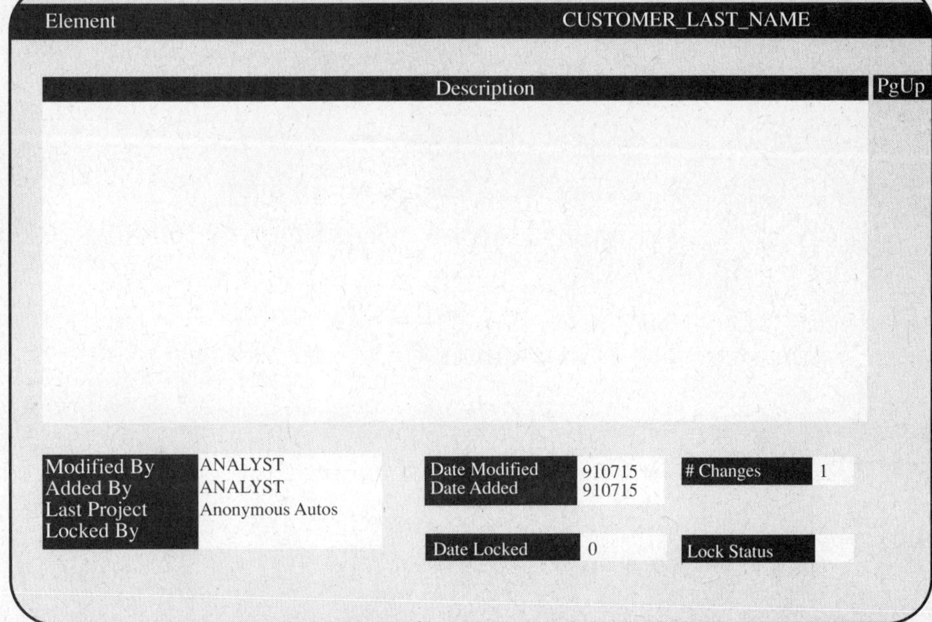

5.2.7 Printing Data Element Descriptions

Data Element descriptions are printed in nearly the same way as Record descriptions. There are only two significant differences between printing Records and Data Elements.

First, you are given a choice of whether or not to underline Data Element description output fields. Underlining these fields is advised because it makes the report easier to read.

Second, condensed print is not required for printing Data Element descriptions as it is for printing Record descriptions. The Data Element output report fits on the page nicely without any special adjustments to your printer.

- Select **X XLDICTIONARY** from Excelerator's Main Menu.
- Select **REC/ELE** from the XLDictionary Menu which appears.
- Select **E Element** REC/ELE Menu.
- Select **Output** from the Element Action Keypad.

A prompt appears near the bottom of the screen asking for the Name Range of the Data Elements(s) you wish to print. Defining name ranges is discussed in **4.2.3 Printing DFD Descriptions**.

- Place the insertion point in the **Name Range** field.
- Press ↵.
- Select **All Entities on Selector List** from the list which appears.
- Type `Y` when asked if output fields should be underlined.
- Select **Printer** with the mouse.

The Data Element descriptions begin printing.

Figure 5.2.7 shows printed output for CUSTOMER_ LAST_ NAME. This report is very similar in layout to the three Data Element description screens. It contains the information from each of those screens in sequence from top to bottom.

Figure 5.2.7
Printed Element Description with Output Fields Underlined

DATE: 25-JUL-91 ELEMENT - OUTPUT PAGE 6
TIME: 08: 33 NAME: * Excelerator / IS

TYPE Element NAME CUSTOMER_LAST_NAME

Alternate Names BUYER LAST NAME

Definition

Input Format X20
Output Format X20
Edit Rules not " "
Storage Type C
Characters left of descimal 20 Characters right of decimal 0

Default
Prompt CUSTOMER LAST NAME:
Column Header CUST LAST NAME
Short Header CUST LN
Base or Derived B
Data Class
Source CUSTOMER

Satisfies Requirement:
Type Name

Associated Entities
Type Name

Description

THIS IS THE LEGAL LAST NAME OF THE PERSON PURCHASING THE NEW VEHICLE

Modified By ANALYST
Added By ANALYST
Last Project Anonymous Aoutos
Locked By

Date Modified 910619 # Changes 2
Date Added 910619
Date Locked 0 Lock Status

5.3

Integrating the Process Model

As shown in Figure 5.3, explosion options for Data Stores and Data Flows in the process model include Records and Elements in the physical data model. When process model objects explode to data structures described in the physical data model, the two models become integrated in the XLDictionary. Data structures describe process model objects.

In the case of the Anonymous Autos process model, the two Data Stores explode to Records and the Data Flows explode either to Records or Elements described in this chapter.

In this section you will explode and index the two Data Stores in the Anonymous Autos process model. You will also explode the Data Flows from all three Data Flow Diagram levels. The result will be the integration of the process and physical data models for the Anonymous Autos system.

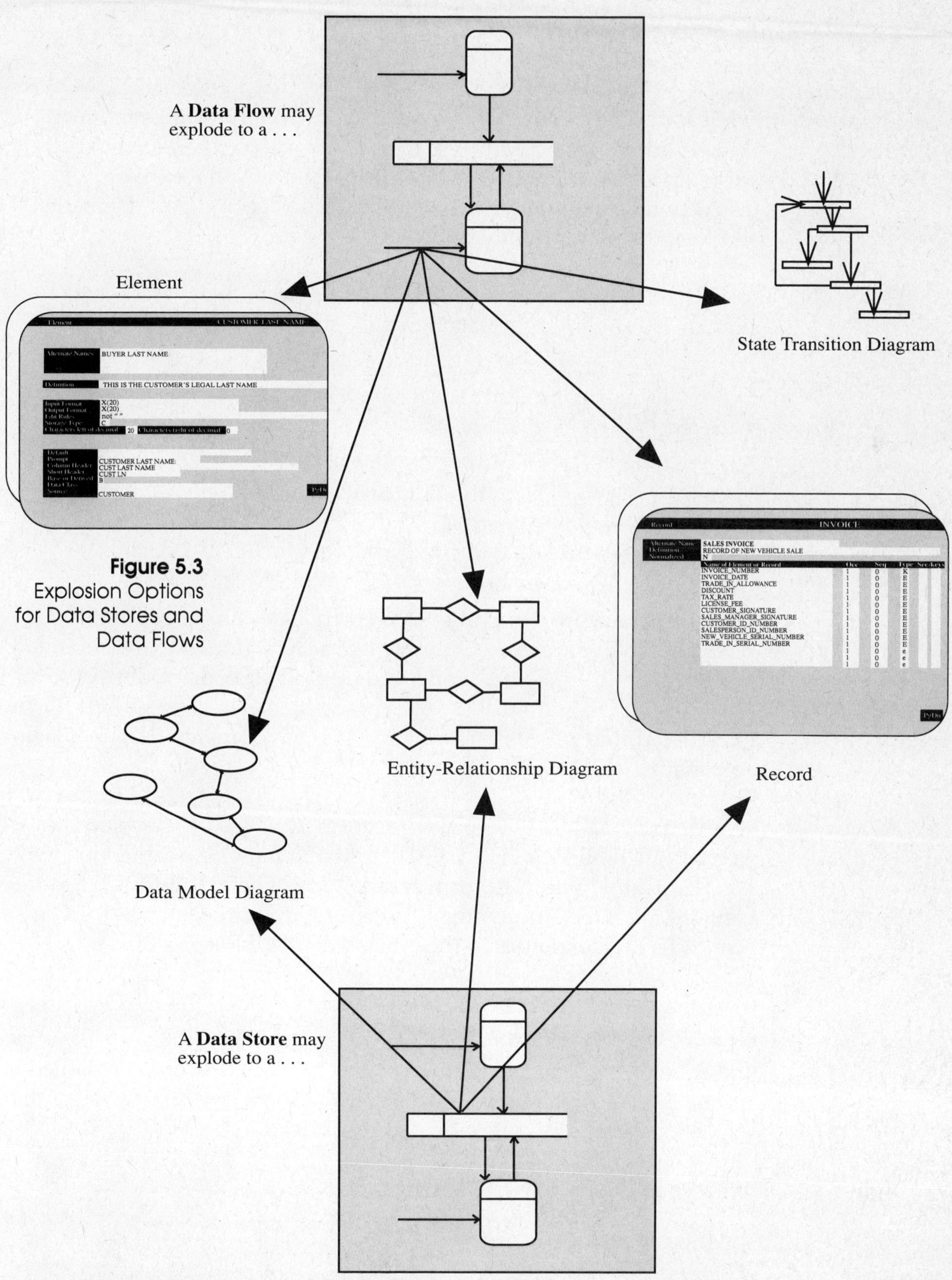

Figure 5.3
Explosion Options for Data Stores and Data Flows

5.3.1 Exploding and Indexing Data Stores

While describing your Data Stores in **4.7.1 Completing Data Store Description Screens**, you were instructed not to complete the fields in Explodes To One Of or Index Elements. The reason for this instruction is that you had not yet identified specific Data Elements and Records in the Anonymous Autos system.

Now that the data has been identified and described, it is time to explode and index your Data Stores.

- Select **X XLDICTIONARY** from Excelerator's Main Menu.
- Select **DATA** from the XLDictionary Menu which appears.
- Select **S Data Store** from the Data Menu.
- Select **Modify** from the Data Store Action Keypad.
- Press ⏎ in the **Name** field.
- Select **VIR** from the Selector List.

The first Data Store description screen appears. As stated on this screen in the **Explodes To One Of** area, a Data Store may be exploded to a Record (REC), a Data Model Diagram (DMD), or an Entity-Relationship Diagram (ERA). To explode the Data Store VIR FILE, you must determine which data structure you have created that details its contents.

The Vehicle Inventory Record (VIR) form, was used to develop the Record called NEW VEHICLE. The Data Elements contained in NEW VEHICLE and in the VIR form are identical. The VIR FILE Data Store contains all of the Anonymous Autos VIRs. This means that the Data Store VIR FILE explodes to the NEW VEHICLE Record.

- Type **`NEW VEHICLE`** in **Record** under Explodes To One Of.

Index Elements are Data Elements used to access Records contained in a Data Store. Primary, secondary, and candidate key Element(s) of the explosion Record are typically used as Index Elements.

With your cursor on NEW VEHICLE,

- Press F4.

The first Record description screen for NEW VEHICLE appears. Find the Record's primary key (denoted by a **K** in the Type field). Also look for candidate keys which might be useful. When you've finished examining the Record,

- Press F3.

Back at the Data Store description screen,

- Position your cursor in the first **Type** field under Index Elements.
- Type **ELE** (This is Excelerator's code for Element.)
- Type **NEW_VEHICLE_SERIAL_NUMBER** in the first **Name** field under Index Elements.

Because the manufacturer's invoice number might also be a useful Index Element for the VIR FILE Data Store,

- Type **ELE** in the second Type field under Index Elements.
- Type **MANUFACTURER_INVOICE_NUMBER** in the second Name field under Index Elements as shown in Figure 5.3.1.
- Press F3 to save and return to the Data Store Action Keypad.

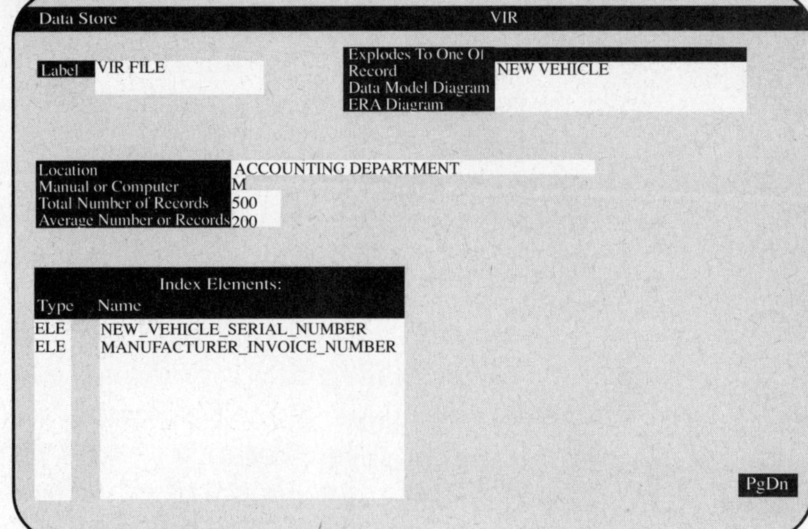

Figure 5.3.1 Explosion and Index Information Completed for VIR FILE

Exercise 5.3.1

Explode and index the INVOICE FILE Data Store.

5.3.2 Exploding Data Flows

While describing Data Flows in **4.5.1 Completing Data Flow Description Screens**, you were instructed not to complete the fields in **Explodes To**. The reason for this instruction is that specific Data Elements and Records in the Anonymous Autos system had not yet been identified.

Now that Data Elements and Records have been identified and described, it is time to explode the Data Flows in the process model.

- Select **X XLDICTIONARY** from Excelerator's Main Menu.
- Select **DATA** from the XLDictionary Menu.
- Select **F Data Flow** from the Data Menu.
- Select **Modify** from the Data Flow Action Keypad.
- Press ⏎ in the **Name** field.
- Select **SD** (this is the ID for Shipping Document) from the list.

The first Data Flow description screen appears. As stated on this screen in the **Explodes To One Of** area, Data Flows may be exploded to a Record (REC), a Data Model Diagram (DMD), Entity-Relationship Diagram (ERA), or a Structure Diagram (STD). To explode the Data Flow called SD (Shipping Document), you must determine which data structure you have created that details its contents.

The accounting department at Anonymous Autos uses the Shipping Document to generate each Vehicle Inventory Record. The data requirements of the Vehicle Inventory Record and the NEW VEHICLE Record are identical. Therefore, data on the Shipping Document which is required by the Anonymous Autos system, is contained in the NEW VEHICLE Record. This means the Data Flow SD (Shipping Document) can be exploded to the Record NEW VEHICLE.

- Type **`REC`** in the **Type** field under Explodes To.
- Type **`NEW VEHICLE`** in the **Name** field under Explodes To.

Your Data Flow description should now resemble Figure 5.3.2.

- Press F3 to save your work and return to the Data Flow Action Keypad.

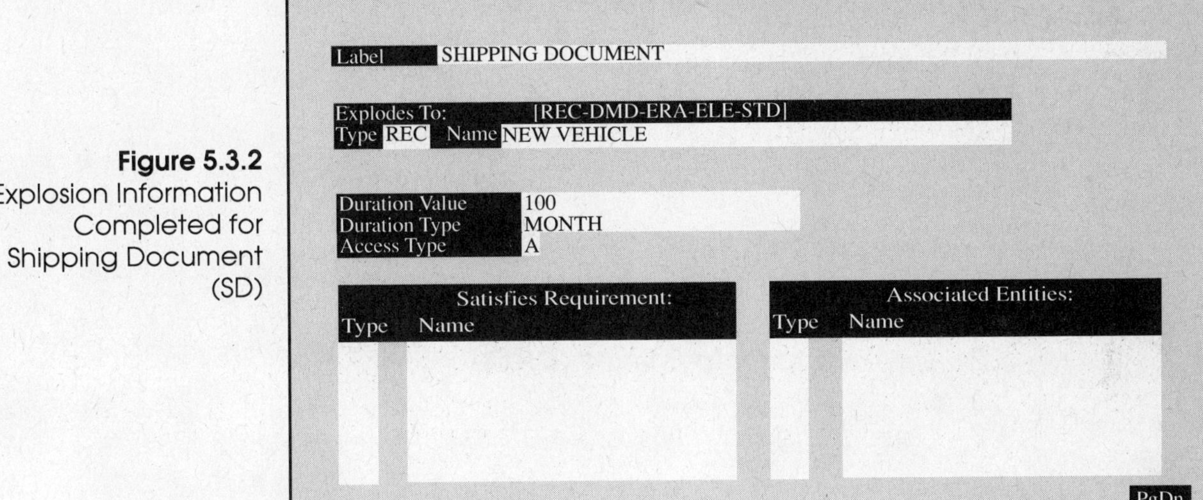

Figure 5.3.2
Explosion Information Completed for Shipping Document (SD)

Exercise 5.3.2

Explode all of the remaining Data Flows in your process model of the current Anonymous Autos system.

MODELING DATA

Entity-Relationship Diagrams (ERAs) are used to develop logical models of system data requirements. As communication tools, ERAs are easy to understand and explain to end-users. They are used to communicate to end-users the developer's interpretation of system data needs. ERAs are graphic models of the interaction among transactions or objects in the business environment. They are used to model the static properties of information important to the continued operation of the enterprise.

Entity-Relationship Diagrams are so useful that many enterprises instruct end-users in the basics of logical data modeling to allow them to participate in designing corporate data models. This not only increases the validity of resulting models, it decreases end-user resistance to new systems. Incorporating end-users into the development of new information systems increases the perception of ownership of the new system.

6.1

Drawing Entity-Relationship Diagrams (ERAs)

Unlike the commonly used acronym ERD, Excelerator's abbreviation for the term Entity-Relationship Diagram is ERA. Because we use Excelerator abbreviations for system components throughout this tutorial, we use ERA instead of ERD in this chapter.

In the top-down method of developing data requirements for an information system, an ERA provides the basis for the physical data model. In the development of the information system for Anonymous Autos, the bottom-up method has been used. This means that data relationships have already been determined in the physical data model.

Drawing ERAs is very similar to other forms of drawing. As shown in Figure 6.1, there are only two object types required in an ERA. Rectangles represent Data Entities and diamonds represent relationships among Data Entities. In Excelerator, ERA relationships are called Data N-ary Relationships (DNRs).

In this section you will create a logical data model for the Anonymous Autos system using Entity-Relationship Diagrams.

Figure 6.1
Entity-Relationship
Diagram Objects

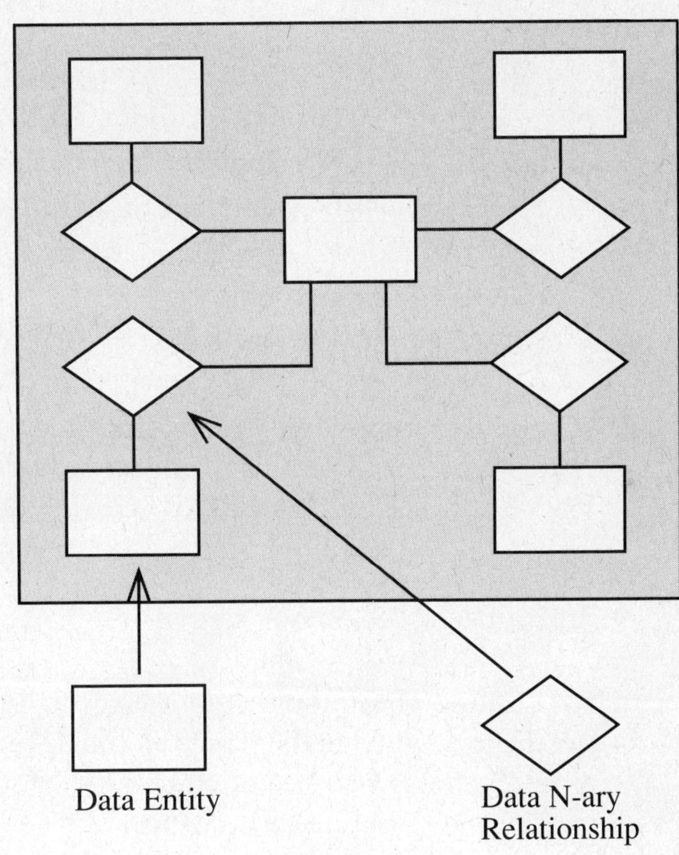

6.1.1 Drawing and Labeling Data Entities

To initiate your Entity-Relationship Diagram, refer to **4.1.1 Initiating Drawings**, substituting **Entity-Relationship Diagram** for **Data Flow Diagram** on the Graphics Menu, and naming the new graph **AA SYSTEM ERA**, as shown in Figure 6.1.1a.

Hint
You will find it helpful to set the GRID to FINE before you begin drawing.

Placing Data Entities and Relationships in the drawing area is accomplished using the same methods explained in **4.1.3 Placing Objects on the Screen** .

- Select **PRINT** from the Command Menu.
- Select **FULL GPH** from the Print options.
- Select **OBJECT** from the Command Menu. (If you have trouble making this selection, press the right button on the mouse and try again.)
- Select **ENTITY** from the list of ERA objects which appears.

If you have completed **5.1 Creating Records (RECs)**, the Anonymous Autos project XLDictionary now contains six Records which represent Data Entities: CUSTOMER, TRADE-IN, INVOICE, NEW VEHICLE, OPTION, and SALESPERSON. (The seventh Record, INSTALLED OPTIONS, represents the relationship between two Data Entities, NEW VEHICLE and OPTION.)

- Position your mouse cursor near the upper left hand corner of the top left page displayed in the drawing area.
- Press the left button on the mouse to select the position, and a Data Entity appears in the location selected.

Hint
Remember to use [Tab] to go from line to line in the label text box, and use [↵] to put the text box away.

Data Entities are labeled using the same methods explained in **4.1.12 Labeling Objects and Connections** .

- Select **LABEL** from the Command Menu.
- Position the mouse cursor on the Data Entity you just created.
- Select the Data Entity by pressing the left button on the mouse, and a label text box appears on the screen.
- Type `CUSTOMER` in the text box.
- Press [↵] or the left button on the mouse, and the label appears in the Data Entity.

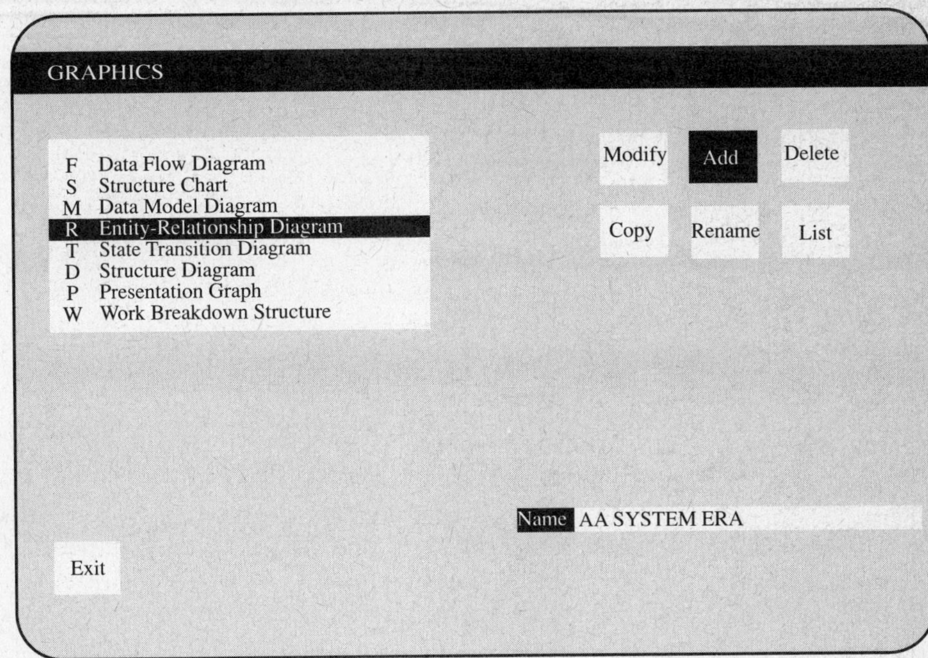

Figure 6.1.1a
Initiating an Entity-Relationship Diagram

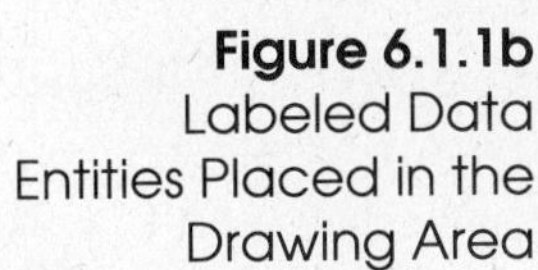

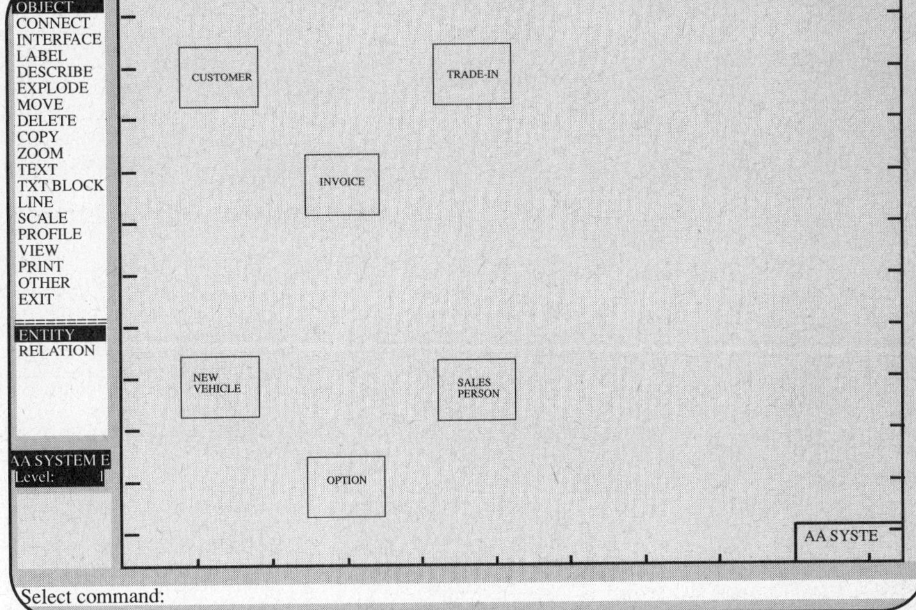

Figure 6.1.1b
Labeled Data Entities Placed in the Drawing Area

Exercise 6.1.1

Draw and label the remaining five Data Entities as shown in Figure 6.1.1b.

6.1.2 Drawing and Labeling Relationships and Connections

If it is not already on your screen, retrieve the AA SYSTEM ERA.

- Select **GRAPHICS** from the Main Menu.
- Select **R Entity-Relationship Diagram** from the Graphics Menu.
- Select **Add** from the ERA Action Keypad.
- Type **AA SYSTEM ERA** in the **Name** field.
- Press ⏎, and your graph appears.
- Select **OBJECT** from the Command Menu.
- Select **RELATION** from the ERA object list which appears.

In Exercise 5.1.8, you determined the relationships between Records in the Anonymous Autos system. You found that INVOICE is related to CUSTOMER, TRADE-IN, NEW VEHICLE, and SALESPERSON. NEW VEHICLE is related to OPTION via a relational record called INSTALLED OPTION. With this information in mind,

- Position the mouse cursor below CUSTOMER and to the left of INVOICE on your graph.
- Select this position by pressing the left button on the mouse.

An ERA object called a Data N-ary Relationship (or Relation for short) appears in the drawing area.

- Select **LABEL** from the Command Menu.
- Position the mouse cursor on the Relation you just created.
- Select the Relation by pressing the left button on the mouse.

The label text box appears on the screen.

- Type `SIGNS` in the text box.
- Press ⏎ or the left button on the mouse.

The label appears in the Relation object.

To connect the Relation to the two Data Entities participating in the relationship, CUSTOMER and INVOICE,

- Select **CONNECT** from the Command Menu.

Hint
To create bends in connections, select the first object, select one or more intermediate locations, then select the second object. Delete legs of the connection by pressing the right button on the mouse one time for each leg to be deleted.

- Position the mouse cursor over the Data Entity labeled CUSTOMER.
- Press the left mouse button to select the Data Entity.
- Position the mouse cursor over the Relation you just created.
- Press the left mouse button to select the Relation.

A line appears connecting CUSTOMER to SIGNS. Using the same method, connect INVOICE to SIGNS, and the relationship is complete.

To label connections,

- Select **LABEL** from the Command Menu.
- Position the mouse cursor on the handle of the connection between INVOICE and SIGNS.
- Select the connection by pressing the left button on the mouse.
- Type **1:M** in the label text box.
- Press ⏎.

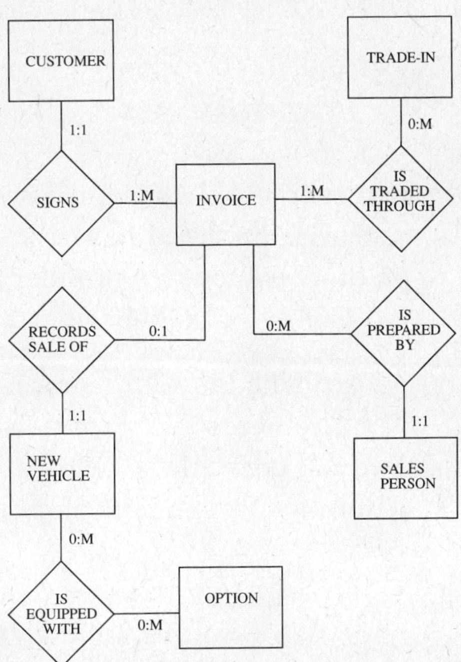

Figure 6.1.2
AA SYSTEM ERA with All Objects and Connections Drawn and Labeled

Exercise 6.1.2

Draw and label the remaining Relations and Connections as shown in Figure 6.1.2.

6.1.3 Completing ERA Description Screens

To initiate the description of AA SYSTEM ERA, refer to **4.2.1 Initiating DFD Descriptions**, selecting **Entity-Relationship Diagram** instead of **Data Flow Diagram** from the Graphs Menu. The first **ERA Description** screen is shown in Figure 6.1.3a. The graph name, AA SYSTEM ERA, appears at the top.

File is an output field providing the name of the file in which the ERA is stored in your Excelerator project subdirectory.

Label is text intended to appear in the graph's title block (see **4.1.17 Using OTHER and EXIT Commands**). In the Label field,

- Type **`ANONYMOUS AUTOS SYSTEM ERA`**.

Short Description should briefly explain what is shown by the ERA.

- Type **`DATA MODEL OF THE ANONYMOUS AUTOS INVOICE AND INVENTORY SYSTEM`** in this field.

Percent Complete is provided for users who wish to indicate the ratio of work completed to work remaining on this ERA. To track progress on this ERA, enter a number here reflecting current completeness of AA CONTEXT DFD. Otherwise, just enter 100.

As explained in **4.2.2 Completing DFD Description Screens**, **Satisfies Requirements** and **Associated Entities** will not be addressed in this tutorial. Leave these fields blank unless User and Engineering requirements were developed.

- Press [Pg Dn], and the second ERA description screen appears.

Use the second ERA description screen shown in Figure 6.1.3b as a guide and complete the **Description** of the AA SYSTEM ERA. When finished,

- Press [F3] to save and return to the ERA Action Keypad.

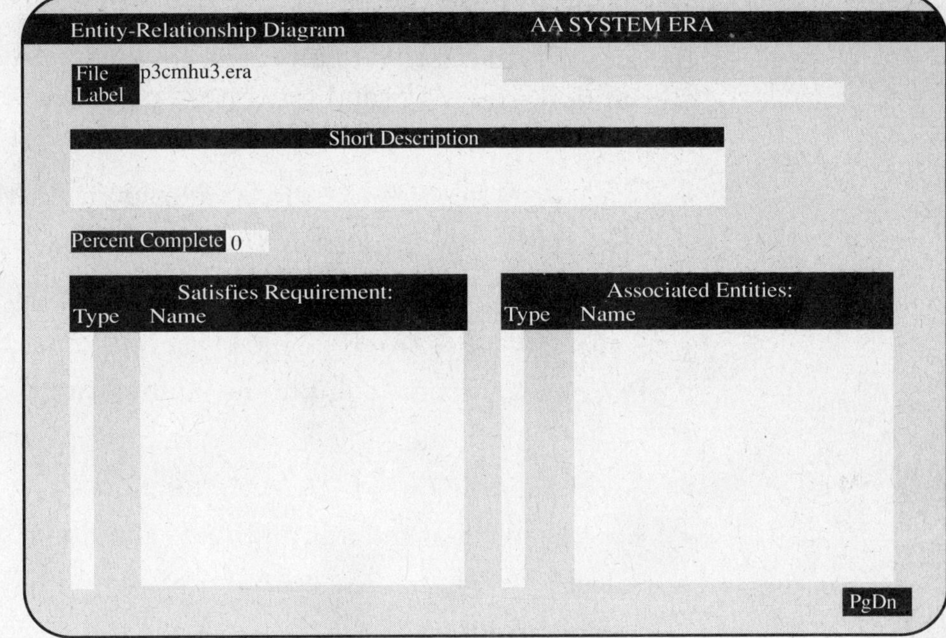

Figure 6.1.3a
First ERA Description Screen Completed for AA SYSTEM ERA

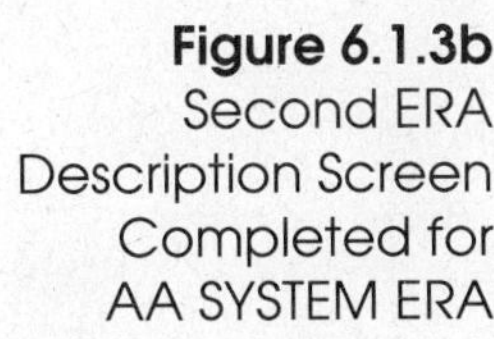

Figure 6.1.3b
Second ERA Description Screen Completed for AA SYSTEM ERA

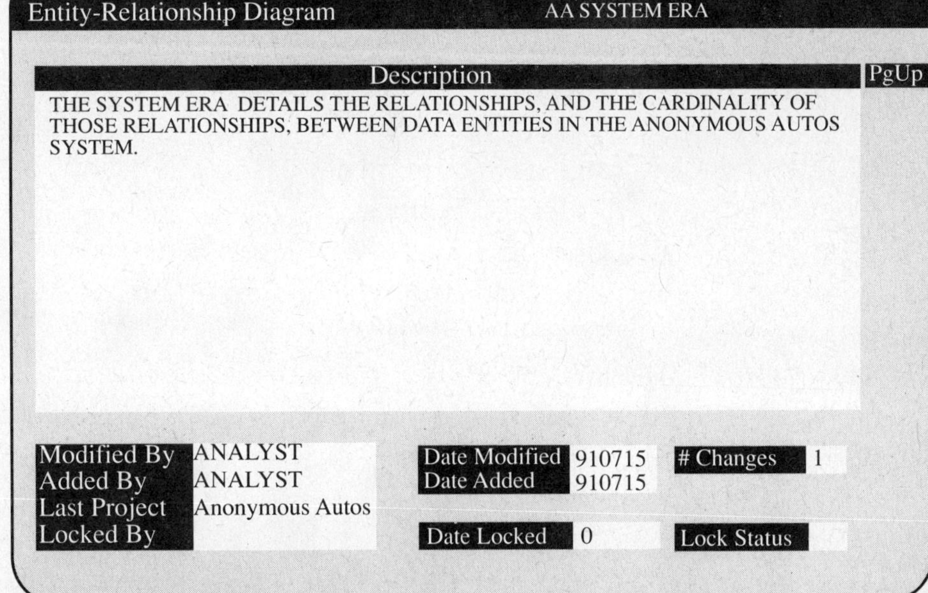

6.1.4 Printing ERA Descriptions

As with the description of any graph, when you've completed an ERA description, you may send it to an output device for printing.

- Select **X XLDICTIONARY** from Excelerator's Main Menu.
- Select **GRAPHS** from the XLDictionary Menu which appears.
- Select **R Entity-Relationship Diagram** from the Graphs Menu.
- Select **Output** from the ERA Action Keypad.
- Place the insertion point in the **Name Range** field.
- Press ⏎ and the XLDictionary Selector List of ERAs appears.
- Select **AA SYSTEM ERA** with the mouse.
- Type `Y` when asked if input fields should be underlined.
- Select **Printer** as the output device, and the ERA description begins printing.

The report Excelerator generates for an ERA closely resembles the Entity-Relationship Diagram description screens. Figure 6.1.4 shows the printed description of AA SYSTEM ERA. Notice that the graph name appears near the top of the page followed by all the other fields from the description screens:

- File
- Label
- Short Description
- Percent Complete
- Satisfies Requirement
- Associated Entities
- Description
- Audit fields from the bottom of the last description screen

The lines on the report are the result of responding affirmatively to Excelerator's question, *Do you want output fields underlined?* during the printing process.

Figure 6.1.4 Printed ERA Description with Output Fields Underlined

DATE: 31-AUG-91 ENTITY-RELATIONSHIP DIAGRAM - OUTPUT PAGE 1
TIME: 10:14 NAME: AA SYSTEM ERA Excelerator / IS

TYPE Entity-Relationship Diagram NAME AA SYSTEM ERA

File p3cmhu3.era
ANONYMOUS AUTOS SYSTEM ERA

Short Description
DATA MODEL OF ANONYMOUS AUTOS INVOICE AND INVENTORY SYSTEM

Percent Complete 0

Satisfies Requirement: Associated Entities
Type Name Type Name

Description

THE SYSTEM ERA DETAILS THE RELATIONSHIPS, AND THE CARDINALITY OF THOSE RELATIONSHIPS, BETWEEN DATA ENTITIES IN THE ANONYMOUS AUTOS SYSTEM.

Modified By ANALYST Date Modified 910825 # Changes 13
Added By ANALYST Date Added 910823
Last Project Anonymous Autos
Locked By Date Locked 0 Lock Status

6.2

Describing Data Entities (DAEs)

A **Data Entity** is anything about which descriptive data is captured by an information system. Examples of Data Entities in the Anonymous Autos system include the following:

- Salesperson
- Customer
- Sales Invoice
- New Vehicle
- Trade-In Vehicle

In an Entity-Relationship Diagram, Data Entities appear as boxes linked to each other through diamond-shaped Relations (short for Data N-ary Relationships). The Data Entities represent **data classes** (multiple instances of the same kind of Data Entity) within the system while Relations describe the relationships among data classes and the cardinality of those relationships.

Data Entities can be exploded to show greater degrees of detail. Figure 6.2 shows that a Data Entity can explode into either a Data Model Diagram, a Entity-Relationship Diagram, or a Record. In the Anonymous Autos system, Data Entities explode to Records described in **5. Identifying Data.**

In this section you will use Excelerator's Data Entity description screens to describe the Date Entities shown on the Entity-Relationship Diagram for the Anonymous Autos system.

Figure 6.2
Data Entity Explosion Options

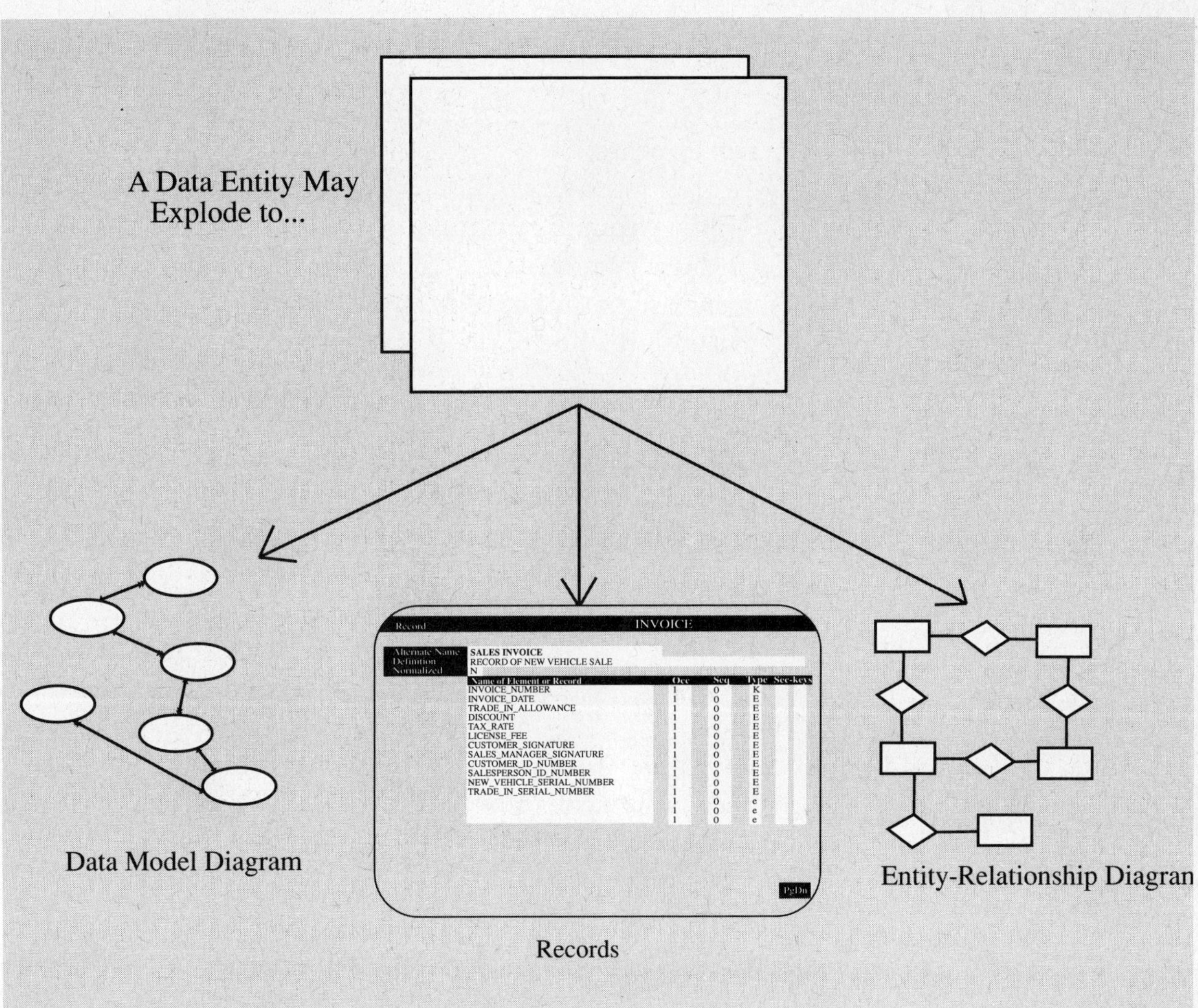

6.2.1 Completing Data Entity Description Screens

If it is not already on your screen, retrieve the AA SYSTEM ERA.

- Select GRAPHICS from the Main Menu.
- Select R Entity-Relationship Diagram from the Graphics Menu.
- Select Modify from the ERA Action Keypad.
- Type **AA SYSTEM ERA** in the **Name** field.
- Press ↵.

When your graph appears,

- Select DESCRIBE from the Command Menu.
- Position the mouse cursor on the Data Entity labeled CUSTOMER.
- Press the left mouse button to select the Data Entity.
- Type **CUS** in the status line at the ID prompt.
- Press ↵.

The first description screen for the Data Entity appears as shown in Figure 6.2.1a. The ID, CUS, appears at the top, and the label you created on the graph itself appears in the **Label** field.

This Data Entity represents the CUSTOMER Record, so

- Type **CUSTOMER** in the **Record** field under **Explodes To One Of**.

Data Entities may satisfy user or engineering requirements. They may also be associated with Excelerator entities. As stated in **4.2.2 Completing DFD Description Screens**, none of these topics are discussed in this tutorial.

- Press Pg Dn, and the second Data Entity description screen appears.

Use the second External Entity description screen shown in Figure 6.2.1b as a guide and complete the long **Description** of CUSTOMER. When you have finished,

- Press F3 to save and return to the drawing screen.

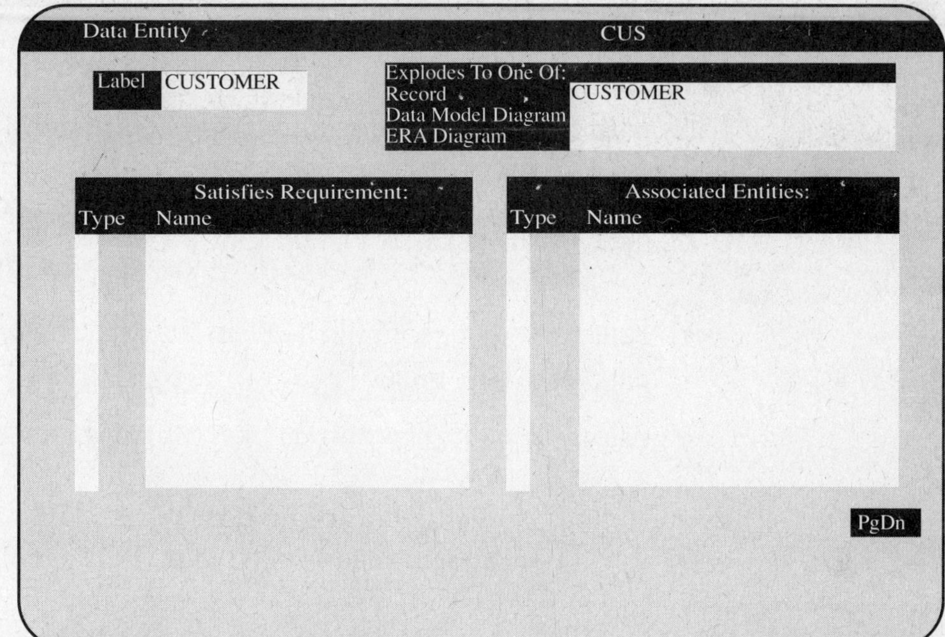

Figure 6.2.1a
First Data Entity Description Screen

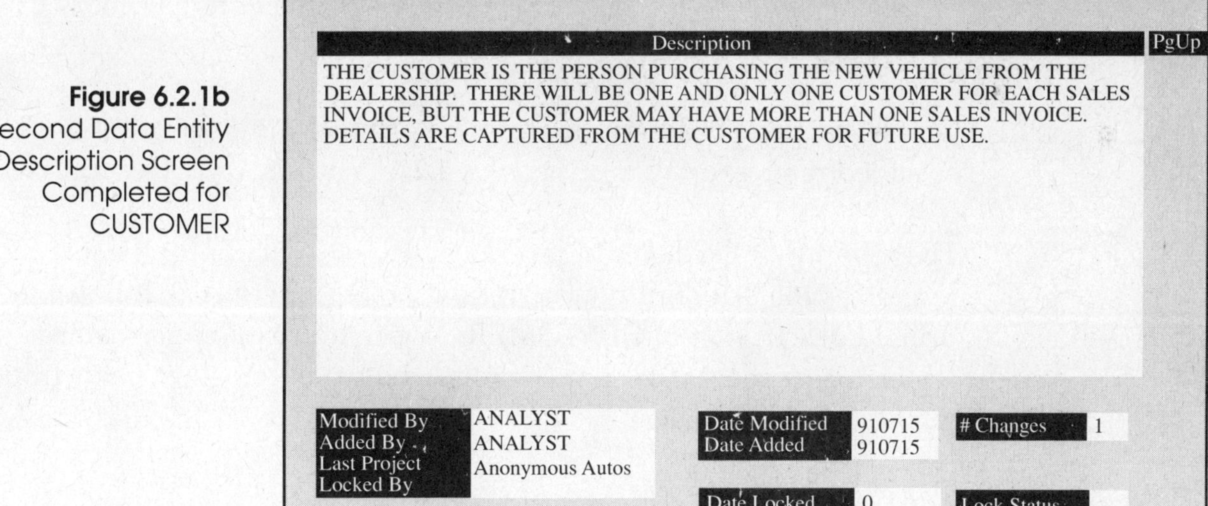

Figure 6.2.1b
Second Data Entity Description Screen Completed for CUSTOMER

Exercise 6.2.1

Describe the remaining five Data Entities on your AA SYSTEM ERA.

6.2.2 Printing Data Entity Descriptions

As with the description of any graph component, when you've completed an External Entity description, you may send it to an output device for printing. Select **XLDictionary** from Excelerator's Main Menu.

- Select **DATA** from the XLDictionary Menu which appears.
- Select **M Data Entity** from the Data Menu.
- Select **Output** from the Data Entity Action Keypad.

The Name Range field appears near the bottom of the screen. With the insertion point positioned in the Name Range field,

- Press ↵, and the XLDictionary list of External Entities appears.
- Select **All Entities on Selector List** with the mouse.
- Type **Y** when asked if output fields should be underlined.
- Select **Printer** as the output device, and the External Entity descriptions begin printing.

Graph component descriptions can be printed one at a time, within specified ranges, or all together. See **4.2.3 Printing DFD Descriptions** .

The report that Excelerator generates for each Data Entity closely resembles the Data Entity description screens. Figure 6.3.2 shows the printed description of CUSTOMER. Notice the Data Entity name appears near the top of the page followed by all the other fields from the description screens:

- Label
- Explodes To One Of
- Satisfies Requirement
- Associated Entities
- Description
- Audit fields from the bottom of the second Data Entity description screen

Figure 6.3.2
Printed Data Entity Description with Output Fields Underlined

DATE: 25-AUG-91 DATA ENTITY - OUTPUT PAGE 1
TIME: 18:52 NAME: * Excelerator / IS

TYPE Data Entity NAME CUS

Label CUSTOMER

Explodes to one of:
Record CUSTOMER
Data Model Diagram
ERA Diagram

Satisfies Requirement:
Type Name

Associated Entities:
Type Name

Description

THE CUSTOMER IS THE PERSON PURCHASING THE NEW VEHICLE FROM THE DEALERSHIP. THERE WILL BE ONE AND ONLY ONE CUSTOMER FOR EACH SALES INVOICE, BUT THE CUSTOMER MAY HAVE MORE THAN ONE SALES INVOICE. DETAILS ARE CAPTURED FROM THE CUSTOMER FOR FUTURE USE.

Modified By ANALYST
Added By ANALYST
Last Project Anonymous Autos
Locked By

Date Modified 910825
Date Added 910823
Date Locked 0

Changes 13
Lock Status

6.2

Describing Data N-ary Relationships (DNRs)

Excelerator refers to a relationship between two or more Data Entities in an ERA as a **Data N-ary Relationship**. The Data N-ary Relationship appears as a diamond-shaped object on the ERA.

The term **N-ary** evolved from Excelerator's ability to create one relationship among up to ten Data Entities. The **N**, therefore stands for a number between one and ten. Commonly used Data N-ary Relationships are as follows:

- **Unary relationship** depicts the relationship between a Data Entity and itself.
- **Binary relationship** shows the relationship between two Data Entities.
- **Trinary relationship** is associates three related Data Entities.

In describing Data N-ary Relationships, cardinality is defined. This cardinality is then used to label connections between Data Entities and Data N-ary Relationship as shown in Figure 6.3.

While Data Entities act as nouns, Data N-ary Relationships act as verbs when expressing associations between Data Entities as sentences. For example, Figure 6.3 shows a binary relationship between CUSTOMER and INVOICE. This relationship can be expressed as a bi-directional statement:

- Reading from the bottom up, Each INVOICE is signed by on and only only one CUSTOMER.
- Reading from the top down, Each CUSTOMER signs one to many INVOICEs.

In this section you will use Excelerator's Data N-ary descriptions screen to describe the Date N-ary Relationships in the Entity-Relationship Diagram for the Anonymous Autos system.

Figure 6.3
Relationship Between the Data Entities CUSTOMER and INVOICE

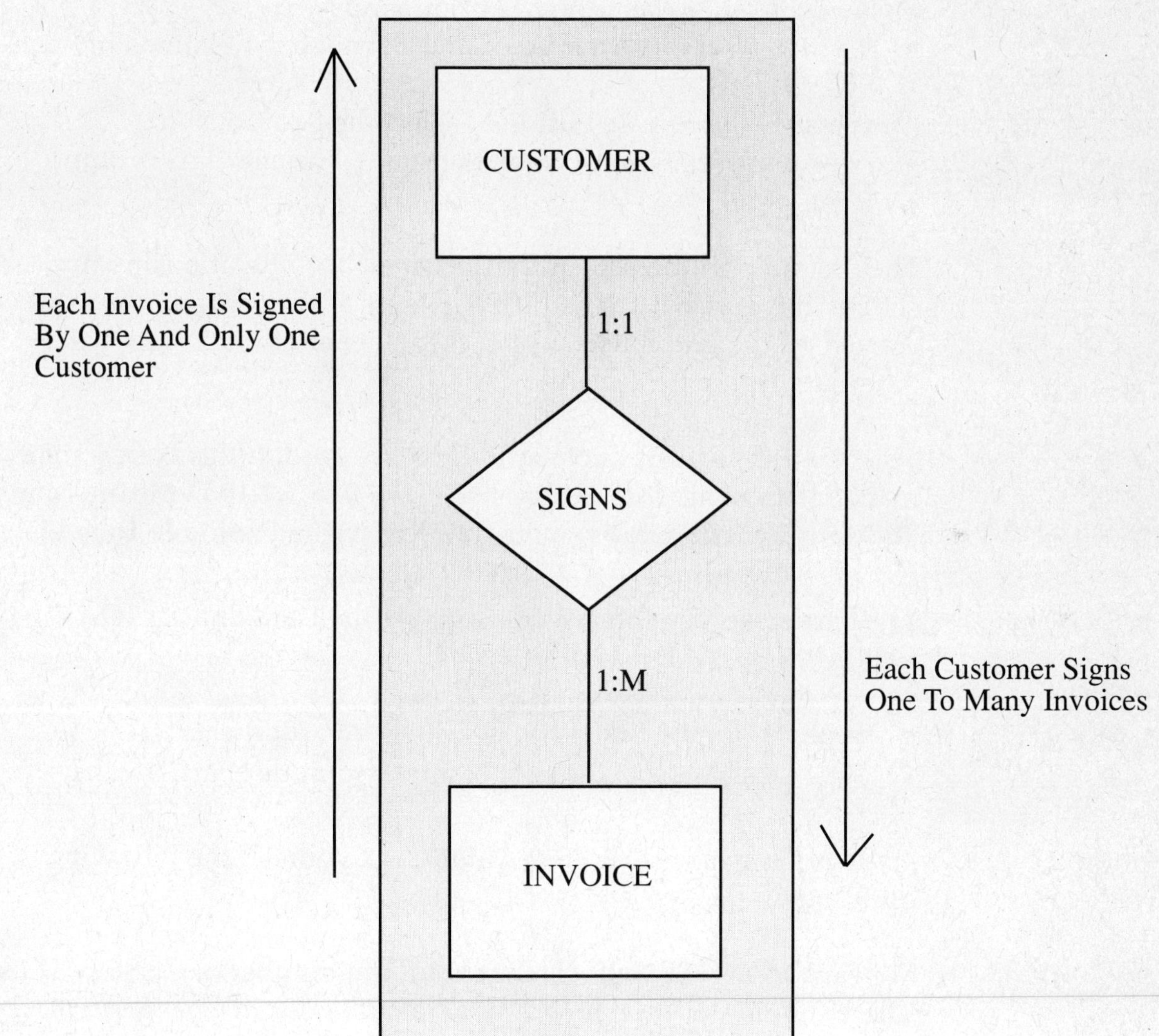

6.3.1 Completing First Data N-ary Relationship Screens

If it is not already on your screen, retrieve the AA SYSTEM ERA. Refer to the instructions at the top of page 176 if necessary. When your graph appears,

- Select **DESCRIBE** from the Command Menu.
- Position the mouse cursor on the Data N-ary Relationship labeled SIGNS.
- Press the left mouse button to select the Relationship.
- Type **S** (short for SIGNS) in the status line at the ID prompt.
- Press ↵.

The first description screen for the Data N-ary Relationship appears as shown in Figure 6.3.1. The ID, S, appears at the top, and the label you created on the graph itself appears in the **Label** field. Leave the **Alternate Name** field blank.

This relationship does not explode to a Record. If this were a many-to-many relationship, the relational Record (see **5.1.10 Defining Many-To-Many Relationships**) would appear in the **Explodes To** fields.

The Participants in this relationship are the Data Entities (DAEs) CUSTOMER and INVOICE.

- Type **DAE** in the first **Type** field under Participants.
- Type **CUSTOMER** in the first **Name** field under Participants.

To determine the Cardinality Values, ask yourself the following questions:

For each INVOICE, what is the minimum number of CUSTOMERs? There should never be fewer than one CUSTOMER per INVOICE, therefore, the answer is 1.

- Type **1** in the first **Min.** field under Cardinality Values.

For each INVOICE, what is the maximum number of CUSTOMERs? There must be no more than 1 CUSTOMER per INVOICE, so

- Type **1** in the first **Max.** field under Cardinality Values.

If you completed Exercise 6.1.2, these cardinality values already appear on your AA SYSTEM ERA graph as connection labels.

The primary Role of the CUSTOMER, in the relationship between CUSTOMER and INVOICE, is to sign the INVOICE.

- Type **SIGNS INVOICE** in the first Role field.

Whenever one of the Cardinality Values is zero, this indicates that the relationship participant is not required. A relationship participant is always Required when its Cardinality Values are both 1 or greater, as is the case with CUSTOMER in its relationship with INVOICE. Without a CUSTOMER, there can be no INVOICE. Without an INVOICE, there can be no CUSTOMER.

- Type **Y** in the first Required field.

Using the same method, enter the second relationship participant, INVOICE, on the next line. When you're done,

- Press Pg Dn, and the second Relationship screen appears.

Figure 6.3.1
First Data N-ary Relationship Description Screen

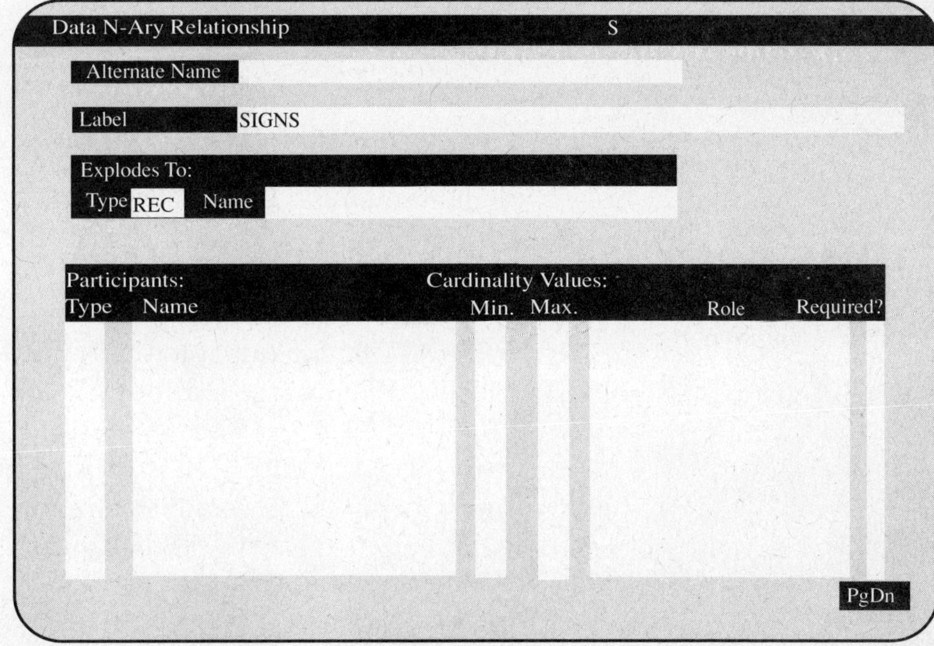

6.3.2 Completing Last Data N-ary Relationship Screens

The second Data N-ary Relationship description screen is shown in Figure 6.3.2a.

As explained in **4.2.2 Completing DFD Description Screens, Satisfies Requirements** and **Associated Entities** are not addressed in this tutorial. Leave these fields blank unless you have developed User and Engineering requirements on your own.

- Press [Pg Dn] and the third Data N-ary Relationship description screen appears.

Use the third Data N-ary Relationship description screen shown in Figure 6.3.2b as a guide and complete the long **Description** of SIGNS. When you've finished,

- Press [F3] to save and return to the drawing screen.

Exercise 6.3.2

Describe the remaining Data N-ary Relationships shown on your AA SYSTEM ERA.

When describing the Data N-ary Relationship labeled IS EQUIPPED WITH, explode it to the Record called INSTALLED OPTION (see **Explodes To** on page 182).

Remember, INSTALLED OPTION is a relational record whose only purpose is to establish a many-to-many relationship between NEW VEHICLE and OPTION.

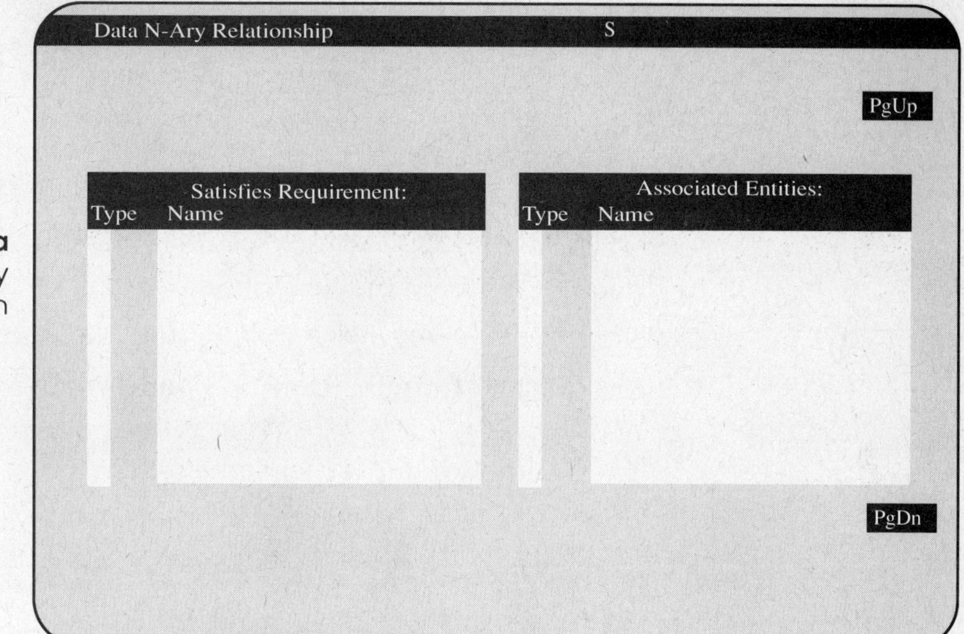

Figure 6.3.2a
Second Data N-ary Description Screen

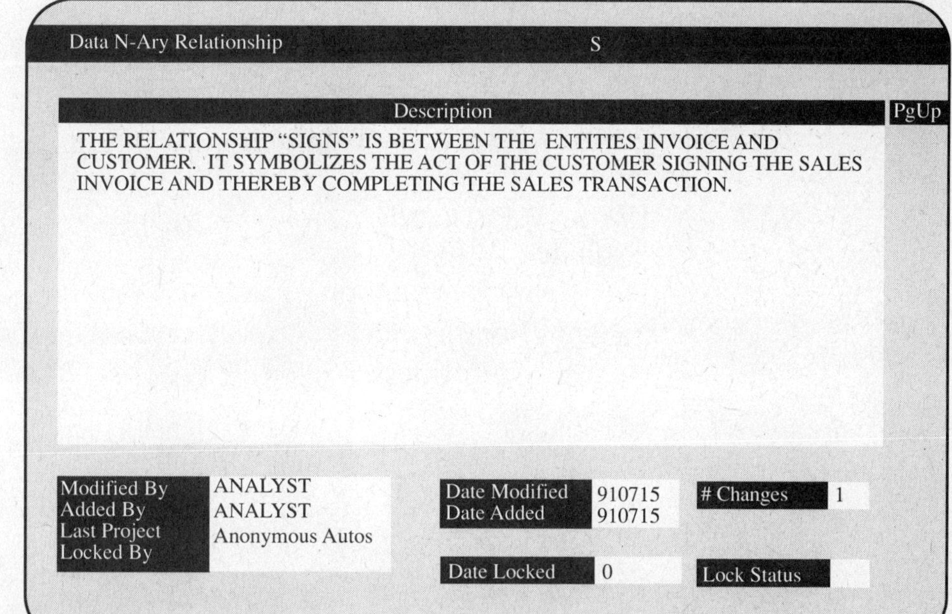

Figure 6.3.2b
Third Data N-ary Description Screen Completed for SIGNS

6.3.3 Printing Data N-ary Relationship Descriptions

As with the description of any graph component, when you have completed an External Entity description, you may send it to an output device for printing.

- Select **X XLDICTIONARY** from Excelerator's Main Menu
- Select **DATA** from the XLDictionary Menu which appears.
- Select **N Data N-Ary Relationship** from the Data Menu.
- Select **Output** from the DNR Action Keypad.

With the insertion point in the Name field,

- Press ⏎, and the XLDictionary list of Data N-ary Relationships appears.
- Select **All Entities on Selector List** with the mouse.
- Type **Y** when asked if input fields should be underlined.
- Select **Printer** as the output device, and the Data N-ary Relationship descriptions begin printing.

The report Excelerator generates for each Data N-ary Relationship closely resembles the Data N-ary Relationship description screens. Figure 6.3.3 shows the printed description of SIGNS. Notice the entity type and Relationship name appear near the top of the page followed by other fields from the description screens:

- Alternate Name
- Label
- Explodes To
- Participant Information
- Satisfies Requirement
- Associated Entities
- Description
- Audit fields from the bottom of the last description screen

Figure 6.3.3
Printed Data N-ary Relationship Description with Output Fields Underlined

DATE: 31-AUG-91 DATA N-ARY RELATIONSHIP - OUTPUT PAGE 1
TIME: 10:14 NAME: * Excelerator / IS

TYPE Data N-Ary Relationship NAME SIGNS

Alternate Name
Label SIGNS

Explodes To:
Type REC Name

Participants: type	Name	Cardinality Values: Min.	Max.	Role	Required?
DAE	CUSTOMER	1	1	SIGNS INVOICE	Y

Satisfies Requirement:
Type Name

Associated Entities
Type Name

Description

THE RELATIONSHIP "SIGNS" IS BETWEEN THE ENTITIES INVOICE AND CUSTOMER
IT SYMBOLIZES THE ACT OF THE CUSTOMER SIGNING THE SALES INVOICE AND
THEREBY COMPLETING THE SALES TRANSACTION

Modified By ANALYST
Added By ANALYST
Last Project Anonymous Autos
Locked By

Date Modified 910825
Date Added 910823
Date Locked 0

Changes 13
Lock Status

DEVELOPING THE END-USER INTERFACE

The concept of the end-user interface has traditionally encompassed the hardware and software through which end-users and computers communicate.

The meaning of the term is changing. It is gradually coming to be equated with the computer screen and system generated reports. The concept is even beginning to address the cognitive and emotional aspects of the end-user's experience. An angry user is not a productive one, and the importance of these issues is paramount in end-user interface design.

The interface should be designed to make contact between humans and computers as effortless and painless as possible. In conceiving the design of the end-user interface for any system, the goal of the designer should be to empower the user, constantly asking the question, What does the user want to do?

End-users frequently find their progress impeded by poor interface design: screens with unclear instructions, menus with mysterious navigational paths, and reports full of useless data.

The end-user interface defines user interaction with, and perception of, an information system. It is the visible part of the system composed of screens, menus, and reports which can be designed and even prototyped using Excelerator's Screen and Report Design facilities.

In this chapter, you will develop the end-user interface for the new Anonymous Autos information system.

7.1 Designing Screens (SCDs)

End-users are generally comfortable with the current system's method for data entry. For this reason, in the design of a new system, **screens** should preserve the look and feel of the old data entry method as much as is practical. This will reduce resistance to the new system and learning time for end-users.

Computer screens are difficult to design due to the physical limitations of many computer monitors. Most monitors show only 25 lines of text at any one time. Each of these lines is usually only 80 columns wide. Systems designers must be careful to avoid the temptation to solve this space limitation problem by creating cluttered screens. It is often helpful to examine some of the screens you deal with every day; understand why you like some displays more than others. Keep notes on what you perceive to be good and bad screen characteristics. This process will aid in the development of easy-to-use screen designs.

Screens are an important factor in the interface between the user and the database. Screens should have all the information required to maintain the database — no more and no less.

The Screen Design facility in Excelerator can be used in conjunction with Data Element definitions to help ensure database integrity. Paths to Excelerator's Screen Design facilities are summarized in Figure 7.1.

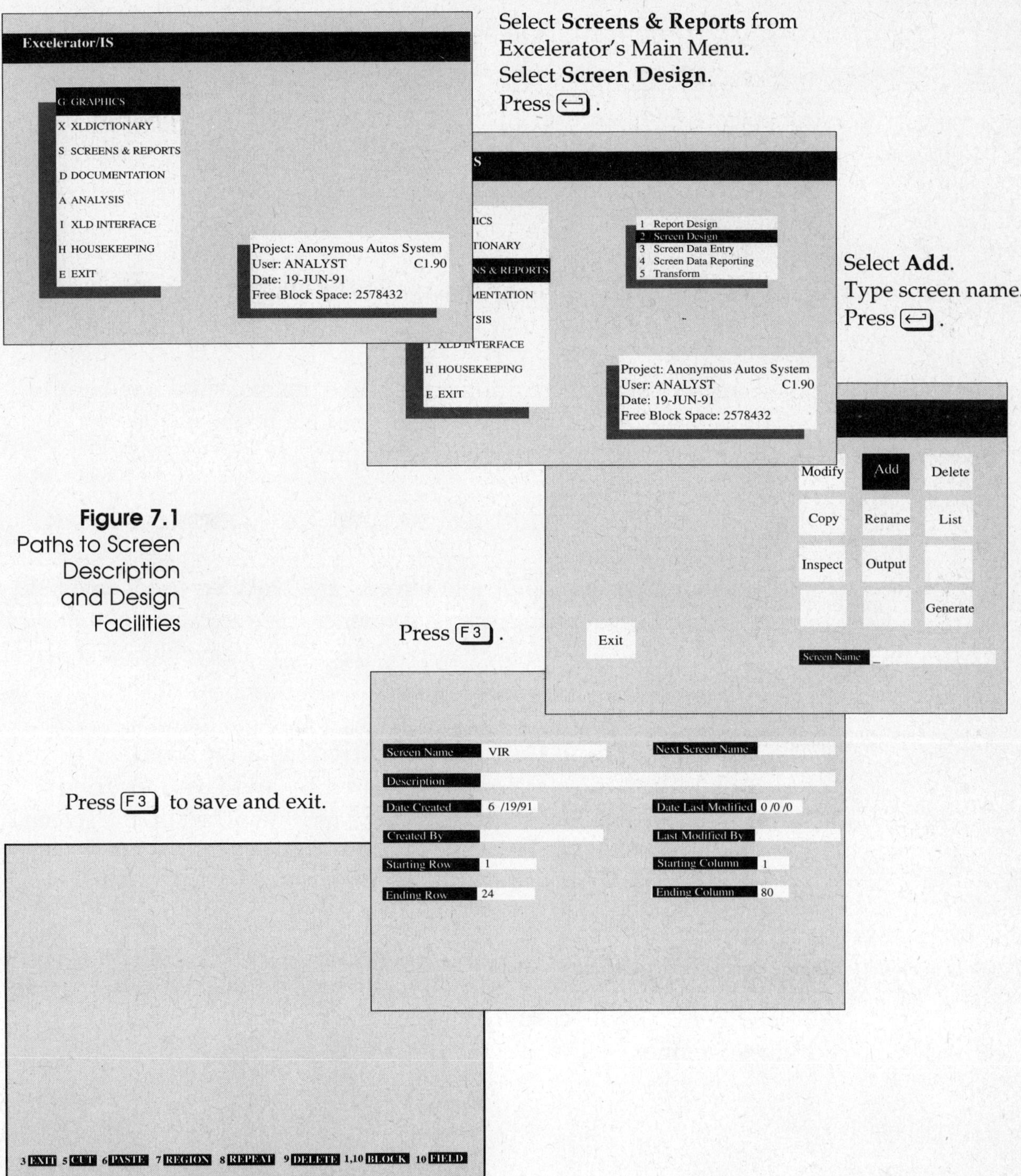

Figure 7.1
Paths to Screen Description and Design Facilities

7.1.1 Describing Screens

To begin the screen development process,

- Select **S SCREENS & REPORTS** from Excelerator's Main Menu.
- Select **2 Screen Design** from the Screens & Reports Menu.
- Select **Add** from the Screen Action Keypad which appears.

The **Screen Name** prompt appears at the bottom of your screen as shown in Figure 7.1.1b.

- Type **`VIR`** (for Vehicle Inventory Record) in the Screen Name field.
- Press ⏎.

The Screen Design description screen, like the one shown in Figure 7.1.1c, appears. VIR appears in the **Screen Name** field. The **Description** field contains the screen's purpose. In this field,

- Type **`VEHICLE INVENTORY RECORD DATA ENTRY SCREEN.`**

For a system involving multiple screens, the **Next Screen Name** field could be used to identify a screen sequence. (See *Excelerator Facilities & Functions Reference Guide* Pages 4-20 & 4-23). Leave the Next Screen Name field blank.

The **Date Created** and **Date Last Modified** fields are filled automatically by Excelerator. The **Created By** and **Last Modified By** fields are used to identify the users who have worked on the screen.

- Type **`ANALYST`** in both of these fields.

The last four fields describe the size of your Screen Design and its physical location. Leave these values alone. You may wish to change them for your own Screen Designs in the future; for now the default values are fine.

Figure 7.1.1a
Main Menu and Screens & Reports Menu

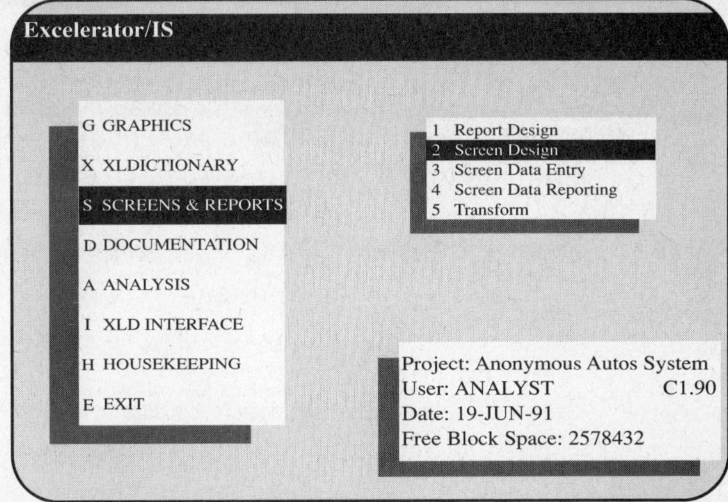

Figure 7.1.1b
Screen Design Action Key Pad

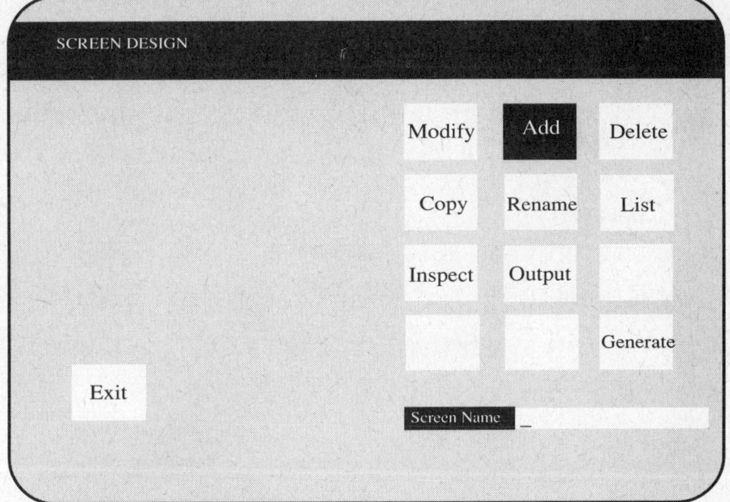

Figure 7.1.1c
Screen Design Description

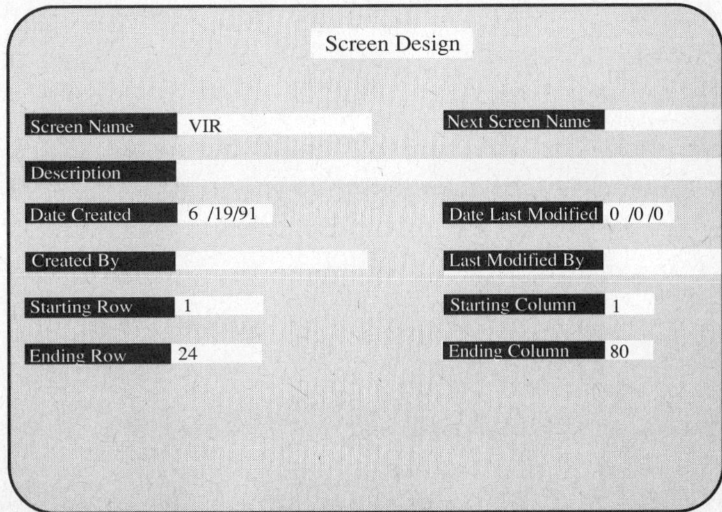

7.1.2 Designing Screen Layout

The first step in designing a screen layout is to decide how the screen is going to look. Everyone will have a slightly different idea about how a particular screen should look. For the purpose of teaching you to use Excelerator's Screen Design facilities, a version of the VIR screen layout appears in Figure 7.1.2b for you to copy. Using it as a reference, begin drawing the screen layout.

While at the Screen Design description screen (refer to **7.1.1 Describing Screens**),

- Press F3.

A blank drawing screen like the one in Figure 7.1.2a appears. The insertion point appears in the upper left-hand corner of the screen. Whenever you begin typing, the characters appear at the insertion point. The insertion point is moved using the arrow keys on your keyboard, or by selecting a position with the mouse and then pressing the left button on the mouse.

To begin drawing the screen in Figure 7.1.2b, position the insertion point near the left-hand side of the screen on the second line from the top.

- Type **DATE:**.

Now move the insertion point to a position about two inches from the right side of the screen on the same line, and

- Type **TIME:**.

You have created prompts for fields which will display the system date and time. The balance of the screen layout is drawn in the same way. Simply position your insertion point and type the desired text.

The next section, **7.1.3 Editing Screen Design**, provides instructions on editing screen layouts. To avoid frustration, read that section before attempting to finish drawing your screen layout.

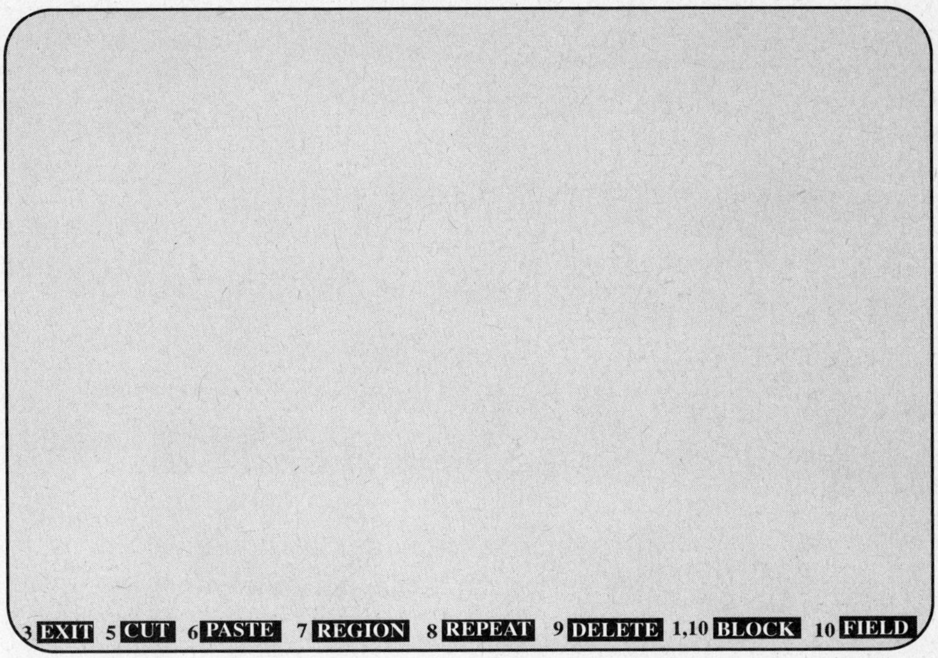

3 EXIT 5 CUT 6 PASTE 7 REGION 8 REPEAT 9 DELETE 1,10 BLOCK 10 FIELD

Figure 7.1.2a
Blank Drawing Screen

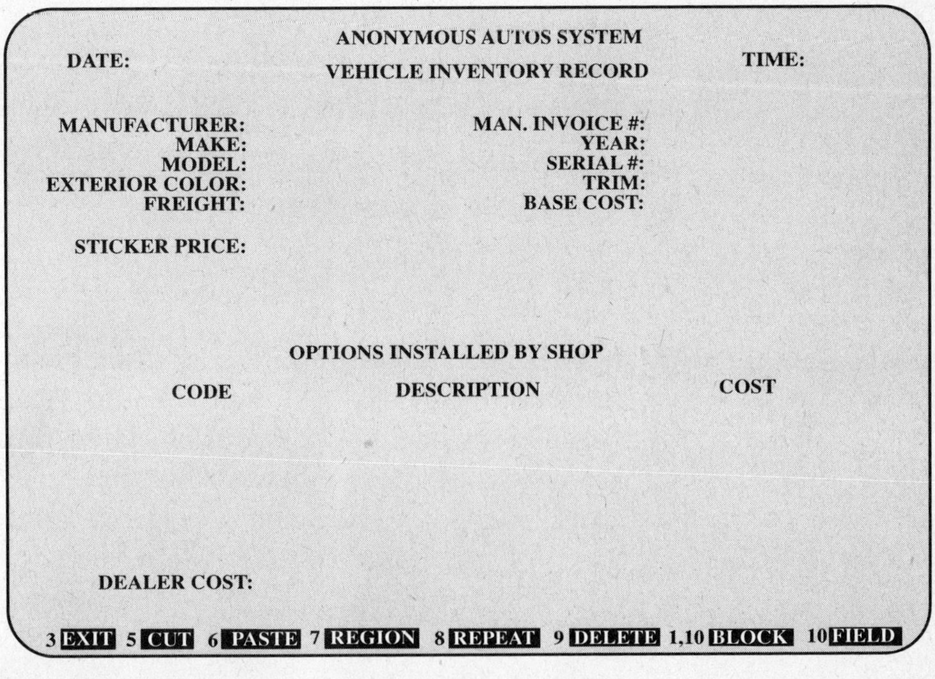

ANONYMOUS AUTOS SYSTEM

DATE: VEHICLE INVENTORY RECORD TIME:

MANUFACTURER: MAN. INVOICE #:
MAKE: YEAR:
MODEL: SERIAL #:
EXTERIOR COLOR: TRIM:
FREIGHT: BASE COST:

STICKER PRICE:

OPTIONS INSTALLED BY SHOP

CODE DESCRIPTION COST

DEALER COST:

3 EXIT 5 CUT 6 PASTE 7 REGION 8 REPEAT 9 DELETE 1,10 BLOCK 10 FIELD

Figure 7.1.2b
Completed Screen Layout

7.1.3 Editing Screen Design

When creating Screen Designs, you may find it necessary to edit your work. Excelerator provides several keyboard commands for moving and changing text and fields.

Retrieve the VIR screen layout. Refer, if necessary, to **7.1.1 Describing Screens**, and substitute **Modify** for **Add** on the Screen Design Action Keypad.

- Place the insertion point somewhere on the top line of the VIR screen layout.
- Type **ANONYMOUS AUTOS SYSTEM.**

This is the screen **header**. It should be centered on the top line. To move the text to the center of the line,

- Place the insertion point to the left of the header on the same line.
- Press [Ins] to move the header away from the insertion point.
- Press [Delete] to move the header closer to the insertion point.

Using [Spacebar] or [Ins] or [Delete], you can change the text by deleting letters or adding spaces.

Refer to Figure 7.1.3 for a complete summary of Excelerator's keyboard commands for designing and editing Screen Designs. This figure also appears inside the back cover of this book.

Exercise 7.1.3

Your Screen Design should now resemble the first lines of the finished screen layout shown in Figure 7.1.2b. With the finished screen layout as your objective, finish drawing your screen layout. Press [F3] when you are done to save your work, and exit to the Screen Design description. You may press [F3] again to exit to the Main Menu.

Figure 7.1.3 Keyboard Commands for Editing Screen Design

Key-Stroke	Result
Backspace	Deletes spaces and characters preceding the insertion point.
Delete	Deletes spaces and characters. Moves text and fields located to the right of insertion point *toward* insertion point.
Ins	Inserts spaces. Moves text and fields located to the right of insertion point *away* from insertion point.
F3 + Backspace	Deletes line from insertion point to *beginning*.
F1 + Delete	Deletes line on which insertion point is positioned. Moves lines located below the insertion point *up*.
F1 + End	Deletes line from the insertion point to the *end*.
F1 + Ins	Inserts lines above the insertion point. Moves lines below the insertion point *down*.
F3	Saves and exits.
F4	Cancels and exits without saving.
F5	Cuts field on which insertion point is positioned.
F6	Pastes most recently cut field.
F7	Creates a region. (See **7.1.9 Creating Scroll Regions**.)
F9	Deletes field on which insertion point is positioned.
F10	Calls the Field Definition Screen.
Spacebar	Deletes characters forward from insertion point.

7.1.4 Initiating Screen Field Definition

Retrieve the VIR screen layout. Refer, if necessary, to **7.1.1 Describing Screens**, and substitute **Modify** for **Add** on the Screen Design Action Keypad.

- Place the insertion point in any blank area on your screen layout.

The position of your insertion point determines where the field you define will appear on the screen. When you have selected a spot,

- Press F10.

The **Field Definition** screen appears in the bottom half of your screen, temporarily covering a portion of your screen layout as shown in Figure 7.1.4.

- Press F3.

The Field Definition screen disappears.

- Press F10 again, and the Field Definition screen reappears.

The Field Definition screen is used to control the display of screen fields, and the data entered in those fields. Use Tab to navigate forward through the Field Definition screen. Hold down Shift and press Tab to navigate backward. You may also use the mouse to position the insertion point by moving the cursor to any field on the Field Definition screen and clicking the left-hand button on the mouse.

In the next section, **7.1.5 Defining Screen Field Attributes**, you will learn what each of the fields on the Field Definition screen means and how each is used.

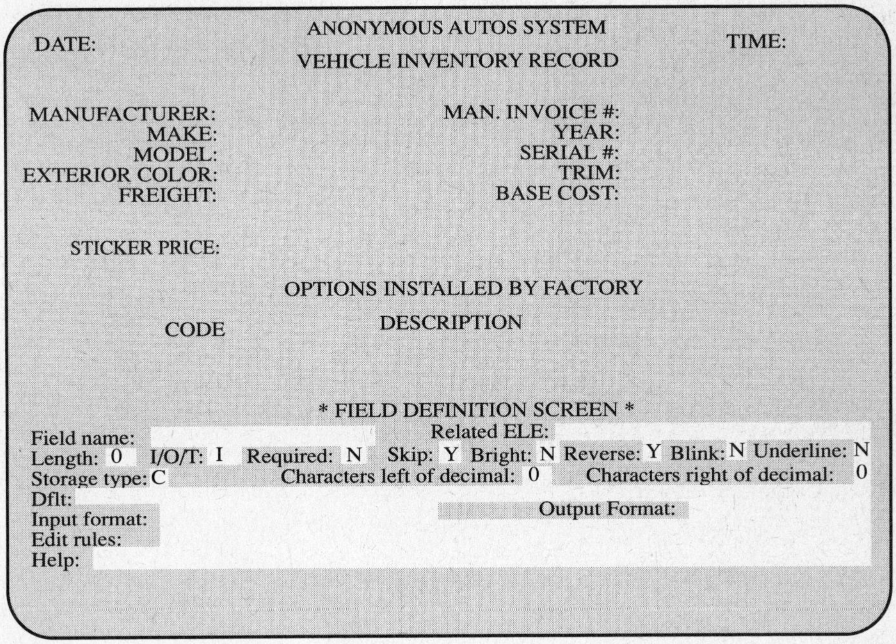

Figure 7.1.4
Field Definition Screen Appearing on the VIR Screen Layout

DATE: ANONYMOUS AUTOS SYSTEM TIME:
VEHICLE INVENTORY RECORD

MANUFACTURER: MAN. INVOICE #:
MAKE: YEAR:
MODEL: SERIAL #:
EXTERIOR COLOR: TRIM:
FREIGHT: BASE COST:

STICKER PRICE:

OPTIONS INSTALLED BY FACTORY
CODE DESCRIPTION

* FIELD DEFINITION SCREEN *
Field name: Related ELE:
Length: 0 I/O/T: I Required: N Skip: Y Bright: N Reverse: Y Blink: N Underline: N
Storage type: C Characters left of decimal: 0 Characters right of decimal: 0
Dflt:
Input format: Output Format:
Edit rules:
Help:

7.1.5 Defining Screen Field Attributes

Figure 7.1.5 explains each screen field attribute provided by Excelerator's Field Definition screen. Since Excelerator places default values in many of the field attributes, you won't have to worry about these values for every screen field you create. Read Figure 7.1.5 carefully though, because many of the attributes can enhance your Screen Designs.

When defining field attributes, avoid Storage Types other than **C** (character) unless you want to read more about them in the Excelerator manuals (see Figure 7.1.5 for Excelerator manual reference). Other storage types will cause you grief if you don't understand how to use them properly. In this tutorial, we deal exclusively with the character storage type.

Experiment with the field attribute options, bearing in mind the information provided in Figure 7.1.5.

Figure 7.1.5
Screen Field Attributes

Field Name: A unique identifier assigned to a field. This may be the same name as the related Data Element.

Related ELE: The name of the Data Element related to the field.

Length: The field length on the screen. Described by the number of characters left of the decimal.

I/O/T: The field type — I (Input), O (Output), or T (Text).
- Input fields accept user-entered data.
- Output fields display system-provided data. Users cannot change the contents of an output field.
- Text fields display character strings on the screen, such as the prompts that precede input fields on the Screen Design. Text fields cannot be altered by users or the system.

Required: Enter "Y" or "N" for "yes" or "no". Your response determines whether the field may be skipped or left blank. A required field may not be left blank. The default value is "N". If you specify that a field is required, you must also specify in an edit rule that blanks are not acceptable using the syntax **not** " ".

Skip: Enter "Y" or "N" for "yes" or "no". Your response determines whether the cursor will move automatically to the next field when the current field is full. This field's default value is "Y".

Bright:
Blink:
Underline:
Reverse Video: These attributes control the way fields and text in the fields look on the screen. Enter "Y" or "N" for "yes" or "no". Not all monitors support these functions, so don't panic if you are unable to implement them. The default value for Bright, Blink, and Underline is "N". The default for Reverse Video is "Y" which makes the field visible on the screen.

Storage Type: This is the format Excelerator uses to store data entered in the field — C (Character), B (Binary), D (Date), F (Floating point), and P (Packed decimal). The default is C.

Characters Left of Decimal:
Characters Right of Decimal: These two fields, in conjunction with the Storage Type, are used to calculate an entry's storage length. Characters Left of Decimal applies to all field types while Characters Right of Decimal applies only to Pack field types. Because we will only be using the Character storage type, leave the Characters Right of Decimal field blank and enter the the field's display length in Characters Left of Decimal (See *Excelerator Facilities & Functions Reference Guide* Page 4-35).

Default: This is a predetermined value for input, output, or text fields. For input fields, the default suggests a valid field value. For output fields, this default should be left blank unless the field value is constant. Since text fields are used as prompts and headers, they should always have a default value.

Input Format: This field contains a description of the valid data input format using a combination of the following characters — B (Blank); S (Positive or negative sign); Y (Year); M (Month); D (Day); , (Comma); . (Period).

Output Format: This is the format of field data display. Use the same values as for Input format plus the following — $ (Dollar sign); +/- (Plus or minus sign); Z (Non-zero digit or a space).

Edit Rules: This is the validation criteria for data entered in this field. For a detailed description of valid Edit Rules, see **5.2.4 Defining Edit Rules**.

Help: This is an explanation of the type of data to be entered in this field. The message displays if you press F2 when you are testing your Screen Design using Inspect.

7.1.6 Creating Unique Screen Fields

A screen field may be defined as unique to the screen and not related to any data Element. Such fields represent data not reflected in the database design, such as the system date or time.

Bring up the VIR screen layout. Refer, if necessary, to **7.1.1 Describing Screens**, and substitute **Modify** for **Add** on the Screen Design Action Keypad.

Your VIR screen layout should resemble the one shown in Figure 7.1.6a.

The **DATE** field on the VIR screen layout should be described as unique because it will contain the system date.

- Place the insertion point just after DATE: on the screen layout.
- Press F10 to bring up the Field Definition screen.
- Type **DATE** in Field Name on the Field Definition screen.

Complete the Field Definition screen for the DATE field using Figure 7.1.6b as a guide. When you have finished,

- Press F3 to save your work and return to the screen layout.

The DATE field is now complete as shown in Figure 7.1.6c. Because you typed N in **Reverse Video** on the Field Definition screen, it is not visible on your screen layout. This can be disconcerting, but the field has been defined properly. If you place your insertion point in the DATE field area and press F10, the Field Definition screen appears showing the DATE field description.

Exercise 7.1.6

Define the TIME field on your VIR Screen Design in the same way you defined the DATE field.

Select insertion point, and press F10.

DATE: ANONYMOUS AUTOS SYSTEM TIME:
VEHICLE INVENTORY RECORD

MANUFACTURER: MAN. INVOICE #:
MAKE: YEAR:
MODEL: SERIAL #:
EXTERIOR COLOR: TRIM:
FREIGHT: BASE COST:

STICKER PRICE:

OPTIONS INSTALLED BY SHOP
CODE DESCRIPTION COST

DEALER COST:

3 EXIT 5 CUT 6 PASTE 7 REGION 8 REPEAT 9 DELETE 1,10 BLOCK 10 FIELD

Figure 7.1.6a
Screen Layout with Insertion Point Selected

Complete Field Definition, and press F3.

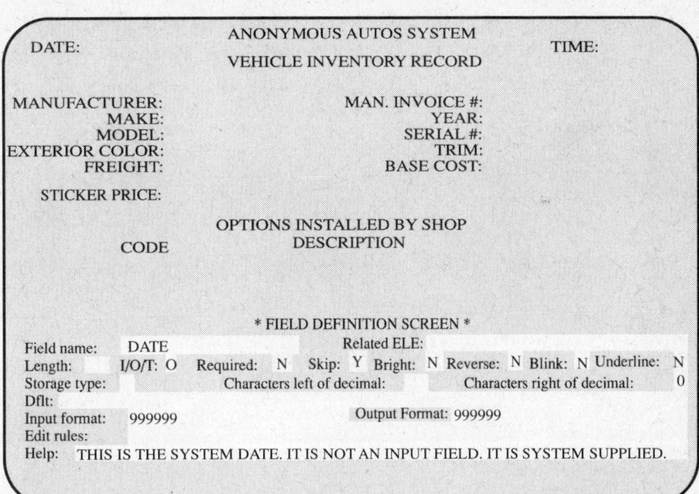

Figure 7.1.6b
Screen Field Definition Screen Completed for DATE

DATE: ANONYMOUS AUTOS SYSTEM TIME:
VEHICLE INVENTORY RECORD

MANUFACTURER: MAN. INVOICE #:
MAKE: YEAR:
MODEL: SERIAL #:
EXTERIOR COLOR: TRIM:
FREIGHT: BASE COST:

STICKER PRICE:

OPTIONS INSTALLED BY SHOP
CODE DESCRIPTION COST

DEALER COST:

3 EXIT 5 CUT 6 PASTE 7 REGION 8 REPEAT 9 DELETE 1,10 BLOCK 10 FIELD

Figure 7.1.6c
DATE Field Defined but Invisible on Screen Layout

7.1.7 Relating Screen Fields to New Elements

A screen field may be related to a new Data Element. That is, it may be related to a Data Element which has not been previously identified or defined in the XLDictionary. Relating screen fields to new Data Elements is usually done when you develop your screens before completing the data model, or when a Data Element omission is noticed during screen development.

If it is not already on your screen, retrieve the VIR screen layout. Refer, if necessary, to **7.1.1 Describing Screens**, and substitute **Modify** for **Add** on the Screen Design Action Keypad.

- Place the insertion point anywhere on the screen layout.
- Press [F10] to bring up the Field Definition screen.
- Type **TESTER** in Field Name and Related ELE.
- Press [F4].

Because TESTER is not a Data Element name described in the XLDictionary, Excelerator gives you a blank Element Description screen on which you may describe this new Data Element. Once the new Data Element is described, press [F3] to save it and return to the Field Definition screen. Then, with the cursor still in the Related ELE field, pressing [F10] will apply the new Data Element attributes to the Field Definition. Figure 7.17 details the command and screen sequence.

Experiment with this function or, while at the Element Description screen, press the right-hand button on your mouse to cancel.

When Excelerator asks if you're sure you want to exit without saving,

- Type **Y** .
- Press [↵].

Once back at the Field Definition screen,

- Press the right-hand button on the mouse to return to your screen layout.

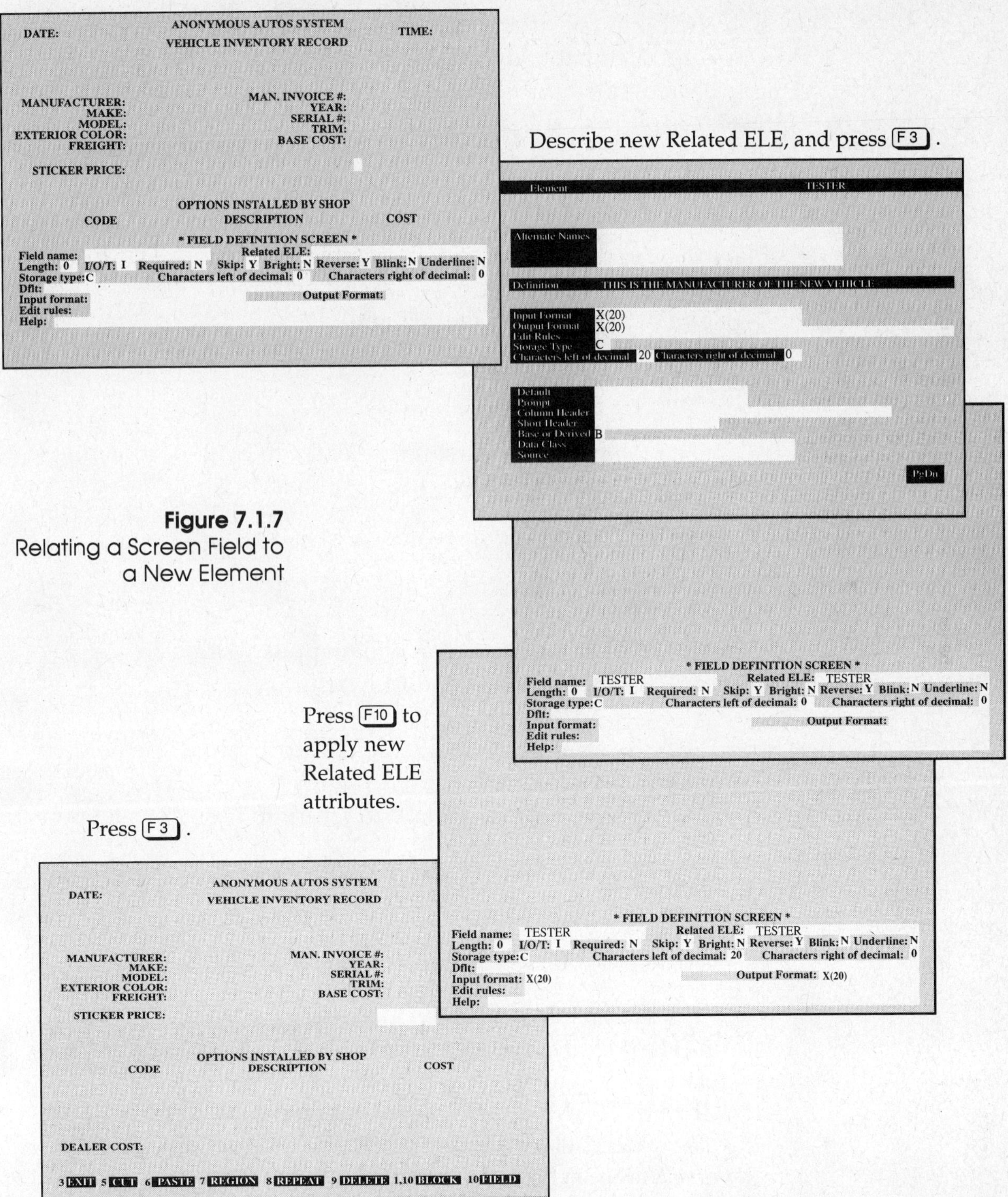

Figure 7.1.7
Relating a Screen Field to a New Element

7.1.8 Relating Screen Fields to Existing Elements

A screen field may be described using the attributes of a related existing Data Element. (An existing Data Element is one that has already been defined in XLDictionary. This process is summarized in Figure 7.1.8.)

On your VIR screen layout,

- Place the insertion point one space after MANUFACTURER:.
- Press F10 to bring up the Field Definition screen.
- Type **MANUFACTURER** in **Field Name**.
- Place the insertion point in the **Related ELE** field.
- Press F4.

Hint
If you know the exact name of the Data Element you want to relate to a field, type the name in Related ELE on the Field Definition Screen. Then press F10 to apply the Data Element attributes to the field. This is a time saver. It bypasses scrolling through your XLDictionary list of Data Elements.

A list of Data Elements appears. If the list is too long to fit on the screen, use Pg Up and Pg Dn (or + and -) to navigate.

- Select the Data Element named MANUFACTURER with the mouse. If selected with the arrow keys, you'll have to press ↵.

The Screen Field Definition screen will reappear with MANUFACTURER in the Related ELE field.

- Press F10 to apply this Data Element's attributes to the field definition.
- Press F3 to save your work and to return to the screen layout.

The new field will be visibly located just after the MANUFACTURER prompt on the screen layout.

Exercise 7.1.8

Define all of the remaining fields on your VIR Screen Design by relating them to existing Data Elements. Define STICKER PRICE and DEALER COST as output fields, and type N in the Reverse Video field. All others input fields should be in Reverse Video. When you are finished, your Screen Design should look something like the third screen shown in Figure 7.1.9a.

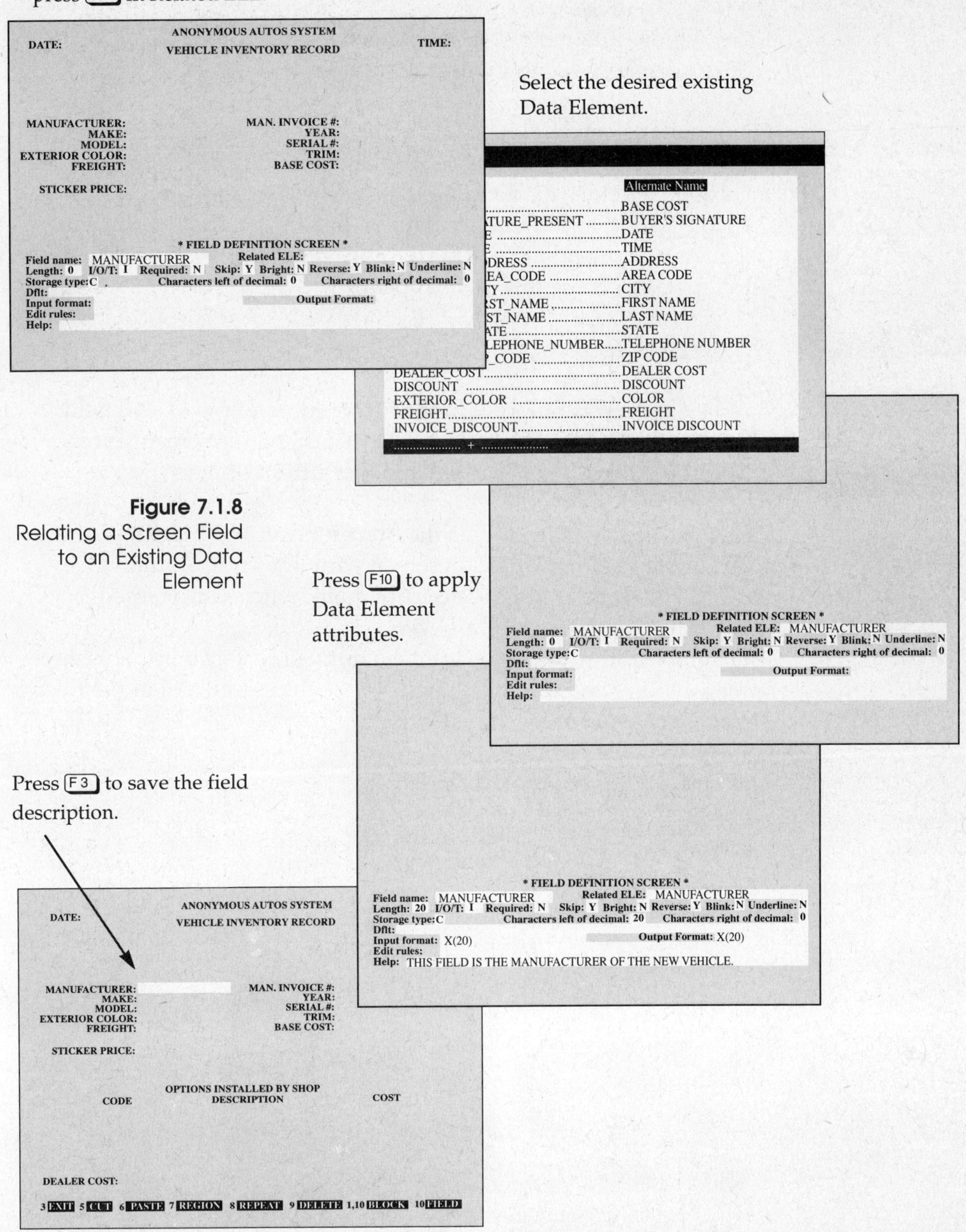

Figure 7.1.8
Relating a Screen Field to an Existing Data Element

7.1.9 Creating Scroll Regions

Scroll regions allow the designer to utilize less screen space for the entry or display of repetitive data.

On the first screen in Figure 7.1.9a, there is only enough room under the OPTIONS INSTALLED BY SHOP column headers for about three lines of data fields. By defining this area as a scroll region, you are able to enter up to 100 lines of data in the same space. As the data fields for CODE and DESCRIPTION are filled, they will appear to scroll up, and empty lines will appear.

On the VIR screen layout,

- Place the insertion point in the first column of the CODE field under OPTIONS INSTALLED BY SHOP on the screen layout.
- Press [F7] to display the **Region Definition** screen.

Excelerator automatically fills the **Starting line** and **Starting column** fields of the Region Definition screen with line and column values based on the position of the insertion point when you pressed F7.

The **Total columns** field contains the number of columns between the insertion point and the right-hand side of the screen. All of the Region Definition fields are explained in Figure 7.1.9b.

On the Region Definition screen,

- Type **`SHOP OPTIONS`** in **Region name**.
- Type **`3`** in **Lines displayed.**
- Type **`100`** in **Total lines.**
- Press [F3] to save the scroll region.

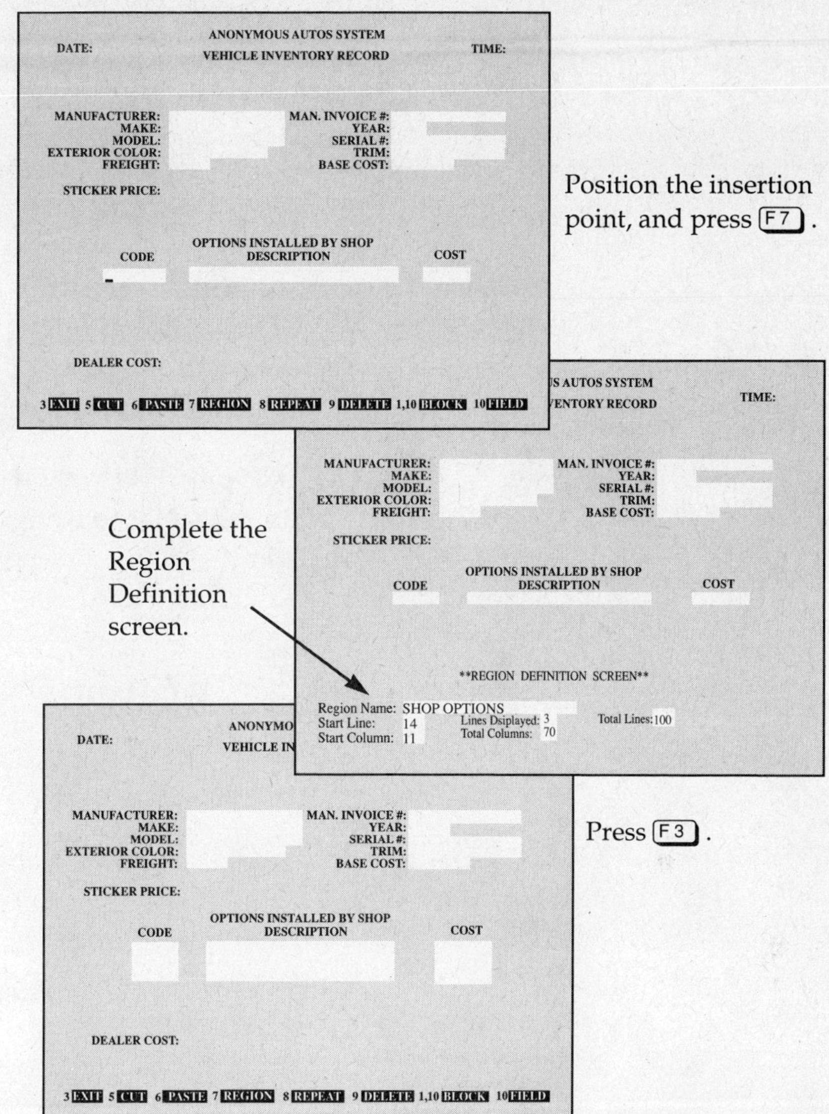

Figure 7.1.9a Creating a Scroll Region on the VIR Screen Design

Figure 7.1.9b Region Definition Screen Fields

Region Name	You may use up to sixteen (16) characters to describe this region. This region name must be unique to this screen.
Start Line	This is the first line in the region. The default value is the place where the insertion point was located when F7 was pressed.
Start Column	This is the first Column in the region. The default value is the place where the insertion point was located when F7 was pressed.
Lines Displayed	Enter the number of lines that you wish to display on the screen. There must be enough room to display those lines.
Total Column	Total number of screen columns included in the region. The default is the total width of the screen minus the starting column of the region.
Total Lines	Total number of lines in the region. The maximum is 100.

7.1.10 Printing Screen Design

When you've completed your screen description and design, you may send it to an output device for printing.

- Select **S SCREENS & REPORTS** from Excelerator's Main Menu.
- Select **2 Screen Design** from the Screens & Reports Menu.
- Select **Output** from the Screen Design Action Keypad.

As shown in Figure 7.1.10a, prompts appear near the bottom of the screen asking for the **Name OR Name Range** of screen(s) you wish to print. Any name entered in the Name field must match one of the screens defined in the XLDictionary.

If the exact name of the desired Screen Design is not known,

- Press ↵.

The XLDictionary list of Screen Designs appears.

- Select the VIR Screen Design with the mouse.

As shown in Figure 7.1.10b, Excelerator now asks where you want the output sent.

- Select **Printer** with the mouse.

The **Screen Design Output** screen appears, as shown in Figure 7.1.10c. You are given options regarding the level of detail the output will provide on your Screen Design. The default settings are just fine.

- Press F4 to print.

As with other Excelerator system components, it is possible to print a specific range of screens rather than just one screen at a time. This is accomplished by using wild cards to define a range. The asterisks is Excelerator's wild card. If, for example, you wanted to print all Screen Designs beginning with the letter **A**, you would type **A*** in the **Name Range** field. Similarly, ***A** indicates all Screen Designs ending with the letter **A**.

Figure 7.1.10a
Output Selection on Screen Design Action Keypad

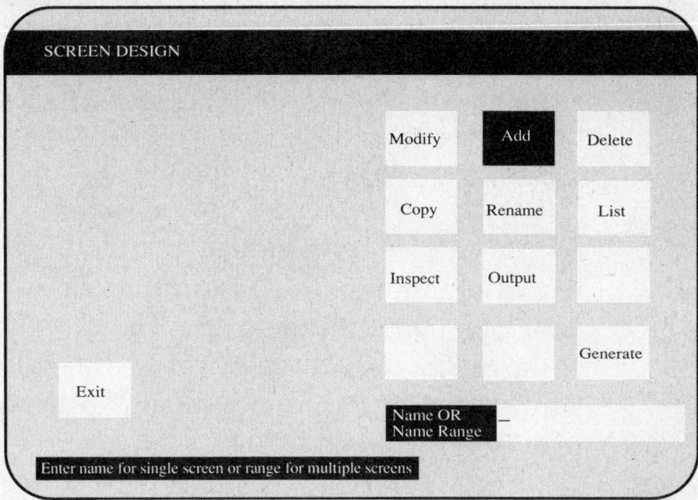

Figure 7.1.10b
List of Screen Designs Available for Output

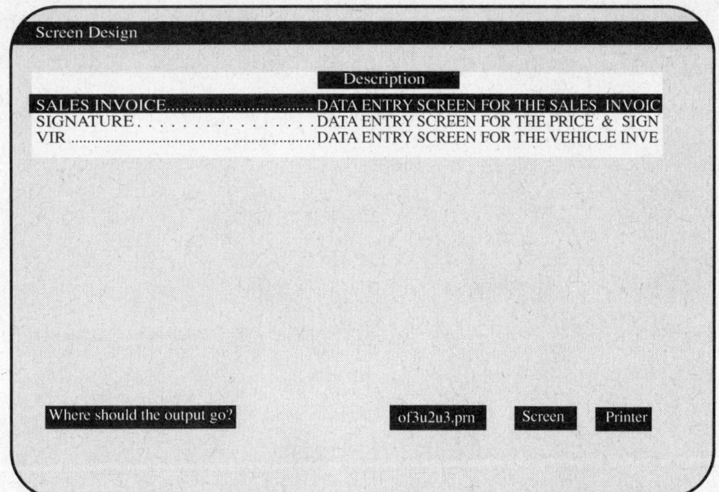

Figure 7.1.10c
Screen Output Description

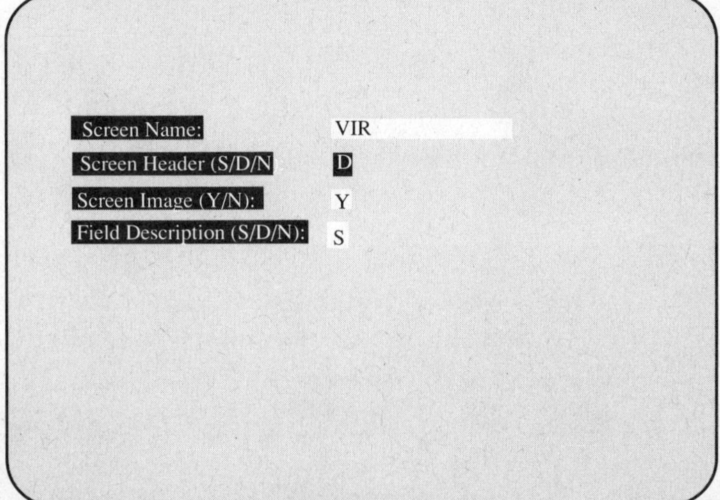

7.1.11 Interpreting Printed Screen Output

Printed screen output consists of three reports: the Screen Design Description, the Field Summary, and the Screen Design.

As you can see from Figure 7.1.11a, the **Screen Design Description** report is similar to the description screen you saw when you first developed your input screen. The block of data on the lower portion of the report provides a count of the various fields that you defined on your screen. The value following **Form map size:** is the number of bytes in this Screen Design.

The **Field Summary**, shown in Figure 7.1.11b, is a tabular summary of all field attributes defined during screen development. This report is a valuable reference tool. It is particularly useful for pointing out errors or inconsistencies in your layout. Each column header corresponds to an attribute chosen during Data Element definition. The column headers are abbreviations for the following terms:

REQ	Required
SKIP	Skip
BRT	Bright
REV	Reverse
BLNK	Blink
UND	Underline
LEN	Length
STYP(S1,S2)	Digits before and after decimal
SLOC	Starting location counter that is incremented by the length of the data field

There are three field type groups listed on the Field Summary: **input**, **output**, and **text**. (Some of the input field have been omitted in Figure 7.1.11b due to the size of the report.)

The actual Screen Design is provided by the **Screen Design** output report shown in Figure 7.1.11c. All labels are shown as they appear on the screen. If you chose to have data fields underlined when you printed this report, then underline characters indicate the location and length of data fields.

Screen Design

Screen Name	VIR	Next Screen Name	
Description	DATA ENTRY SCREEN FOR THE VEHICLE INVENTORY RECORD		
Date Created	6 /19/91	Date Last Modified	7 /9/ 91
Created By	ANALYST	Last Modified By	
Starting Row	1	Starting Column	1
Ending Row	24	Ending Column	80

Nbr of groups:

Total fields:

Field descriptors by field type:
- Input fields: 24
- Output fields: 4
- Text fields: 20

Form map size: 404

Chain map size: 404

Figure 7.1.11a Screen Design Description for the VIR Screen

Field groups

None

Field Descriptions

(row,col)	---- name ----	Req	Skip	Brt	Rev	Blnk	Und	Len	styp(s1,s2) : sloc
(4,56)	'MFGR INVOICE # '	N	Y	N	Y	N	N	15	C(15, 0): 12
(5,17)	'MAKE '	N	Y	N	Y	N	N	20	C(20, 0): 27
(5,56)	'YEAR '	N	Y	N	Y	N	N	4	C(4, 0): 47
(6,17)	'MODEL '	N	Y	N	Y	N	N	20	C(20, 0): 51
(6,56)	'SERIAL '	N	Y	N	Y	N	N	20	C(20, 0): 71
(7,17)	'COLOR '	N	Y	N	Y	N	N	15	C(15, 0): 91
(7,56)	'TRIM '	N	Y	N	Y	N	N	20	C(20, 0): 106
(8,17)	'FREIGHT '	N	Y	N	Y	N	N	7	C(5, 2): 126
(8,56)	'BASE COST '	N	Y	N	Y	N	N	8	C(6, 2): 131
(12,11)	'SHOP OPT. CODE 1 '	N	Y	N	Y	N	N	10	C(10, 0): 137
(12,27)	'SHOP OPT. DESC 1 '	N	Y	N	Y	N	N	30	C(30, 0): 147
(13,11)	'OPTION COST 1 '	N	Y	N	Y	N	N	7	C(7, 0): 177
(13,27)	'SHOP OPT. CODE 2 '	N	Y	N	Y	N	N	10	C(10, 0): 187

Output Fields

(row,col)	name	Req	Skip	Brt	Rev	Blnk	Und	Len	styp(s1,s2) : sloc
(2, 7)	' '	N	Y	N	N	N	N	6	C(6, 0) : 0
(2,75)	'CURRENT TIME '	N	Y	N	N	N	N	6	C(6, 0) : 6
(16,16)	'STICKER PRICE '	N	Y	N	N	N	N	8	C(6, 2) : 257
(23,16)	'DEALER COST '	N	Y	N	N	N	N	8	C(6, 2) : 398

Text Fields

(row,col)	name	Req	Skip	Brt	Rev	Blnk	Und
(1,28)	'ANONYMOUS AUTOS'	N	N	N	N	N	N
(2, 1)	'DATE: '	N	N	N	N	N	N
(2,27)	'VEHICLE INVENTOR '	N	N	N	N	N	N
(4, 3)	'MANUFACTURER: '	N	N	N	N	N	N
(4,17)	' '	N	N	N	N	N	N
(4,40)	'MAN. INVOICE #: '	N	N	N	N	N	N
(5,11)	'MAKE: '	N	N	N	N	N	N
(5,50)	'YEAR: '	N	N	N	N	N	N
(6,10)	'MODEL: '	N	N	N	N	N	N
(6,46)	'SERIAL #: '	N	N	N	N	N	N
(7, 1)	'EXTERIOR COLOR: '	N	N	N	N	N	N
(7,50)	'TRIM: '	N	N	N	N	N	N

Figure 7.1.11b Field Summary for the VIR Screen

```
Form <VIR        > (as of 23-JUL-91)
--------------------------------------------------------------------------------
                        ANONYMOUS AUTOS SYSTEM
DATE: ~~~~~~           VEHICLE INVENTORY RECORD                     TIME: ~~~~~~

     MANUFACTURER: ______________        MAN. INVOICE #: __________
             MAKE: ______________                  YEAR: ____
            MODEL: ______________              SERIAL #: __________________
   EXTERIOR COLOR: ___________                     TRIM: __________________
          FREIGHT: _______                    BASE COST: _________

        STICKER PRICE: ~~~~~~
                                   SHOP INSTALLED OPTIONS
               CODE                     DESCRIPTION

          __________   ______________________________
          __________   ______________________________
          __________   ______________________________

         DEALER COST: ~~~~~~

--------------------------------------------------------------------------------
```

Figure 7.1.11c Screen Design for the VIR Screen

Excelerating Your Skills ... in Screen Design

In working your way through the **Designing Screens** section, you have successfully completed the **Vehicle Inventory Record (VIR)** screen for Rich Royce's new Anonymous Autos information system. You are now ready to develop the remaining screens required for the new system.

This is a good time to go back and re-read **3. The Anonymous Autos Project**. As you read, watch for screen requirements.

The Sales Invoice shown on the opposite page is clearly one screen requirement. All of the information on the Sales Invoice must be entered into the automated system. A **Sales Invoice** screen will facilitate that data entry process.

Think about your VIR screen and its resemblance to the original Vehicle Inventory Record form shown on the opposite page. Develop your Sales Invoice screen to look as much like the one presently in use at Anonymous Autos as possible. While defining fields, study fields like **Tax & License Fee** carefully, Tax & License Fee involves variable values: tax rate and license fee. Perhaps it should be defined as more than one field.

The sales staff at Anonymous Autos changes frequently The need to add, delete and modify salesperson records must be considered. How will this be accomplished? Is there a need for a **Salesperson Information** screen? Obtain the data requirements for this screen from your XLDictionary. What Data Elements are in the Salesperson record? Because the screen will facilitate the capture of those Data Elements, they must be defined as fields on your Salesperson Information screen.

Describe and design the Sales Invoice and Salesperson Information screens.

The Anonymous Autos Current Sales Invoice Form

Sales Invoice

Invoice #: ____________ **Date:** ___/___/___

SOLD TO: Name: ____________
Address: ____________
____

City: ____________ State: _____ Zip: ____________
Telephone:(___) ___ –______

SOLD BY ____________

NEW CAR: Make: ____________ Year: ____________
Model: ____________ Serial #: ____________

OPTIONS:

Code	Description	Price

TRADE-IN: Make: ____________ Year: ____________
Model: ____________ Serial #: ____________

Sticker Price + : ____________
Total Option Price + : ____________
Discount - : ____________
Total Price = : ____________
Trade-In Allowance - : ____________
Tax & License Fee + : ____________
Total Due = : ____________

BUYER SIGNATURE

____

SALES MANAGER SIGNATURE

____

7.2

Designing Reports (REDs)

Information reporting is a natural extension of the data capture which occurs through input screens. Data captured and stored through system screens can be processed and output in a form useful to end-users.

Reports are especially useful to management because they can be tailored to provide specific information. Reports can turn raw data captured by the system into useful information by presenting processed data in a user-defined format.

The careful design of reports is crucial to ensure usability. Information should be displayed in an orderly, uncluttered, and easy-to-read format.

Excelerator provides Report Design facilities accessed by following the paths illustrated in Figure 7.2.

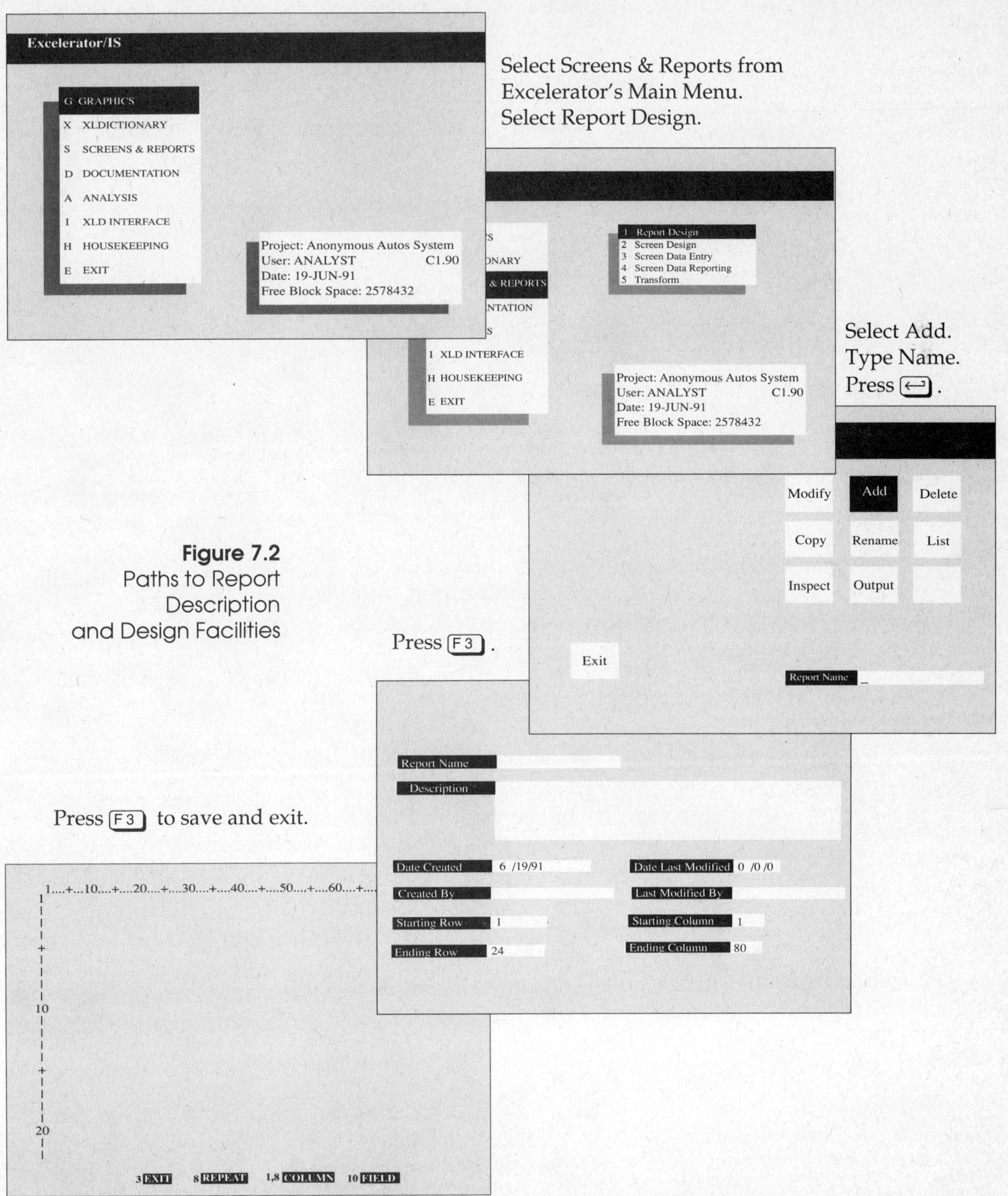

Figure 7.2
Paths to Report Description and Design Facilities

7.2.1 Describing Reports

As shown in Figure 7.2.1a, initiate the report description.

- Select **S SCREENS & REPORTS** from Excelerator's Main Menu.
- Select **1 Report Design** from the Screens & Reports Menu.
- Select **Add** from the Report Design Action Keypad.

The **Report Name** prompt appears at the bottom of your screen as shown in Figure 7.2.1b.

- Type **`AUTO SALES BY MAKE`** in the Report Name field.
- Press ⏎.

The **Report Design** description screen, like the one shown in Figure 7.2.1c, is displayed. Your report's name will be in the **Report Name** field. The **Description** field contains the purpose of the report. In this field,

- Type **`THIS IS A REPORT OF AUTO SALES GROUPING THE SALES BY MAKE OF AUTO.`**

The **Date Created** and **Date Last Modified** fields are filled automatically by Excelerator. The **Created By** and **Last Modified By** fields are used to identify the users who have worked on the report.

- Type **`ANALYST`** in both of these fields.

The last four fields describe the size of your Report Design and its physical location on the page. Leave these values alone. You may wish to change them for your own Report Designs, but for now the default values are fine.

Go now to the next section, **7.2.2 Designing Report Layout**, to begin designing your report.

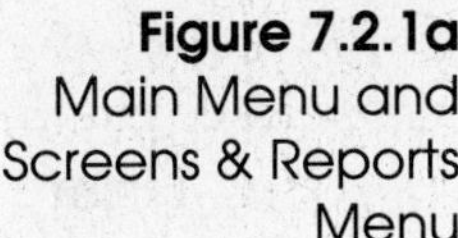

Figure 7.2.1a
Main Menu and Screens & Reports Menu

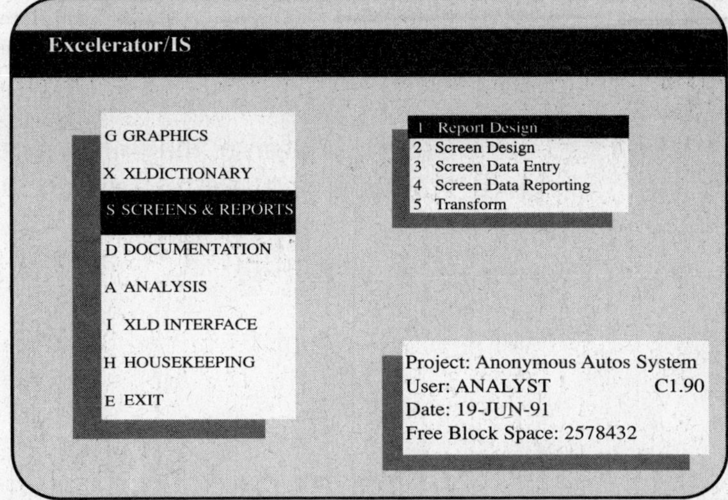

Figure 7.2.1b
Report Design Action Key Pad

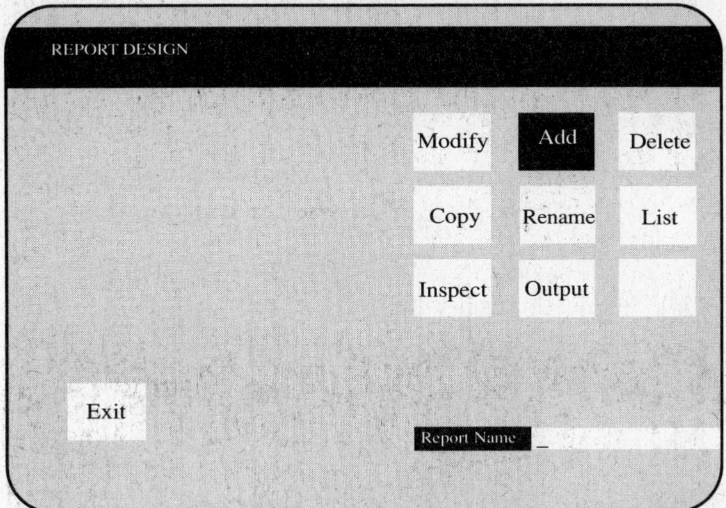

Figure 7.2.1c
Report Design Description

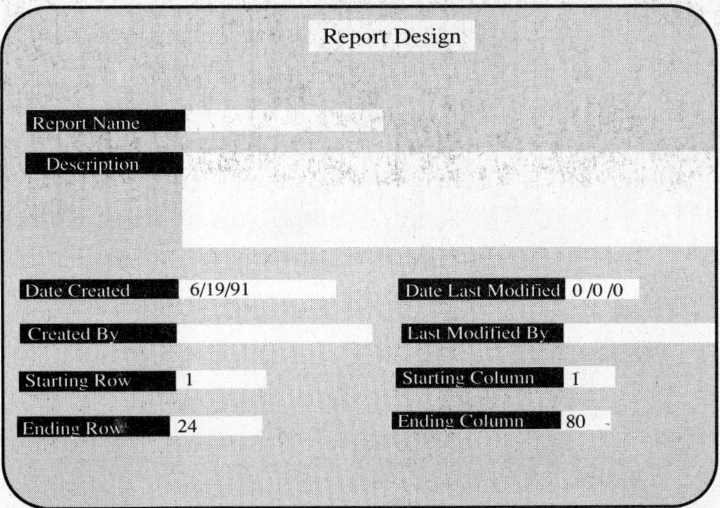

7.2.2 Designing Report Layout

As with Screen Design, the first step in designing a report layout is deciding how you want the report to look. A version of the Auto Sales by Make report layout appears in Figure 7.2.2b. Using Figure 7.2.2b as a reference, begin drawing your report layout.

While at the Report Description screen (refer to **7.2.1 Describing Reports**),

- Press F3.

A blank report drawing screen like the one in Figure 7.2.2a appears. Look for the tiny flashing box, called the insertion point, in the upper left-hand corner of the screen. The insertion point is moved by using the arrow keys on your keyboard or by selecting a position with the left button on the mouse.

To begin drawing the report in Figure 7.2.2b, position the insertion point on the top line at around the 30th column.

- Type **`AUTO SALES BY MAKE.`**

On the very next line, centered below the header you just created,

- Type **`Report Date:`**.

Now move the insertion point to the fourth line near the left side of the screen.

- Type **`MAKE:`** .

The next section, **7.2.3 Editing Report Layout**, gives instructions on editing report layouts. To avoid frustration, read that section before attempting to finish drawing your report layout.

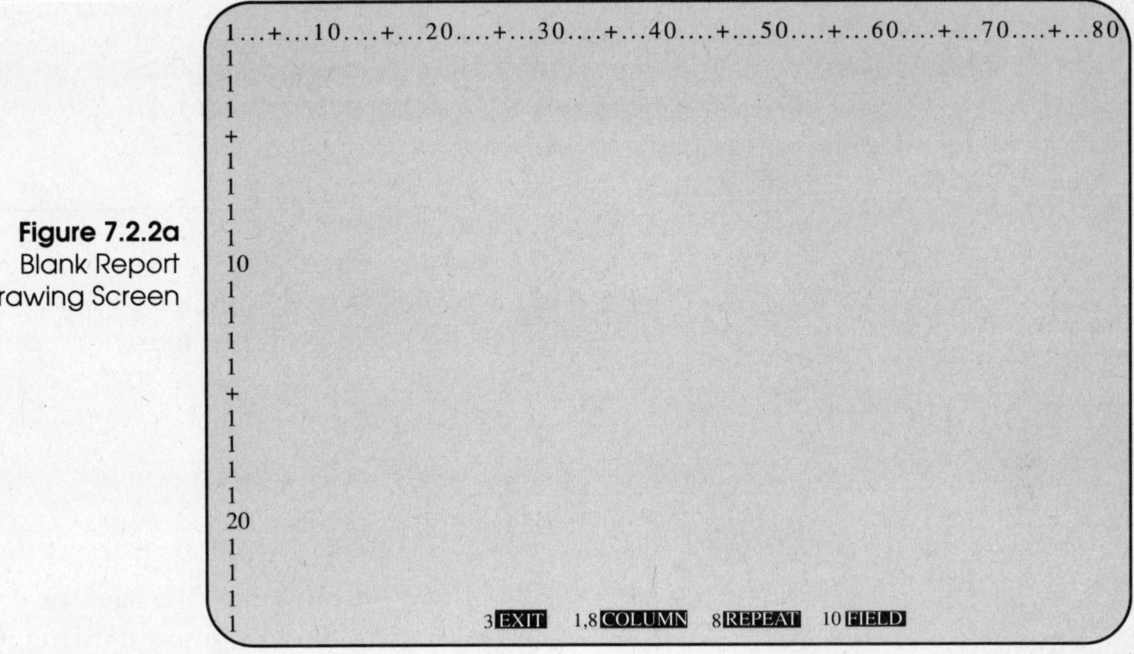

Figure 7.2.2a
Blank Report Drawing Screen

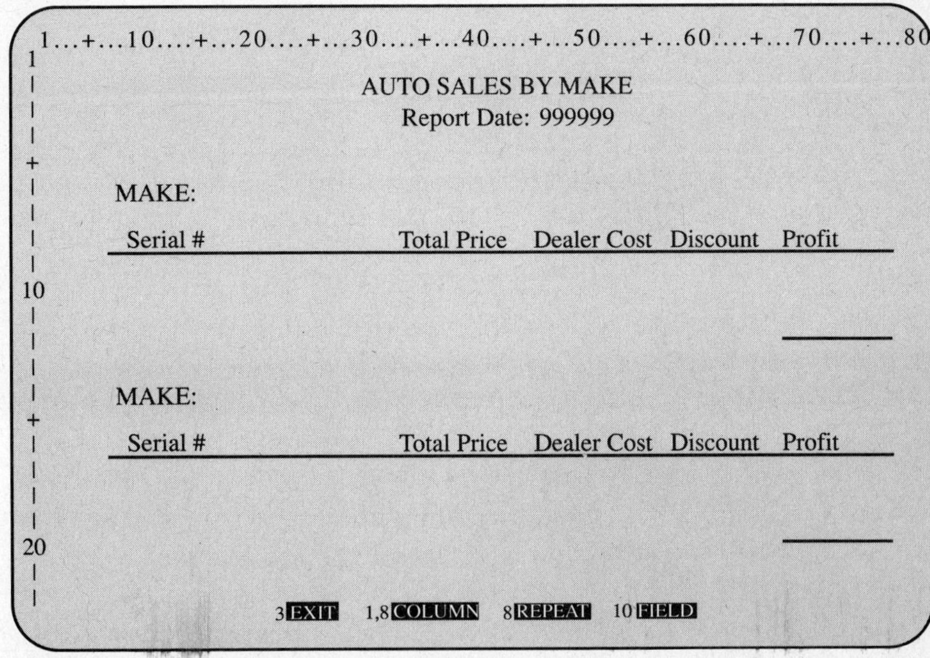

Figure 7.2.2b
Completed Auto Sales by Make Report Layout

7.2.3 Editing Report Layout

When creating Report Designs, you may find it necessary to edit your work. Excelerator provides several keyboard commands for moving and changing text and fields.

To practice moving text around on the line,

- Place the insertion point to the left of the report header.
- Press [Ins] to move the header away from the insertion point.
- Press [Delete] to move the header closer to the insertion point.

Using [Spacebar] or [Ins] or [Delete], allows changes to the text by adding spaces, inserting new characters, or deleting unwanted characters.

Refer to Figure 7.2.3 for a complete summary of Excelerator's keyboard commands for designing and editing reports. This summary is nearly identical to the one shown in **7.1.3 Editing Screen Design** .

Exercise 7.2.3

Your Report Design should now resemble the first few lines of the finished report layout shown in Figure 7.2.2b. With Figure 7.2.2b as your objective, finish drawing your report layout.

Use the hyphen key to achieve the underlines shown in Figure 7.2.2b.

Press [F3] when you are finished to save your work and exit to the Report Design Action Keypad.

Figure 7.2.3 Keyboard Commands for Report Design

Key-Stroke	**Result**
Backspace	Deletes spaces and characters preceding the insertion point.
Delete	Deletes spaces and characters. Moves text and fields located to the right of insertion point *toward* insertion point.
Ins	Inserts spaces. Moves text and fields located to the right of insertion point *away* from insertion point.
F 3 + Backspace	Deletes a characters from the insertion point to the *beginning* of the line.
F1 + Delete	Deletes the line on which the insertion point is positioned. Moves lines located below the insertion point *up*.
F1 + End	Deletes characters from the insertion point to the *end* of the line.
F1 + Ins	Inserts lines above the insertion point. Moves lines below the insertion point *down*.
F 3	Saves and exits.
F 4	Cancels and exits without saving.
F 5	Cuts the field on which insertion point is positioned.
F 6	Pastes most recently cut field.
F 8	Create a column. (See **7.2.7 Creating Repeating Field Columns.**)
F 9	Deletes the field on which the insertion point is positioned.
F10	Calls the Field Definition screen.
Spacebar	Deletes characters forward from insertion point.

7.2.4 Initiating Report Field Definition

When you have completed Exercise 7.2.3, your report layout should resemble the one in Figure 7.2.2b. The next step in the report development process is positioning and initiating the definition of report fields.

Retrieve the Auto Sales by Make Report Design. Refer, if necessary, to **7.2.1 Describing Reports**, and substitute **Modify** for **Add** on the Report Design Action Keypad.

- Place the insertion point in any blank area on your report layout.

The position of your insertion point determines where the field you define will appear on the screen. When you've selected a good spot,

- Press F10.

The **Field Definition** screen appears in the bottom half of your screen, as shown in Figure 7.2.4. This Field Definition screen is used to control the position and attributes of report fields.

The **Line** and **Column** fields are filled automatically by Excelerator with values based on the position of the insertion point when you pressed F10.

- Press F3 to return to the Report Layout.

In the next sections, **7.2.5 Relating Report Fields to New Elements** and **7.2.6 Relating Report Fields to Existing Elements**, you learn how to use the Field Definition screen in concert with the XLDictionary.

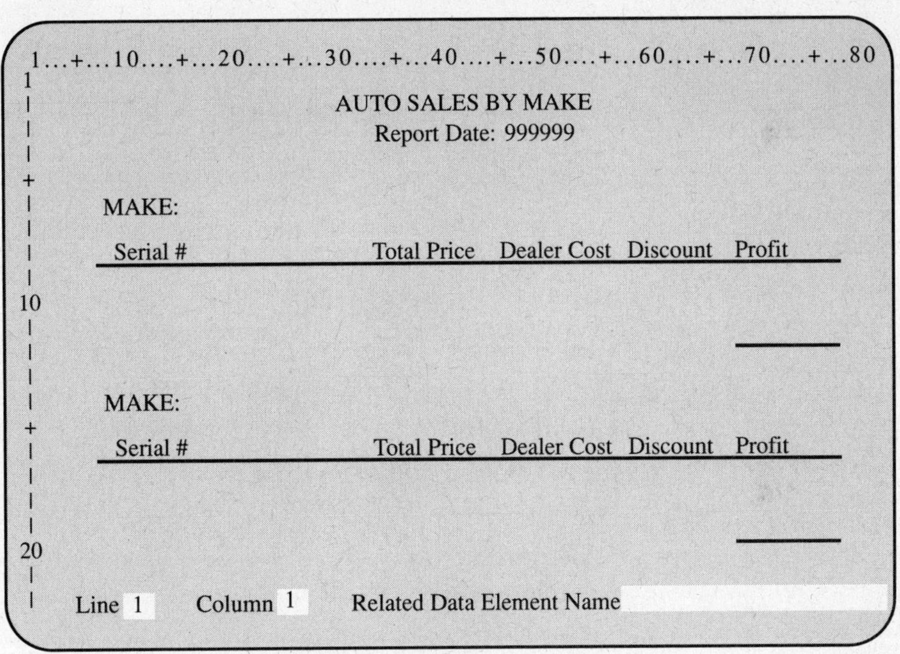

Figure 7.2.4
Report Field Definition Screen Appearing on the Auto Sales by Make Report Layout

7.2.5 Relating Report Fields to New Elements

As with screen fields, report fields may be related to new Data Elements. That is, they may be related to Data Elements which have not been previously identified or defined in the XLDictionary. This is usually done when you develop your reports before completing the data model, or when a Data Element omission is noticed during report development.

On the Auto Sales by Make Report Design,

- Place the insertion point anywhere on the report layout.
- Press F10 to bring up the Field Definition screen.
- Type `TEST 2` in the **Related Data Element Name** field.
- Press F4.

Because TEST 2 is not an Data Element name described in the XLDictionary, Excelerator displays a blank Data Element description screen on which you can describe this new data element. (Once a new element is described, pressing F3 to saves it and returns you to the Field Definition screen. Then, when F3 is pressed again, the new report field appears on the report layout.)

- Press the right-hand button on your mouse to cancel the new Data Element description.

When Excelerator asks if you're sure you want to exit without saving,

- Type `Y`.

The Field Definition screen displays,

- Press the right-hand button on the mouse to get back to your screen layout.

It is important to understand how this type of field definition is accomplished. The process is summarized in Figure 7.2.7. Since you have described the Data Elements for the Anonymous Autos project, it is not necessary for you to relate report fields to new Data Elements in the exercises in this book.

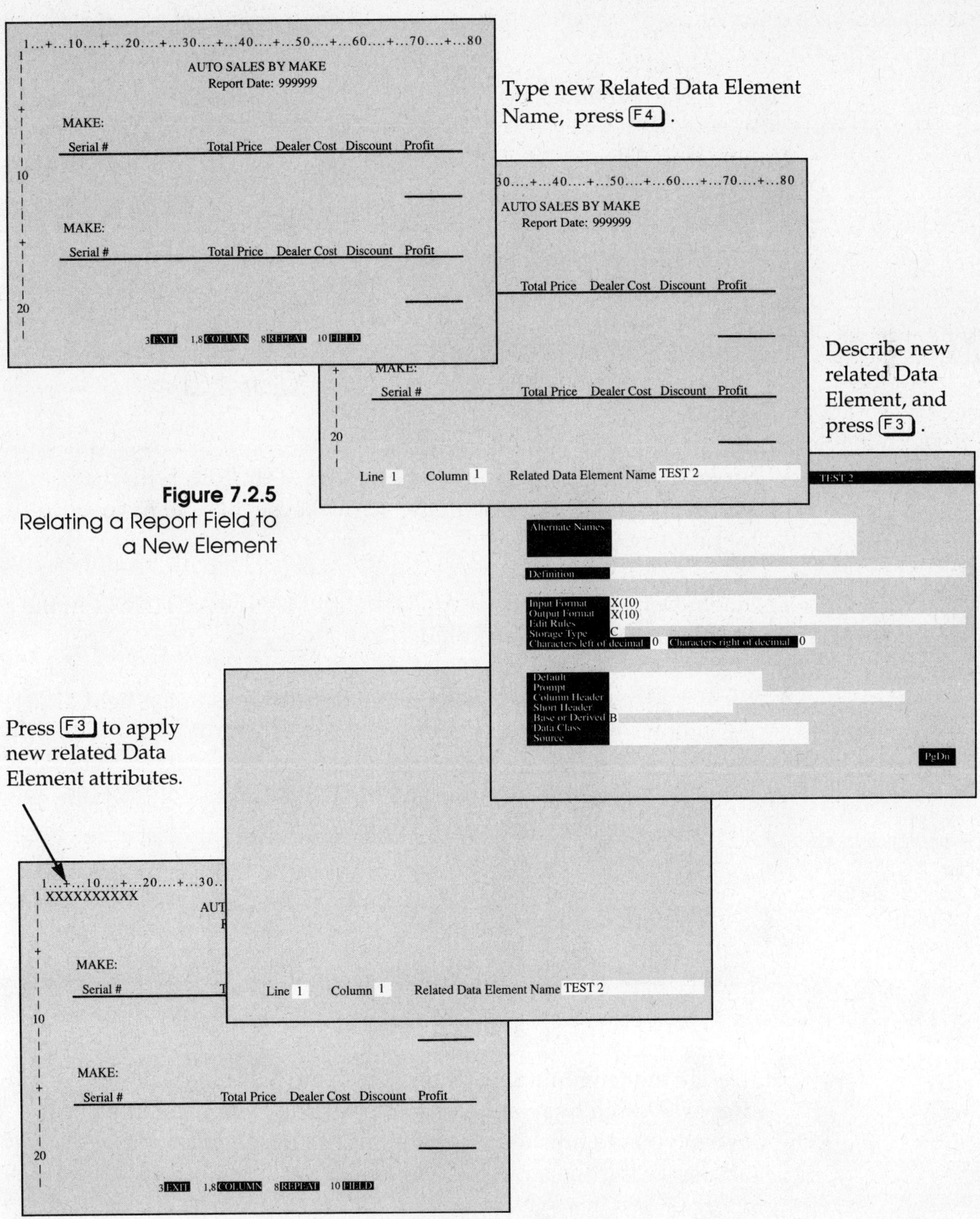

Figure 7.2.5
Relating a Report Field to a New Element

7.2.6 Relating Report Fields to Existing Elements

A report field may be described using the attributes of a related existing Data Element as shown in Figure 7.2.6. An existing Data Element is one that has been defined in the XLDictionary.

On the Auto Sales by Make Report Design,

- Place the insertion point one space after MAKE:.
- Press F10 to bring up the Field Definition screen.
- Press F4.

Hint
If you know the exact name of the Data Element you want to relate to a field, type the name in the Related Data Element Name field on the Field Definition screen. Then press F3 to apply the Data Element attributes to the field. This is a time-saver. It bypasses scrolling through your XLDictionary list of Data Elements.

You will see a list of Data Elements in the XLDictionary. If the list is too long to fit on the screen, use Pg Up and Pg Dn (or + and -) to navigate.

- Select the Data Element named MANUFACTURER with the mouse. (If you selected with the arrow keys, you will have to press ↵ afterward.)

The Field Definition screen reappears with MANUFACTURER in the Related Data Element Name field.

- Press F3 to apply this Data Element's attributes to the field definition.

The new field is visible just after the MAKE prompt on the report layout as shown at the bottom of Figure 7.2.6.

Exercise 7.2.6

Define the remaining fields on your Auto Sales by Make Report Design by relating them to existing Data Elements. When you are finished, your Report Design should look similar to the one shown in Figure 7.2.7a.

Select field position with mouse, and press F10 .

```
1...+...10....+...20....+...30....+...40....+...50....+...60....+...70....+...80
                    AUTO SALES BY MAKE
                    Report Date: 999999

MAKE:
 Serial #              Total Price  Dealer Cost  Discount  Profit

MAKE:
 Serial #              Total Price  Dealer Cost  Discount  Profit

3 EXIT   1,8 COLUMN   8 REPEAT   10 FIELD
```

With insertion point in Related Data Element Field, press F4 .

```
+...30....+...40....+...50....+...60....+...70....+...80
          AUTO SALES BY MAKE
          Report Date: 999999

           Total Price  Dealer Cost  Discount  Profit

MAKE:
 Serial #  Total Price  Dealer Cost  Discount  Profit

Line 7   Column 15   Related Data Element Name
```

Select desired existing Data Element.

```
Entity Name                                  Alternate Name
BASE_COST....................................BASE COST
BUYER'S_SIGNATURE_PRESENT....................BUYER'S SIGNATURE
CURRENT_DATE.................................DATE
CURRENT_TIME.................................TIME
CUSTOMER_ADDRESS.............................ADDRESS
CUSTOMER_AREA_CODE...........................AREA CODE
CUSTOMER_CITY................................CITY
CUSTOMER_FIRST_NAME..........................FIRST NAME
CUSTOMER_LAST_NAME...........................LAST NAME
CUSTOMER_STATE...............................STATE
CUSTOMER_TELEPHONE_NUMBER....................TELEPHONE NUMBER
CUSTOMER_ZIP_CODE............................ZIP CODE
DEALER_COST..................................DEALER COST
DISCOUNT.....................................DISCOUNT
EXTERIOR_COLOR...............................COLOR
FREIGHT......................................FREIGHT
INVOICE_DISCOUNT.............................INVOICE DISCOUNT
.................... + ....................
```

Figure 7.2.6
Relating a Report Field to an Existing Element

```
Line 7   Column 15   Related Data Element Name  MANUFACTURER
```

Press F3 to apply Data Element attributes.

```
1...+...10....+...20....+...30....+...40....+...50....+
                    AUTO SALES BY MAKE
                    Report Date: 999999

MAKE: XXXXXXXXXXXXXXXXXXXX
 Serial #              Total Price  Dealer Cost  Discount  Profit

MAKE:
 Serial #              Total Price  Dealer Cost  Discount  Profit

3 EXIT   1,8 COLUMN   8 REPEAT   10 FIELD
```

7.2.8 Printing Report Designs

When you've completed your report description and design, you may send it to an output device for printing.

- Select **S SCREENS & REPORTS** from Excelerator's Main Menu.
- Select **1 Report Design** from the Screens & Reports Menu which appears to the right of the Main Menu.
- Select **Output** from the Report Design Action Key Pad.

As shown in Figure 7.2.8a, prompts appear near the bottom of the screen asking for the **Name OR Name Range** of reports(s) you wish to print. Any name entered in the Name field must match one of the reports defined in the XLDictionary.

If the exact name of the desired Report Design is not known,

- Place the insertion point in the Name field.
- Press ↵.

The XLDictionary list of Report Designs appears.

- Select the AUTO SALES BY MAKE Report Design with the mouse.

As shown in Figure 7.2.8b, Excelerator now asks where you want the output sent.

- Select **Printer** with the mouse.

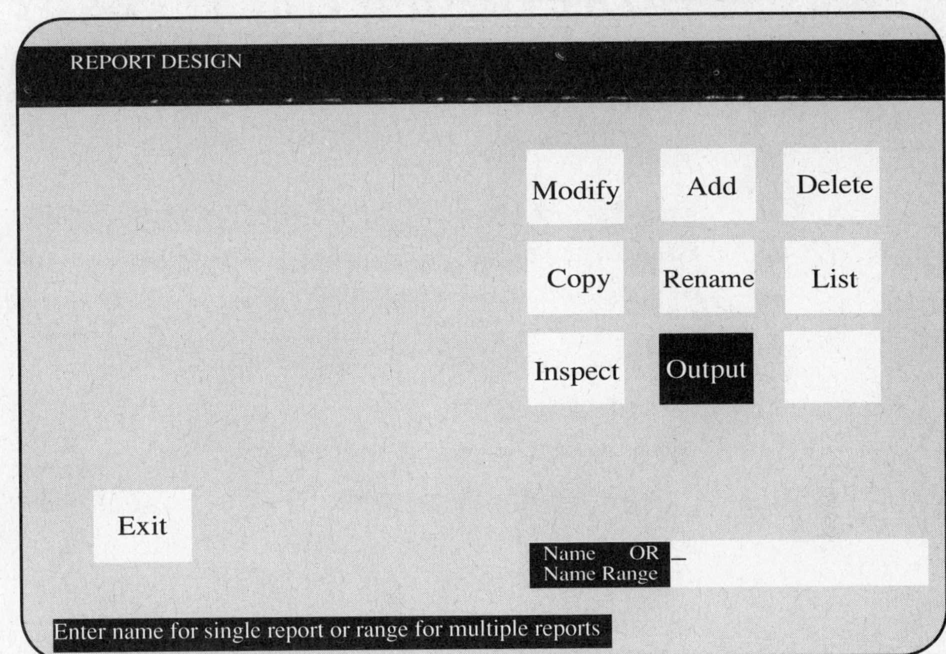

Figure 7.2.8a
Output Selection on Report Design Action Keypad

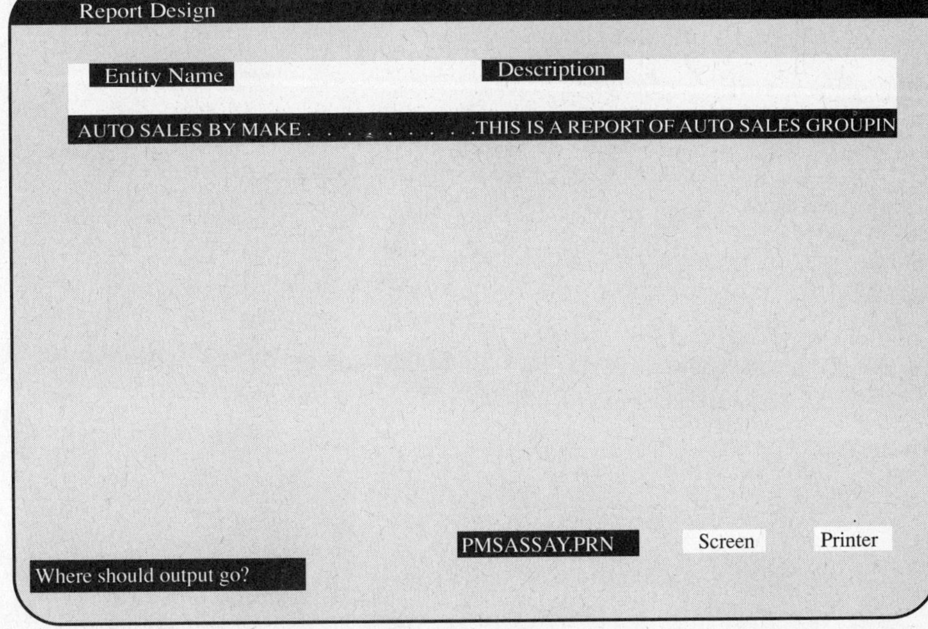

Figure 7.2.8b
List of Report Designs Available for Output

7.2.9 Interpreting Printed Report Output

Printed report output consists of two reports: the Report Design Description and the Report Design.

The **Report Design Description**, shown in Figure 7.2.9a, is a report based on the Report Description screen. It gives the report name, description, dates of creation and last modification, size, and location.

The **Report Design**, shown in Figure 7.2.9b, shows the actual layout of the proposed report. It is the printed version of the report you designed on the computer screen.

Report Design

Report Name AUTO SALES BY MAKE

Description THIS IS A REPORT OF AUTO SALES GROUPING THE SALES BY MAKE OF AUTO.

Date Created:	6 /25/91	Date Last Modified:	7 /11/91
Created By:	ANALYST	Last Modified By:	ANALYST
Starting Line:	1	Starting Column:	1
Ending Line:	24	Ending Column:	80

Figure 7.2.9a
Report Design Description Output for Auto Sales by Make

AUTO SALES BY MAKE
Report Date: 999999

MAKE: XXXXXXXXXXXXXXXXXXXX

Serial #	Total Price	Dealer Cost	Discount	Profit
XXXXXXXXXXXXXXXXXXXX	999,999.99	999,999.99	999,999.99	999,999.99
XXXXXXXXXXXXXXXXXXXX	999,999.99	999,999.99	999,999.99	999,999.99
XXXXXXXXXXXXXXXXXXXX	999,999.99	999,999.99	999,999.99	999,999.99

MAKE: XXXXXXXXXXXXXXXXXXXX

Serial #	Total Price	Dealer Cost	Discount	Profit
XXXXXXXXXXXXXXXXXXXX	999,999.99	999,999.99	999,999.99	999,999.99
XXXXXXXXXXXXXXXXXXXX	999,999.99	999,999.99	999,999.99	999,999.99
XXXXXXXXXXXXXXXXXXXX	999,999.99	999,999.99	999,999.99	999,999.99

Figure 7.2.9b
Report Design Output for Auto Sales by Make

Excelerating Your Skills ... in Report Design

In working your way through the **Designing Reports** section, you have successfully completed the **Auto Sales by Make** report for Rich Royce's new Anonymous Autos information system. Now you're ready to develop the remaining reports required for the new system. Once again, go back and re-read **3. The Anonymous Autos Project**. This time, look for report requirements.

The **Commissions Report**, shown on the opposite page, is clearly a screen requirement. All of the information on the Commissions Report has been captured through or can be calculated from the Vehicle Inventory Record and Sales Invoice. The addition of a Commissions Report to the automated system will facilitate the computer generation of this report.

Think about your Auto Sales by Make report and its resemblance to the original report shown in **3. The Anonymous Autos Project**. Develop your Commissions Report to look as much like the one already in use at Anonymous Autos as possible.

Rich Royce wants a report listing the options installed by his shop on each car. All of the information for this **Shop Options Report** is captured through screens you've already designed. Think about what specific information Rich Royce may find useful. For instance, will he want to know the cost of each option? Will he want to know the profit he made on each option? How much information will he want on each car? Unfortunately, he's out of the country on a buying trip, so you can't ask him. You must design this new report on your own.

Describe and design the Commissions Report and Shop Options Report.

Anonymous Autos' Current Commissions Report

Commissions Report

Salesman: D.J. Anders

Serial #	Profit	Commission	
1078834	1,458	247.86	
4077654	5,040	856.80	**Total=** $1,104.66

Salesman: J.R. Carlston

Serial #	Profit	Commission	
4674575	10,465	1,779.05	
1020034	1,570	266.90	**Total=** $2,045.95

Salesman: H.I. Hanley

Serial #	Profit	Commission	
4098333	6,860	1,166.20	
7639736	8,770	1,490.90	**Total=** $2,657.10

Salesman: F.R. Williams

Serial #	Profit	Commission	
6576767	5,455	927.35	
4025056	4,305	731.85	**Total=** $1,659.20

7.3 Designing Menus

The user's first impression of the information system comes from the **terminal dialogue**. The term terminal dialogue refers to the methods used by the system designer to guide the user to and from various system functions.

A common dialogue method is the use of **menus**. Menus are screens that provide the user with several options. A menu option can be chosen by entering a character in a field, by pointing and clicking with a mouse, or some by other selection process. When a menu selection is made, the system displays another screen, either a menu or an activity screen. The user is commonly led through the system in this manner. Because the terminal dialogue is crucial to the success or failure of an information system design, time spent in the design of effective dialogues is never wasted.

As shown in Figure 7.3, the terminal dialogue for the new Anonymous Autos system is menu-driven. In this section Excelerator's Screen Design facilities are used to develop the menus and navigational screens required to access the data capture screens you have already created.

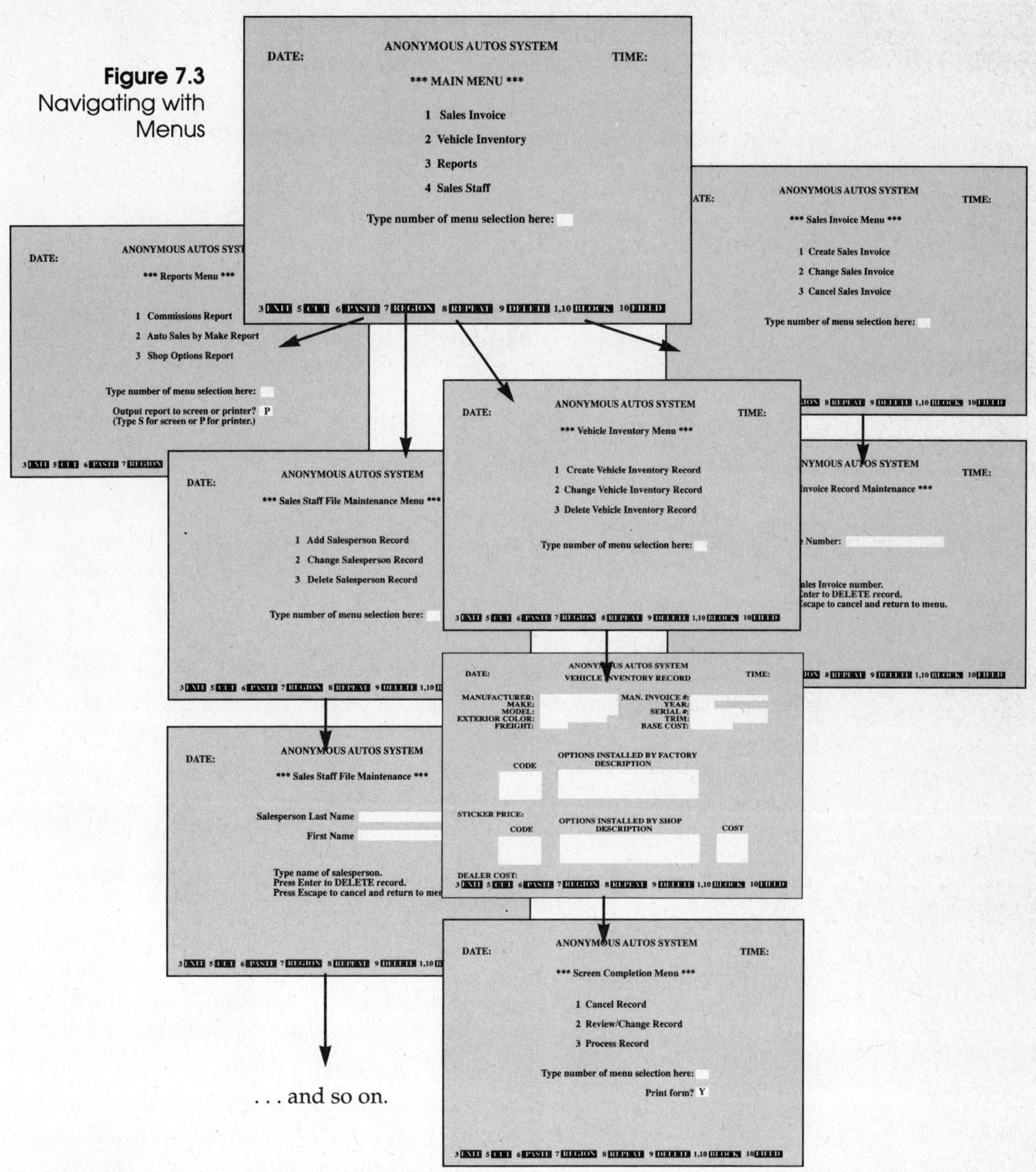

Figure 7.3
Navigating with Menus

7.3.1 Designing the Screen Sequence

The screen sequence or **dialogue**, is the order in which screens occur, and the circumstances under which screens occur. To illustrate this concept, we use a tool called the **dialogue chart** to depict the Anonymous Autos system screen sequence.

Figure 7.3.1 shows the beginning of the Anonymous Autos dialogue chart. It describes the new system's Main Menu, its four options, and the screen which will appear when each option is selected. It also shows the screen sequence following the Main Menu's Vehicle Inventory option.

Each box on the chart is divided into three sections:

- The top section contains the screen reference number
- The middle section contains the screen description or name.
- The bottom section names possible shortcuts or escapes available to the user from a given point in the screen sequence.

Lines connecting the boxes indicate a bi-directional flow between screens. Users are usually allowed to move both backwards and forwards through screen sequences.

Although the dialogue chart is not generated with Excelerator, it is a valuable tool when thinking about the screen sequence for your system. Even if you choose not to use dialogue charts, you have to design your screen sequence before designing your menus. Otherwise, how will you know what menus your system requires? How will you know what options each menu should contain? And how will you know what happens when each option is selected?

This screen sequence design is not necessarily the right one; it is one possible version. If you have ideas on how to improve it, that's great. The exercises in this section are based on our screen sequence design. If you prefer your own design, develop your version's menu screens instead.

With the system's Main Menu in mind, go on to the next section, **7.3.2 Designing the Main Menu Screen**, to design your first menu.

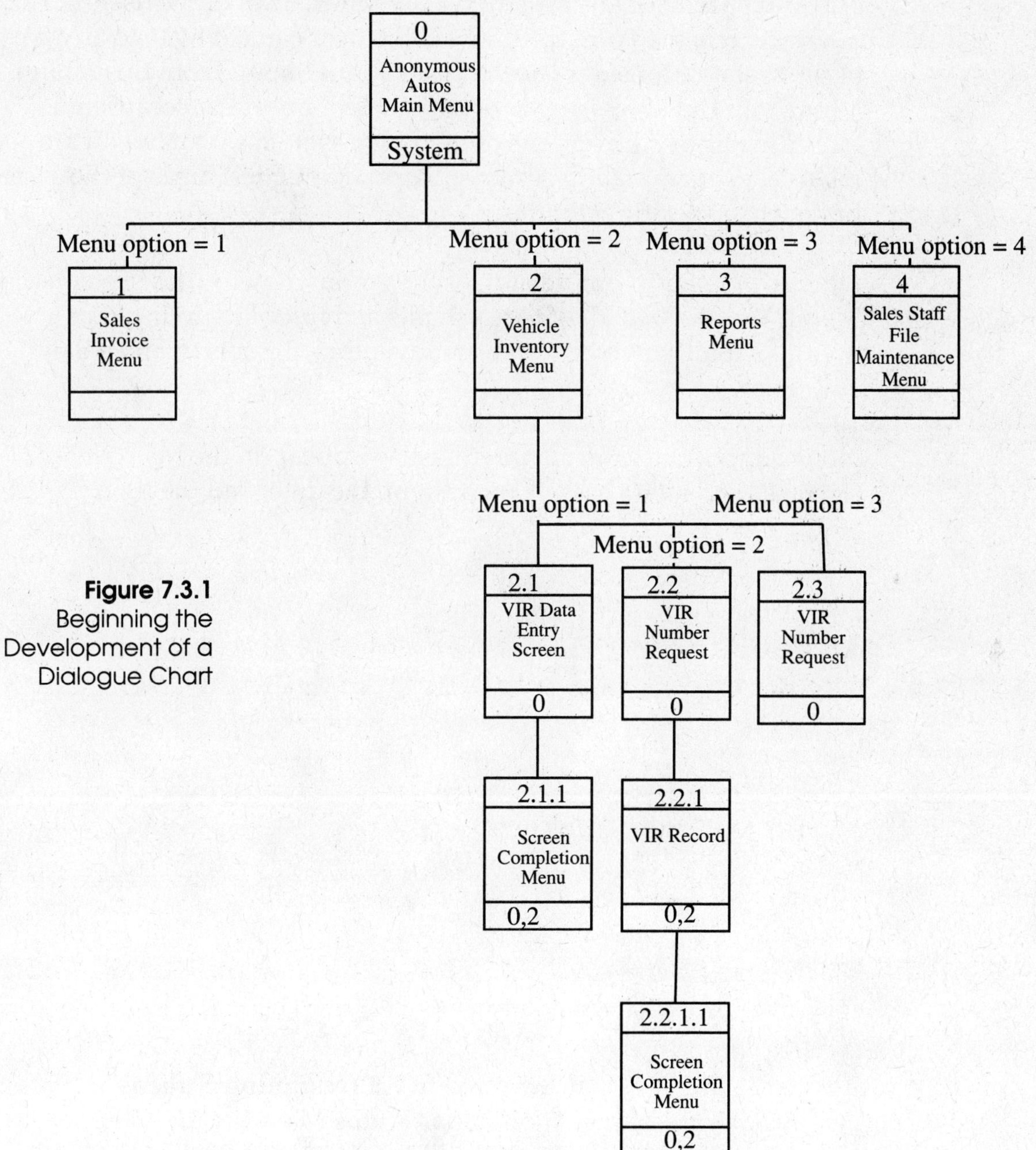

Figure 7.3.1
Beginning the Development of a Dialogue Chart

7.3.2 Designing the Main Menu Screen

The Main Menu of any system is the highest level of the user interface. It is the point from which the user can navigate to any part of the system. Consider Excelerator's Main Menu. From this Main Menu, you can access any activity Excelerator offers. Because it is global in nature, the options offered by a system's main menu are relatively general. The Main Menu options suggest areas of the system rather than specific activities.

Figure 7.3.2 shows our version of the Anonymous Autos system Main Menu. We grouped all of the system's activities into four menu options: 1 Sales Invoice, 2 Vehicle Inventory, 3 Reports, and 4 Sales Staff Files.

Notice important information that also appear on the Main Menu screen such as the name of the system, the date, and the time.

Exercise 7.3.2

Using the skills you acquired in **7.2 Designing Screens (SCDs)**, create the Anonymous Autos Main Menu screen shown in Figure 7.3.2. Remember what you learned about defining the system date and time fields. Define them as unique to the screen. The only other field on the screen is the one in which the user types the menu option choice. This is also a screen unique field.

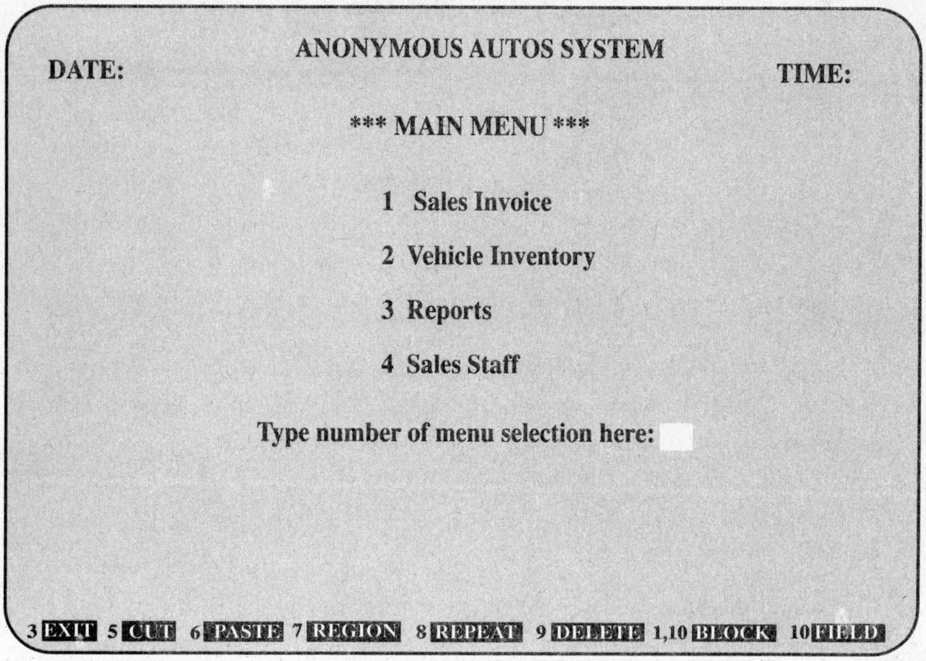

ANONYMOUS AUTOS SYSTEM

DATE: TIME:

*** MAIN MENU ***

1 Sales Invoice

2 Vehicle Inventory

3 Reports

4 Sales Staff

Type number of menu selection here:

3 EXIT 5 CUT 6 PASTE 7 REGION 8 REPEAT 9 DELETE 1,10 BLOCK 10 FIELD

Figure 7.3.2
The Anonymous Autos System Main Menu

7.3.3 Designing Lower Level Menu Screens

Figure 7.3.3 shows a version of the Anonymous Autos system Vehicle Inventory Record (VIR) Menu, indicated by the dialogue chart on Page 241.

Lower level menus generally offer more specific options related to functions rather than system areas. Our version of the VIR Menu offers the user three options:

1 Create a Vehicle Inventory Record
2 Change a Vehicle Inventory Record
3 Delete a Vehicle Inventory Record

Functions such as delete, modify, or cancel are ones to which management may wish to restrict access. Another way to handle such options, however, would be to access them through a restricted access option on the Main Menu.

Exercise 7.3.3

Using the skills you acquired in **7.2 Designing Screens (SCDs)**, create the Anonymous Autos VIR Menu screen shown in Figure 7.3.3. Again, the system date and time fields are unique to the screen. The only other field on the screen is the one in which the user types the menu option choice. This is also a screen unique field.

ANONYMOUS AUTOS SYSTEM

DATE: TIME:

*** Vehicle Inventory Menu ***

1 Create Vehicle Inventory Record

2 Change Vehicle Inventory Record

3 Delete Vehicle Inventory Record

Type number of menu selection here:

3 EXIT 5 CUT 6 PASTE 7 REGION 8 REPEAT 9 DELETE 1,10 BLOCK 10 FIELD

Figure 7.3.3 The Vehicle Inventory Record (VIR) Menu

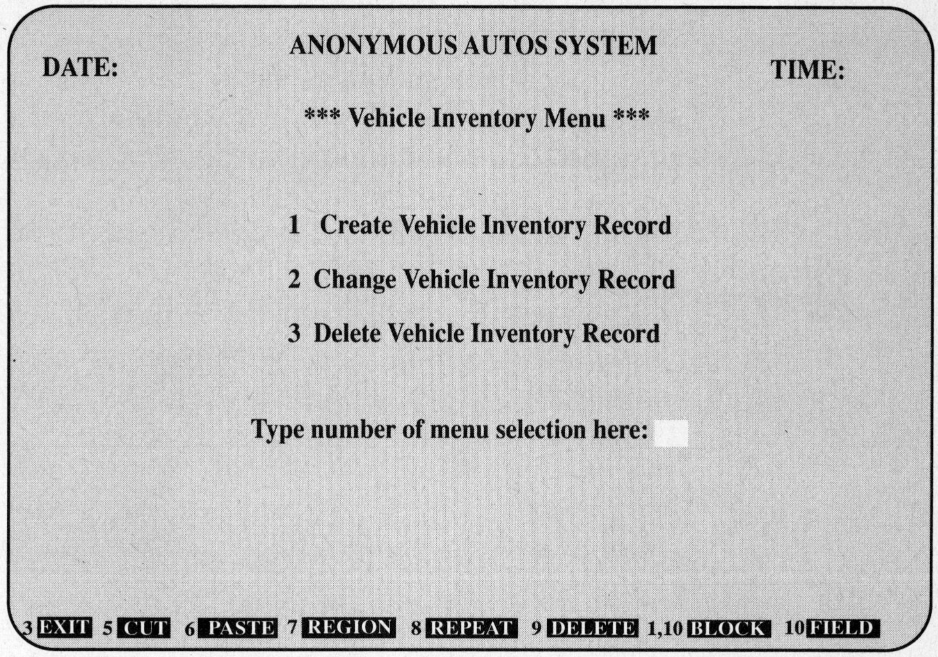

7.3.4 Designing Other Navigational Screens

Navigational screens are screens that ask the user a question or require the user to make a choice. Any input screen can be defined as a navigational screen.

So far, you have designed primary data entry screens and menu screens to access the data entry screens. During the screen sequence development process system designers often discover the need for additional screens to be used exclusively to get the user from the menu to the desired data entry screen.

The input screen shown in Figure 7.3.4 is an example of such a purely navigational screen. We developed this screen after asking ourselves a few questions about the system's screen sequence design:

What happens when the user selects option 2 Change VIR from the VIR Menu? The first thing the computer will need to know is which VIR the user wants to change. This leads to another question: How does the user specify the desired VIR?

Our answer to these questions is illustrated in Figure 7.3.4. When the user selects option 2 from the VIR Menu, a screen appears prompting the user to supply the VIR number. The user then types the VIR number, and the related VIR data appears on the VIR screen.

As you ask yourself what-happens-when questions about screen sequence, the importance of careful screen sequence design will become clearer.

Exercise 7.3.4

Using the skills you acquired in **Designing Screens**, create the VIR number request screen shown in Figure 7.3.4. Remember what you learned about defining the system date and time fields. Define them as being unique to the screen. The only other field on the screen is the one in which the user types the VIR number. This field is related to the NEW_VEHICLE_SERIAL_ NUMBER Data Element.

ANONYMOUS AUTOS SYSTEM

DATE: TIME:

*** Vehicle Inventory Record Maintenance ***

Vehicle Inventory Record (VIR) Number:

Type VIR number.
Press Enter to REVIEW/CHANGE record.
Press Escape to cancel and return to menu.

3 EXIT 5 CUT 6 PASTE 7 REGION 8 REPEAT 9 DELETE 1,10 BLOCK 10 FIELD

Figure 7.3.4
Navigational Screen Which Appears When **2 Change VIR** is Selected from the VIR Menu

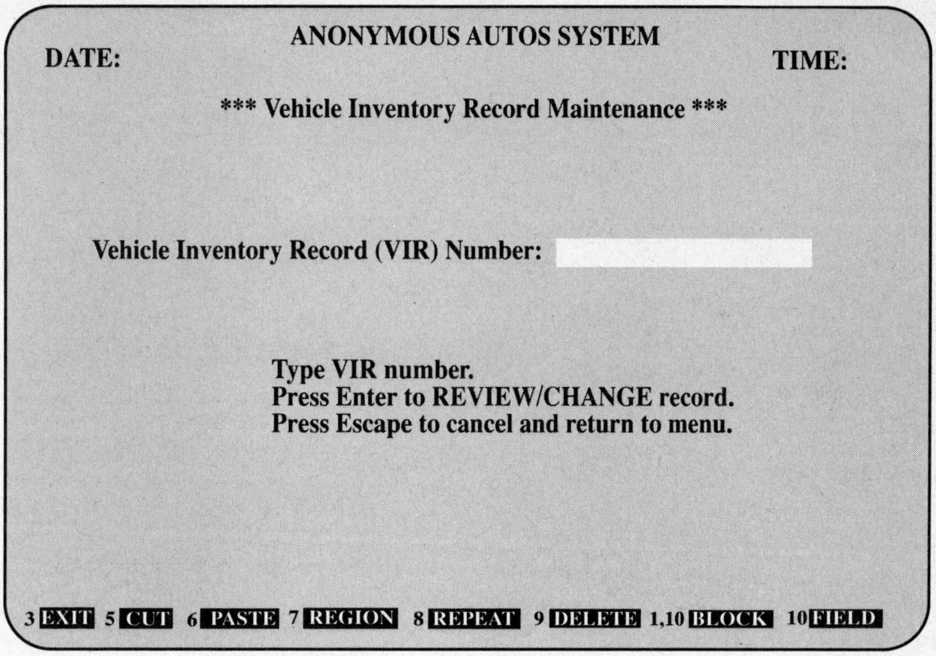

DESIGNING SYSTEM STRUCTURE

If the information system is fully developed, software modules must be designed that provide system functionality as defined during systems analysis. Development of system structure can be accomplished using **structured design**, a methodology that provides a disciplined approach to the development of software.

Through modularization, structured design facilitates the rapid production of reliable systems which are flexible and easy to maintain. Such systems are easy to understand and easy to modify.

In this chapter, the structure design for the Anonymous Autos system is developed. Structure Charts are drawn and their components are labeled and described.

8.1

Drawing Structure Charts (STCs)

Structure Charts (STCs) are a design tool used to modularize software development. By breaking down operations and processing procedures into discrete portions, system designers are able to create software modules that perform a single task. These modules are reusable. They are easy to maintain, and provide the programmer with a highly detailed explanation of the designer's needs and expectations.

Structure Charts contain the following objects:

- Function
- Library Function
- Data or Control Symbols or Flags
- Connections
- Interface Connections

As shown in Figure 8.1, Structure Charts are built in a top down fashion. The connections between the Functions represent the paths that data takes from Function to Function. The directional arrows along the connections denote individual pieces of data or control flags being passed from one Function to another. The Library Function is a shared module used in many different programs and systems. It is part of a Library of modules available to the developer.

Each function performs a single task. It may retrieve a record from a file, calculate a value, or perform an error check. In each case it should perform a single operation with as little interaction with other functions as possible.

In this section a Structure Chart named PRODUCE VIR is developed for the new Anonymous Autos system.

Figure 8.1
Structure Charts and Components

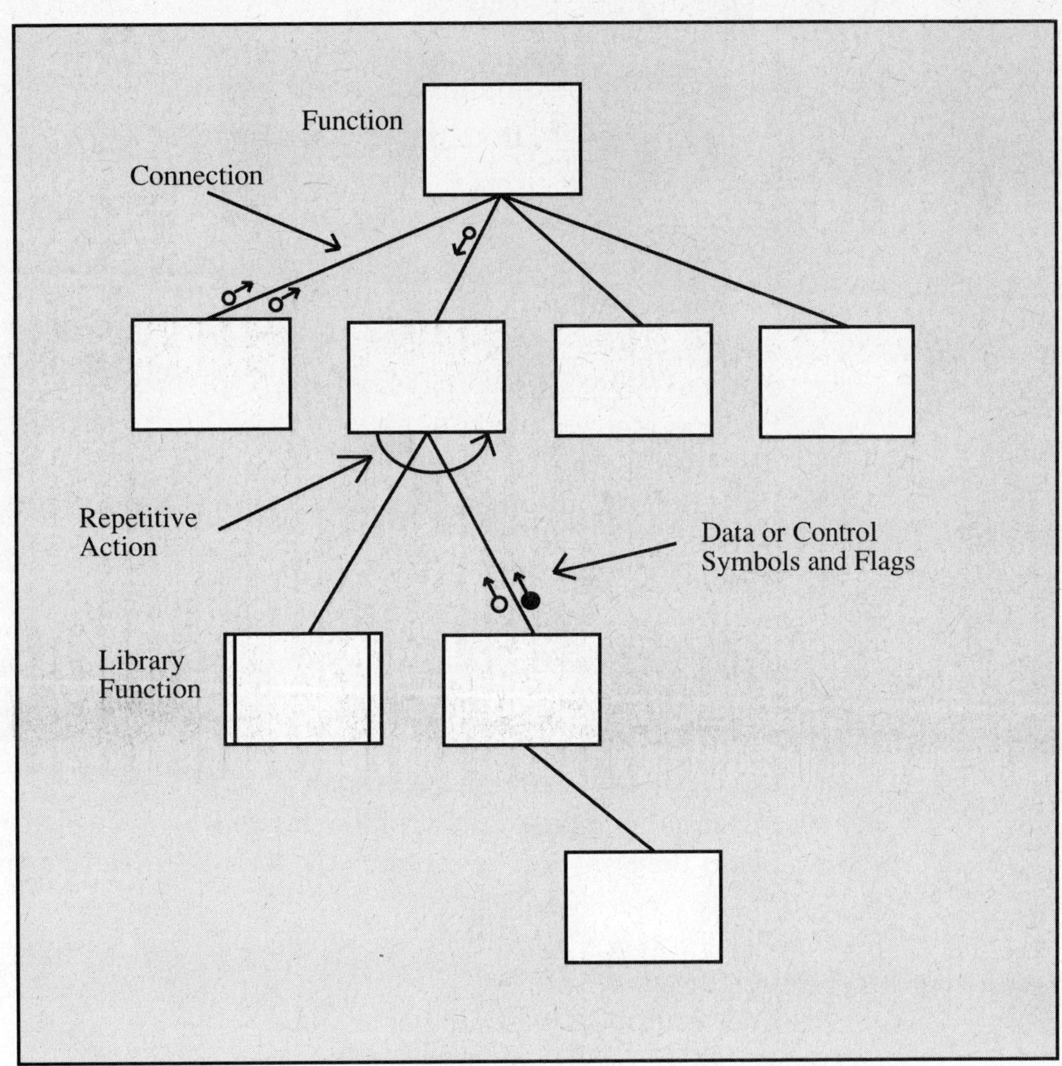

8.1.1 Drawing and Labeling Functions

To initiate a Structure Chart, refer to **4.1.1 Initiating Drawings**, substituting Structure Chart for Data Flow Diagram from the Graphics Menu, and naming the new graph **PRODUCE VIR**, as shown in Figure 8.1.1a.

When the drawing screen appears,

- Select **PRINT** from the Command Menu.
- Select **FULL GPH** from the Print Commands.
- Select **OBJECT** from the Command Menu.

A list of Structure Chart objects appears at the bottom of the Command Menu.

Hint
You will find it helpful to set the GRID to FINE before you begin drawing.

- Select **FUNCTION** from the list of STC objects.
- Position your mouse cursor near top of the top left page displayed in the drawing area.
- Press the left button on the mouse to select the position.

A Function appears in the location selected.

Functions are labeled using the same methods explained in **4.1.12 Labeling Objects and Connections**.

- Select **LABEL** from the Command Menu.
- Position the mouse cursor on the Function you just created.
- Select the Function by pressing the left button on the mouse.

The label text box appears on the screen.

- Type **PRODUCE VIR** in the text box.
- Press ↵ or the left button on the mouse.

The first few letters of the label appear in the Function.

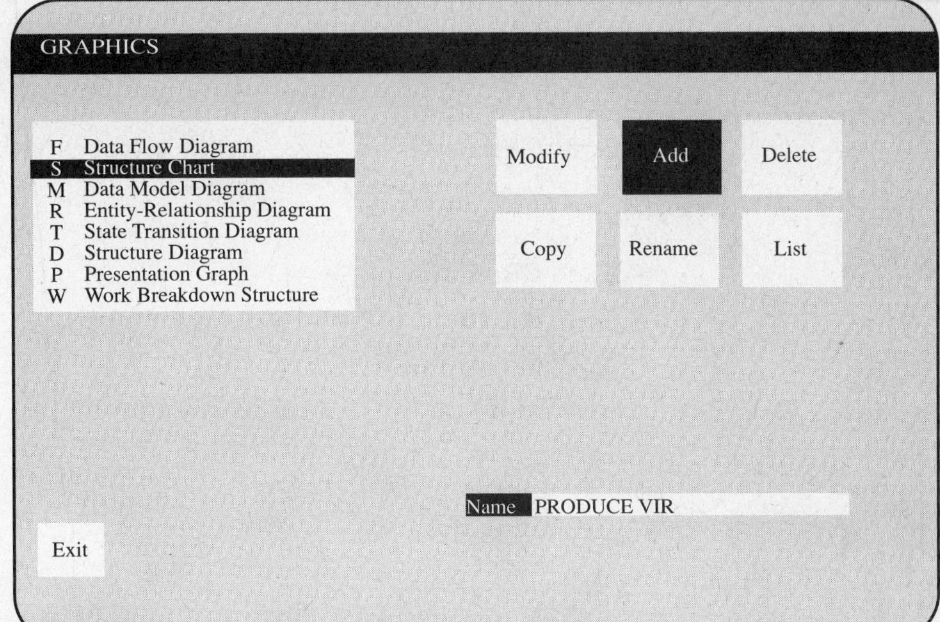

Figure 8.1.1a
Initiating a Structure Chart

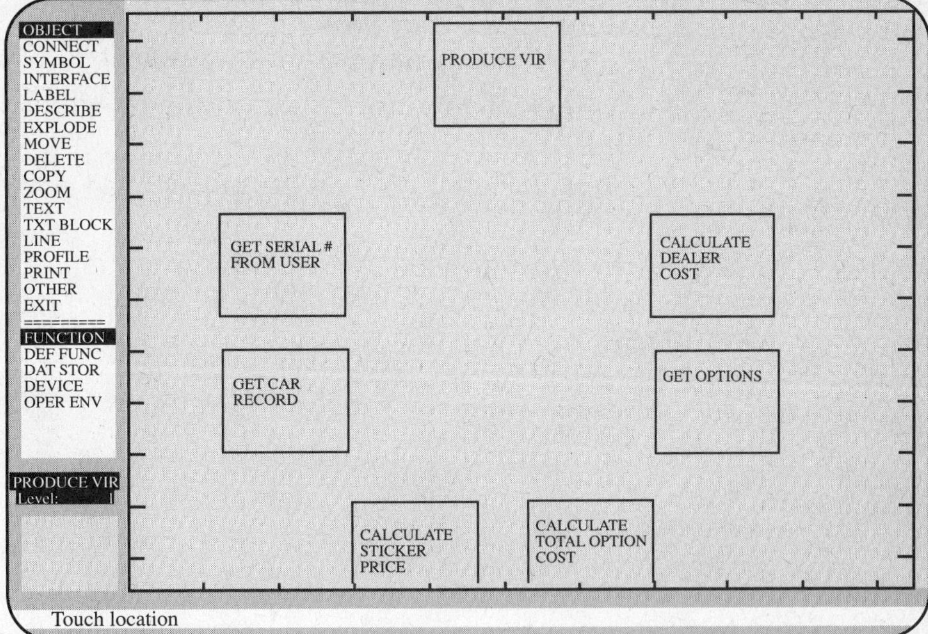

Figure 8.1.1b
Functions Placed in the Drawing Area

Exercise 8.1.1

Draw and label the remaining six Functions. Figure 8.1.1b shows the labeled Functions at CLOSE UP magnification. Remember to use Tab to go from line to line in the label text box, and use ↵ to apply the label to the object.

8.1.2 Connecting Functions

If it is not already on your screen, retrieve the PRODUCE VIR Structure Chart.

- Select **GRAPHICS** from the Main Menu.
- Select **S Structure Chart** from the Graphics Menu.
- Select **Modify** from the Graphics Action Keypad.
- Type **PRODUCE VIR** in the Name field.
- Press ↵.

When your graph appears,

- Select **CONNECT** from the Command Menu.
- Position the mouse cursor on the Function labeled PRODUCE VIR at the top of your Structure Chart.
- Select the Function by pressing the left button on the mouse.
- Position the mouse cursor on the Function labeled GET VEHICLE SERIAL # FROM USER.
- Press the left button on the mouse.

A line appears connecting the two Functions. Using the same method, connect PRODUCE VIR to the other five Functions on the Structure Chart, as shown in Figure 8.1.2.

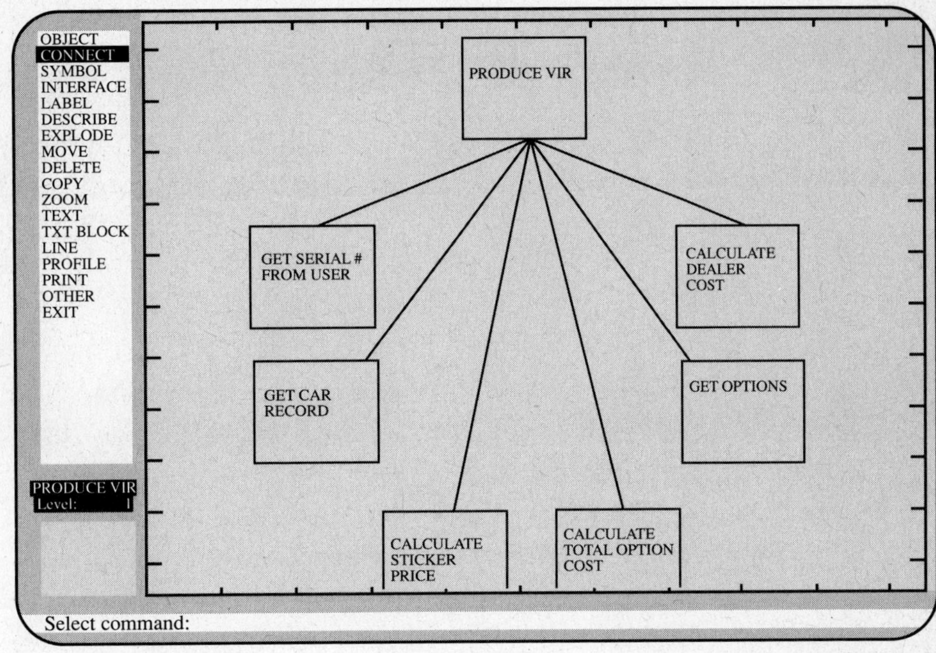

Figure 8.1.2
Structure Chart Functions Connected

8.1.3 Drawing and Labeling STC Symbols

If it is not already on your screen, retrieve the PRODUCE VIR Structure Chart.

- Select **SYMBOL** from the drawing screen Command Menu.

A list of Structure Chart symbols appears at the bottom of the Command Menu. Structure Chart symbol choices are **Diamond** (Decision Diamond), **Data Up**, **Data Dwn** (Data Down), **Ctrl Up** (Control Up), and **Ctrl Dwn** (Control Down), **Rep Loop** (Repetition Loop), **Lex Incl** (Lexical Inclusion).

- Select **DATA UP** from the list of STC symbols.
- Position your mouse cursor on the handle of the connection between PRODUCE VIR and GET VEHICLE SERIAL # FROM USER.
- Press the left button on the mouse.

Hint
Use ZOOM and CLOSE UP to get a better look at what you are doing.

A Data Up symbol appears beside the connection pointing up toward PRODUCE VIR.

STC Symbols are labeled using the same methods explained in **4.1.12 Labeling Objects and Connections** .

- Select **LABEL** from the Command Menu.
- Position the mouse cursor in the circle on the symbol you just created.
- Select the symbol by pressing the left button on the mouse.

The label text box appears on the screen.

- Type **NEW VEHICLE SERIAL #** in the text box.
- Press ⏎ or the left button on the mouse.

A truncated version of the label appears near the symbol. Unlike other objects and labels, symbols and their labels cannot be moved.

Figure 8.1.3
PRODUCE VIR Structure Chart with All Symbols and Labels

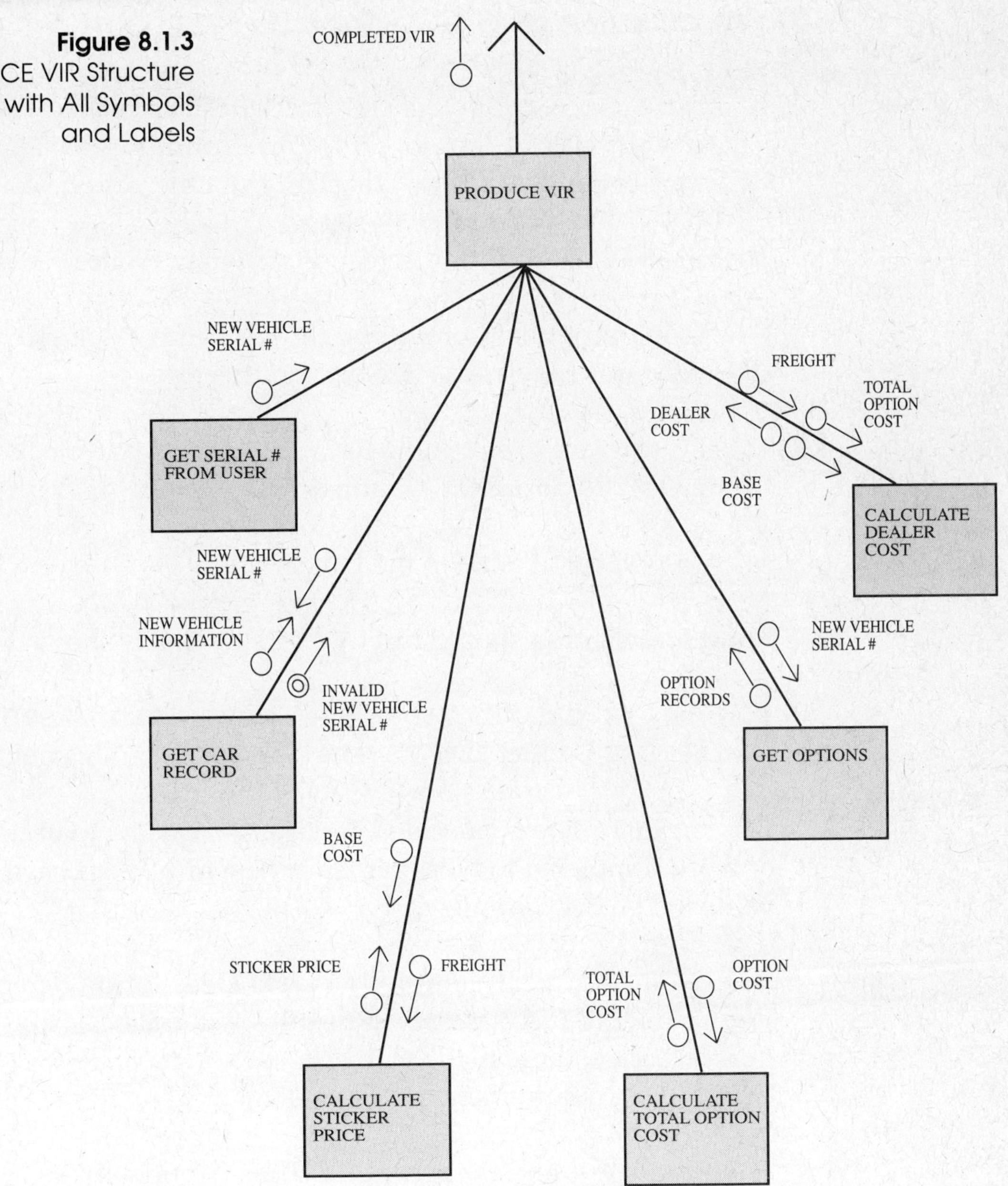

Exercise 8.1.3

Using Data Up, Data Down, and Control Up symbols, draw and label the remaining symbols on the PRODUCE VIR Structure Chart as shown in Figure 8.1.3. Note that the symbol labeled INVALID NEW VEHICLE SERIAL # is drawn using Control Up.

8.1.5 Completing STC Description Screens

To initiate the description of the Structure Chart called PRODUCE VIR, refer to **4.2.1 Initiating DFD Descriptions**, selecting **Structure Chart** instead of **Data Flow Diagram** from the Graph Menu.

The first **STC Description** screen is shown in Figure 8.1.5a.

File, is an output field providing the file name in which the STC is stored in your Excelerator project subdirectory.

Label is text you wish to appear in the graph's title block (See **4.1.17 Using OTHER and EXIT Commands**.)

- Type **`PRODUCE VIR`** in the Label field.

Short Description should briefly explain what is shown by the STC.

- Type **`VIR CALCULATIONS ARE PERFORMED BASED ON CAPTURED VEHICLE INVENTORY DATA`** in this field.

Percent Complete is provided for users who wish to indicate the ratio of work completed to work remaining on this STC. Leave the default value in Percent Complete.

As explained in **4.2.2 Completing DFD Description Screens, Satisfies Requirements** and **Associated Entities** will not be addressed in this tutorial. Leave these fields blank unless you have developed User and Engineering requirements on your own.

- Press [Pg Dn], and the second STC Description screen appears.

Use the second STC Description screen shown in Figure 8.1.5b as a guide and complete the **Description** of the PRODUCE VIR Structure Chart. When you finish,

- Press [F3] to save and return to the STC Action Keypad.

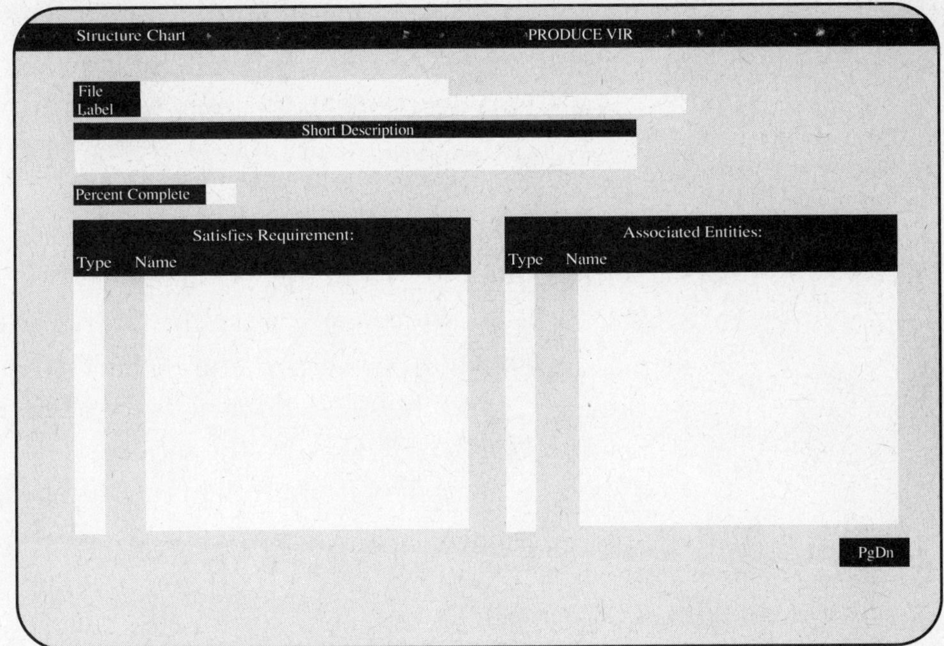

Figure 8.1.5a First STC Description Screen Completed for PRODUCE VIR

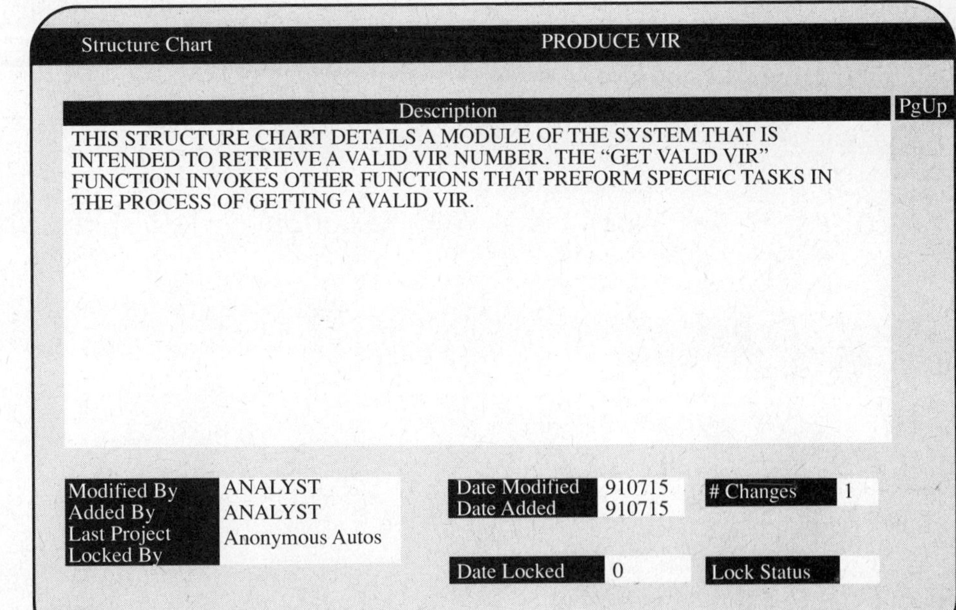

Figure 8.1.5b Second STC Description Screen Completed for PRODUCE VIR

8.1.6 Printing STC Descriptions

As with the description of any graph, when you have completed a Structure Chart description, you may send it to an output device for printing.

- Select **X XLDICTIONARY** from Excelerator's Main Menu.
- Select **GRAPHS** from the XLDictionary Menu which appears.
- Select **S Structure Chart** from the Graphs Menu.
- Select **Output** from the Structure Chart Action Keypad.
- Press ↵, and the XLDictionary list of STCs appears.
- Select **PRODUCE VIR** with the mouse.
- Type `Y` when asked if input fields should be underlined.
- Select **Printer** as the output device.

The report Excelerator generates for a STC closely resembles the Structure Chart Description screens. Figure 8.1.6 shows the printed description of PRODUCE VIR. Notice that the entity type and graph name appear near the top of the page followed by other fields from the description screens:

- File
- Label
- Short Description
- Percent Complete
- Satisfies Requirement
- Associated Entities
- Description
- Audit fields from the bottom of the last description screen

Figure 8.1.6 Printed STC Description of PRODUCE VIR with Output Fields Underlined

DATE: 29-AUG-91 STRUCTURE CHART - OUTPUT PAGE 1
TIME: 11:17 NAME: PRODUCE VIR Excelerator / IS

TYPE Structure Chart NAME PRODUCE VIR

File pzamo5.stc
Label PRODUCE VIR

Short Description

VIR CALCULATIONS ARE PERFORMED BASED ON CAPTURED VEHICLE INVENTORY DATA

Percent Complete 100

Satisfies Requirement:
Type Name

Associated Entities
Type Name

Description

THIS STRUCTURE CHART DETAILS A MODULE OF THE SYSTEM THAT IS INTENDED TO RETRIEVE A VALID VIR NUMBER. THE "GET VALID VIR" FUNCTION INVOKES OTHER FUNCTIONS THAT PREFORM SPECIFIC TASKS IN THE PROCESS OF GETTING A VALID VIR.

Modified By ANALYST
Added By ANALYST
Last Project Anonymous Autos
Locked By

Date Modified 910825
Date Added 910823
Date Locked 0

Changes 13
Lock Status

8.2

Describing Functions (FUNs)

Functions (FUNs) are used in Structure Charts to represent the activities required by the system. As shown in Figure 8.2, each Function can be decomposed further to another graph (Structure Chart or Structure Diagram) or described by a Module.

The Function description contains a list of input and output variables and a free-form or structured English specification for the Function.

In this section, the Functions you placed on the Structure Chart called PRODUCE VIR are described using Excelerator's Function description screens. A textual description defining the purpose of the Function is developed, and printing procedures for the Function description are discussed.

Figure 8.2
Function Explosion Options

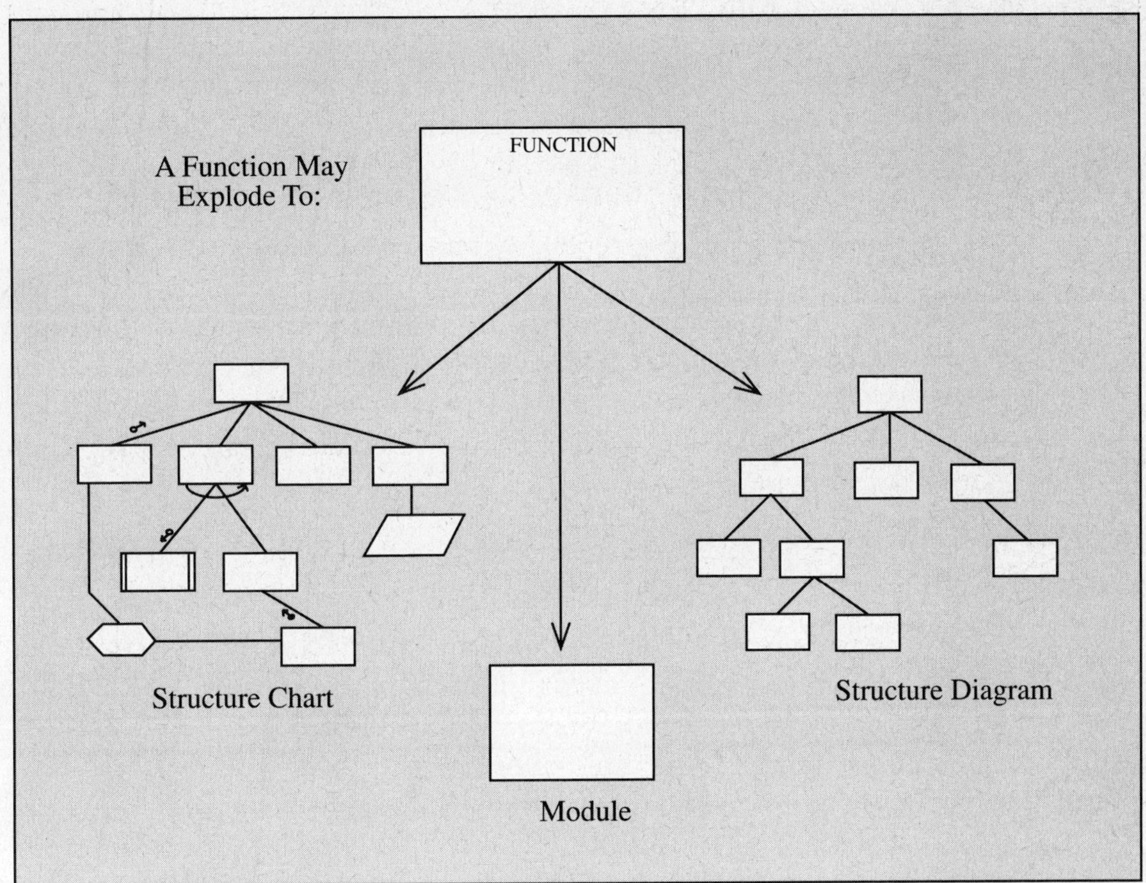

8.2.1 Completing Function Description Screens

If it is not already on your screen, retrieve the PRODUCE VIR Structure Chart.

- Select DESCRIBE from the Command Menu.
- Position the mouse cursor on the Function labeled CALCULATE STICKER PRICE.
- Press the left button on the mouse to select the Function.
- Type **CSP** in the status line at the ID prompt.
- Press ⏎, and the first Function description screen is displayed as in Figure 8.2.1a.

Functions can be exploded to show a more detailed picture of activities. Function explosion options are Structure Charts, Structure Diagrams, or Modules. Functions are not exploded in this tutorial so leave the **Explodes To One Of** fields blank.

Location is where the Function takes place. It can be a department, person, machine, or program.

Type **INVENTORY SUBSYSTEM** in Location.

Duration Value is the maximum expected number of times the Function occurs for each unit of time in **Duration Type**. STICKER PRICE is calculated every time a VIR is produced on the screen. Make an estimate of the number of times a VIR is produced each day.

- Type **250** in Duration Value.
- Type **DAY** in Duration Type.

As explained in **4.2.2 Completing DFD Description Screens, Satisfies Requirements** and **Associated Entities** will not be addressed in this tutorial.

- Press Pg Dn, and the second Function description screen appears.

Description is for a detailed, free-form explanation of Function activities. Complete this screen using Figure 8.2.1b as a guide.

- Press F3 when you finish to save and return to your graph.

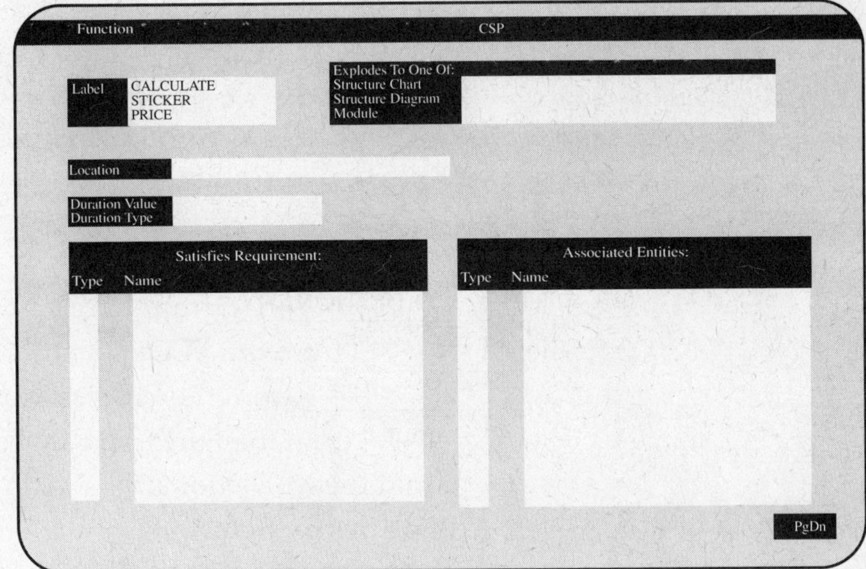

Figure 8.2.1a First Function Description Screen

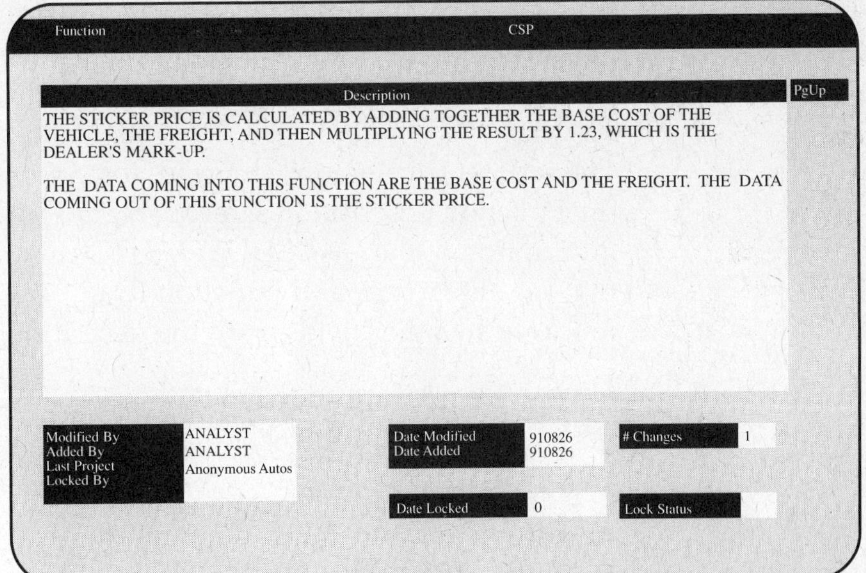

Figure 8.2.1b Second Function Description Screen

Exercise 8.2.1

Describe the remaining Functions on PRODUCE VIR. It may be helpful to refer back to **3. The Anonymous Autos Project** to refresh your memory about the calculations being made. When assigning IDs, make them meaningful. Acronyms of Function labels work well.

8.2.2 Printing Function Descriptions

As with the description of any graph component, when you have completed a Process description, you may send it to an output device for printing.

- Select **X XLDICTIONARY** from Excelerator's Main Menu.
- Select **Process** from the XLDictionary Menu which appears.
- Select **F Function** from the Process Menu.
- Select **Output** from the Function Key Pad.
- Press ↵, and the XLDictionary list of Functions appears.
- Select **All Entities on Selector List** with the mouse.
- Type `Y` when asked if input fields should be underlined.
- Select **Printer** as the output device.

Graph component descriptions can be printed one at a time, within specified ranges, or all together. See **4.2.3 Printing DFD Descriptions** .

The reports Excelerator generates for your Functions closely resemble the Function description screens. Figure 8.2.2 shows the printed description of the CALCULATE STICKER PRICE Function. Notice that the entity type and Function ID appear near the top of the page followed by other fields from the description screens:

- Label
- Explodes To
- Location
- Duration Value
- Duration Type
- Satisfies Requirement
- Associated Entities
- Description
- Audit fields from the bottom of the second Function Description screen

Figure 8.2.2
Printed Function Description for CALCULATE STICKER PRICE (CSP) with Output Fields Underlined

DATE: 25-AUG-91 FUNCTION - OUTPUT PAGE 1
TIME: 18:52 NAME: * Excelerator / IS

TYPE FUNCTION NAME CSP

Label CALCULATE STICKER PRICE

Explodes to one of:
Structure Chart ______
Structure Diagram ______
Module ______

Location INVENTORY SUBSYSTEM

Duration Value 250
Duration Type DAY

Satisfies Requirement:
Type Name

Associated Entities
Type Name

Description

THE STICKER PRICE IS CALCULATED BY ADDING THE BASE COST OF THE VEHICLE, THE FREIGHT, AND THEN MULTIPLYING THE RESULT BY 1.23, WHICH IS THE DEALER'S MARK-UP.

THE DATA COMING INTO THIS FUNCTION ARE THE BASE COST AND THE FREIGHT. THE DATA COMING OUT OF THIS FUNCTION IS THE STICKER PRICE.

Modified By ANALYST Date Modified 910814 # Changes 13
Added By ANALYST Date Added 910814
Last Project Anonymous Autos
Locked By ______ Date Locked 0 Lock Status ______

8.3

Describing Structure Graph Connections (SGCs)

Structure Graph Connections (SGCs) show the flow of Data Elements and control flags from Function to Function on the Structure Graph

Structure Graph Connections carry the following symbols as shown in Figure 8.3:

- Data Up
- Data Down
- Control Flag Up
- Control Flag Down

Communication between Functions occurs as these Data Elements and Control Flags move up and down Structure Graph Connections.

Although Structure Graph Connections are not exploded in this tutorial, Excelerator allows them to be exploded to Records from the data model.

In this section, you will describe and print the Structure Graph Connections shown on the Structure Graph for the Anonymous Autos system called PRODUCE VIR.

Figure 8.3
Structure Graph Connections Carrying Symbols between Functions

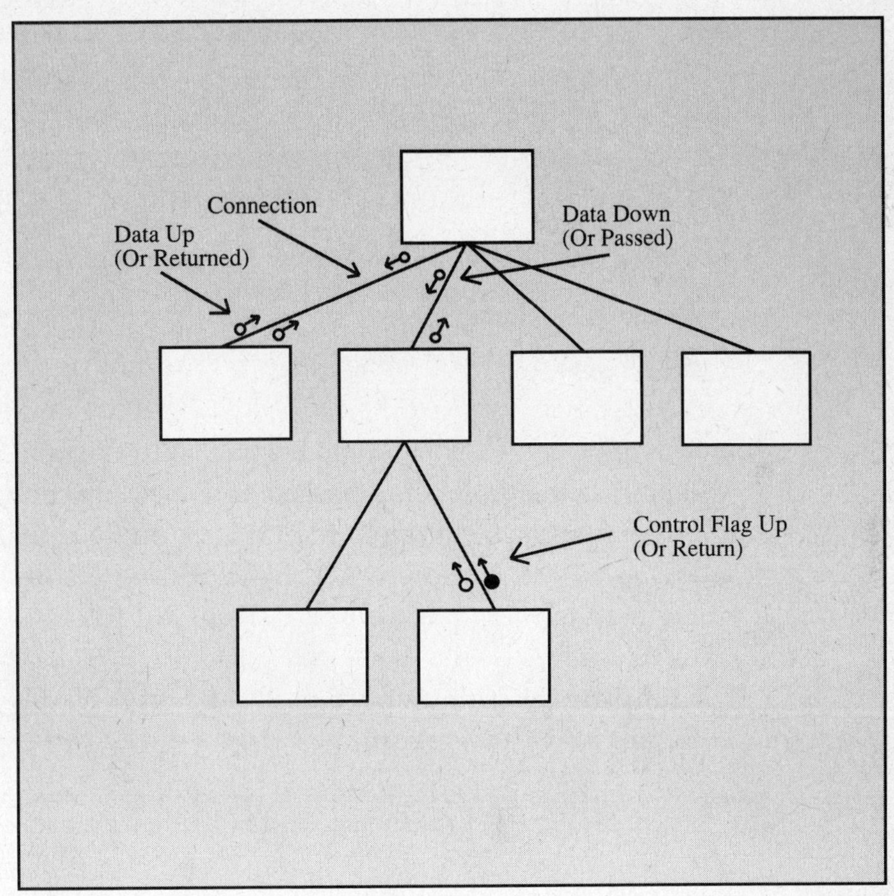

8.3.1 Completing SGC Description Screens

If it is not already on your screen, retrieve the PRODUCE VIR Structure Chart.

- Select **DESCRIBE** from the Command Menu.
- Position the mouse cursor on the handle of the SGC connecting the Functions labeled PRODUCE VIR and CALCULATE STICKER PRICE.
- Press the left button on the mouse to select the SGC.
- Type **GSP** (short for Get Sticker Price) in the status line at the ID prompt.
- Press ↵, and the first SGC description screen is displayed as in Figure 8.3.1a.

Because SGCs are not exploded in this tutorial, leave the **Explodes To** field blank.

The remaining fields on the first SGC description screen are for detailing the data being passed between Functions. Look at the Structure Chart shown in Figure 8.1.3 on Page 257. Two Data Elements are being passed down: BASE_COST and FREIGHT. One Data Element is being passed up: STICKER_PRICE.

Complete the bottom portion of the first SGC description screen using Figure 8.3.1a as a guide.

- Press Pg Dn, and the second SGC description screen appears.

As explained in **4.4.2 Completing DFD Description Screens, Satisfies Requirements** and **Associated Entities** will not be addressed in this tutorial.

- Press Pg Dn, and the third SGC description screen appears.

Description on this last screen is for a detailed, free-form explanation of SGC activities. Complete this screen using Figure 8.3.1b as a guide.

- Press F3 when you finish to save and return to your graph.

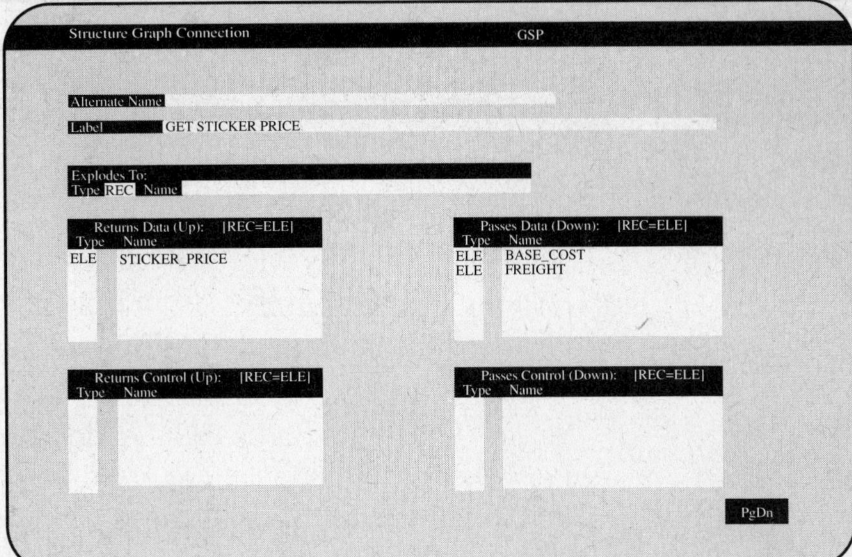

Figure 8.3.1a
First SGC Description Screen

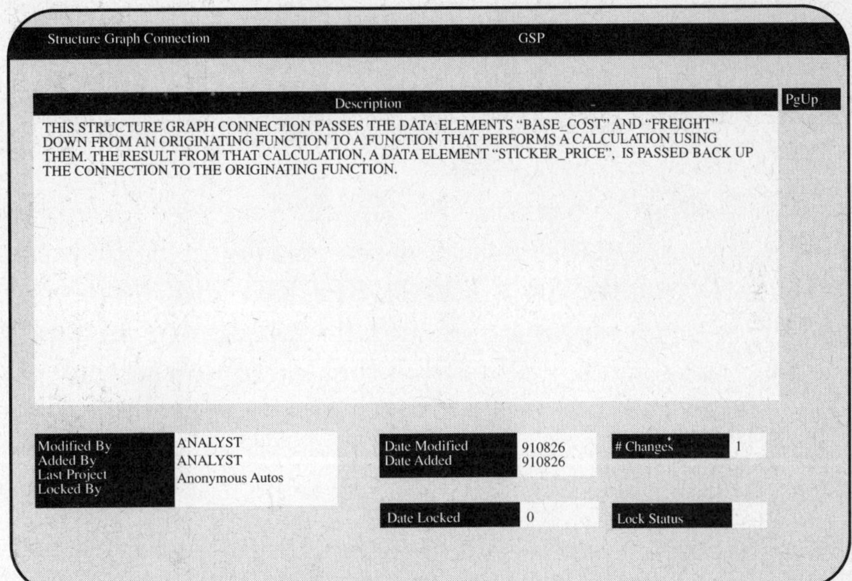

Figure 8.3.1b
Third SGC Description Screen

Exercise 8.3.1

Describe the remaining SGCs on the PRODUCE VIR Structure Chart. When assigning IDs, make them meaningful. Acronyms of SGC labels work well.

When this exercise is finished, your Structure Graph will be complete. Print the finished Structure Chart, PRODUCE VIR. (See **4.1.16 Using PRINT Options** if necessary.)

8.3.2 Printing SGC Descriptions

As with the description of other graph components, when you've completed a Structure Graph Connection (SGC) description, you may send it to an output device for printing.

- Select **X XLDICTIONARY** from Excelerator's Main Menu.
- Select **Process** from the XLDictionary Menu which appears.
- Select **S Structure Graph Connection** from the Process Menu.
- Select **Output** from the SGC Action Keypad.
- Press ↵ and the XLDictionary list of SGCs appears.
- Select **All Entities on Selector List** with the mouse.
- Type **Y** when asked if input fields should be underlined.
- Select **Printer** as the output device.

Graph component descriptions can be printed one at a time, within specified ranges, or all together. See **4.2.3 Printing DFD Descriptions**.

The reports Excelerator generates for your SGCs closely resemble the SGC description screens. Figure 8.3.2 shows the printed description of the CALCULATE STICKER PRICE Function. Notice that the entity type and Function ID appear near the top of the page followed by other fields from the description screens:

- Label
- Explodes To
- Location
- Duration Value
- Duration Type
- Satisfies Requirement
- Associated Entities
- Description
- Audit fields from the bottom of the second Function description screen

Figure 8.3.2
Printed SGC Description for GET STICKER PRICE (GSP) with Output Fields Underlined

DATE: 29-AUG-91 STRUCTURE GRAPH CONNECTION - OUTPUT PAGE 1
TIME: 10:17 NAME: * Excelerator / IS

TYPE STRUCTURE GRAPH CONNECTION NAME GSP

Alternate Name

Label GET STICKER PRICE

Explodes To:
Type REC Name

Returns Data (Up) : [REC-ELE]

Type	Name
ELE	STICKER_PRICE

PASSES Data (Down) : [REC-ELE]

Type	Name
ELE	BASE_COST
ELE	FREIGHT

Returns Control (Up) : [REC-ELE]
Type Name

PASSES Control (Down) : [REC-ELE]
Type Name

Satisfies Requirement:
Type Name

Associated Entities
Type Name

Description

THIS STRUCTURE GRAPH CONNECTION PASSES THE DATA ELEMENTS "BASE_COST" AND "FREIGHT" DOWN FROM AN ORIGINATING FUNCTION TO A FUNCTION THAT PERFORMS A CALCULATION USING THEM. THE RESULT FROM THAT CALCULATION, A DATA ELEMENT "STICKER_PRICE", IS PASSED BACK UP THE CONNECTION TO THE ORIGINATING FUNCTION.

Modified By ANALYST Date Modified 910814 # Changes 13
Added By ANALYST Date Added 910814
Last Project Anonymous Autos
Locked By Date Locked 0 Lock Status

Excelerating Your Skills ... in Structure Design

The Anonymous Autos system is nearly complete. All that remains is the completion and integration of the system's Structure Charts with the process and data models.

The Structure Chart you created in this chapter, PRODUCE VIR, is actually a detailed graphical representation of a Process you described in Chapter 4. The low-level Data Flow Diagram shown at the top of the opposite page called 1.0 INVENTORY SUBSYSTEM was created in Exercise 4.6.2. This DFD contains a Process called 1.2 PRODUCE COMPLETED VIR. Your Structure Chart called PRODUCE VIR describes in detail the activities taking place within that Process.

Retrieve the first Description screen for Process 1.2 PRODUCE VIR and complete the **Explodes To** Type and Name fields with STC and PRODUCE VIR respectively. By doing this, you have begun integrating the Structure Design and Process Model of the Anonymous Autos project.

Integration of the Structure Design and Data Model began when you completed the Structure Graph Connection (SGC) Descriptions, indicating the movement up and down of Data Elements and Records from the Data Model.

Create Structure Charts for all remaining low-level processes which you feel STCs can further describe. Integrate these Structure Charts with the Process Model by exploding low-level Process to STCs. Integrate the Data Model by indicating the movement of described Data Elements and Records up and down Structure Graph Connections (SGCs).

When you are finished, print out all the Structure Charts, their descriptions, and their component descriptions. Also, re-print low-level Process descriptions with new explosion information.

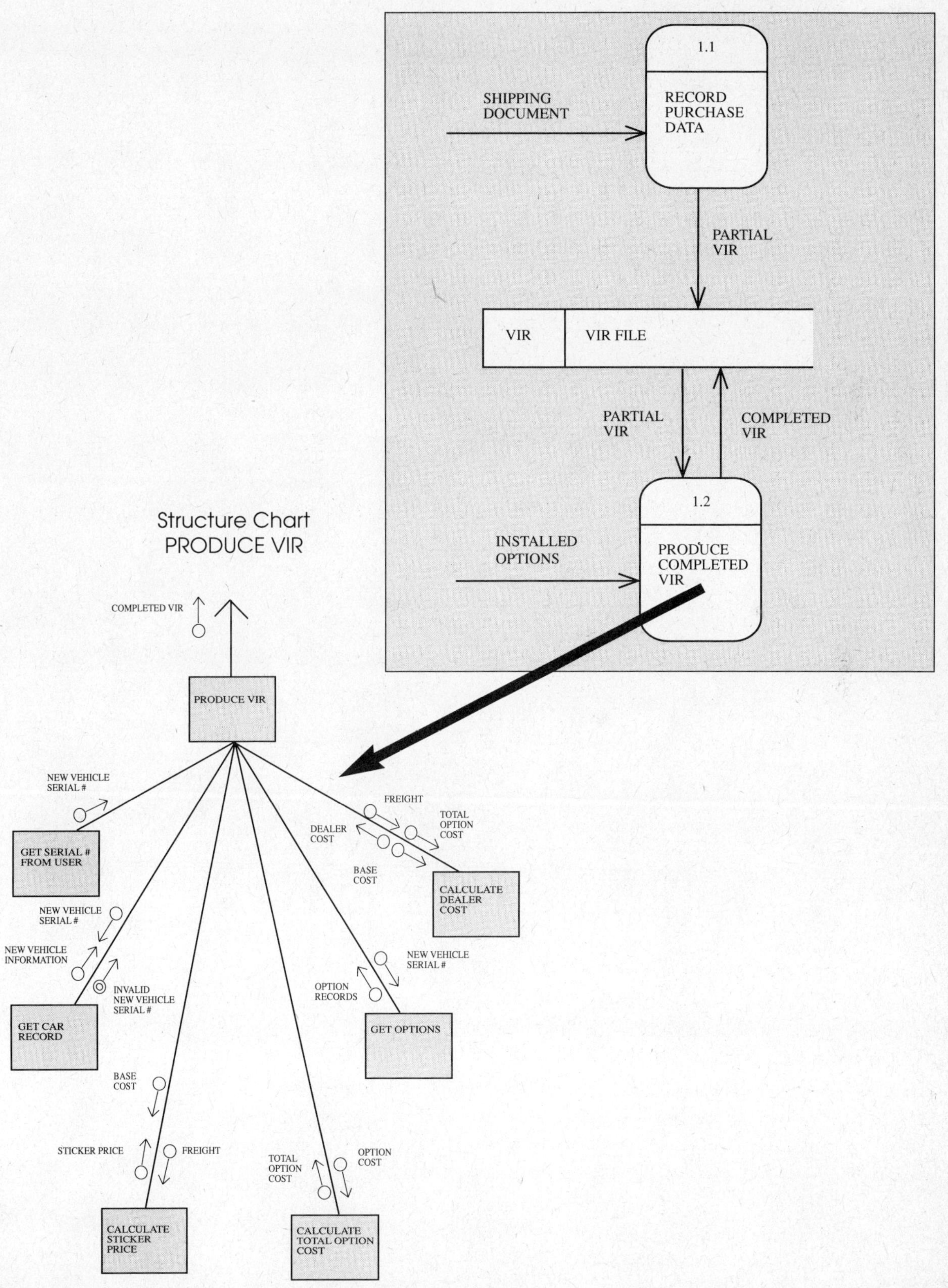
Data Flow Diagram
1.2 PRODUCE COMPLETED VIR
1.1
RECORD PURCHASE DATA
SHIPPING DOCUMENT
PARTIAL VIR
VIR
VIR FILE
PARTIAL VIR
COMPLETED VIR
1.2
PRODUCE COMPLETED VIR
INSTALLED OPTIONS
Structure Chart
PRODUCE VIR
COMPLETED VIR
PRODUCE VIR
NEW VEHICLE SERIAL #
GET SERIAL # FROM USER
NEW VEHICLE SERIAL #
NEW VEHICLE INFORMATION
INVALID NEW VEHICLE SERIAL #
GET CAR RECORD
BASE COST
STICKER PRICE
FREIGHT
CALCULATE STICKER PRICE
TOTAL OPTION COST
OPTION COST
CALCULATE TOTAL OPTION COST
FREIGHT
DEALER COST
TOTAL OPTION COST
BASE COST
CALCULATE DEALER COST
NEW VEHICLE SERIAL #
OPTION RECORDS
GET OPTIONS

INDEX

Sales Invoice, 26-27, 94, 116-118, 120, 122, 130, 132-133, 174, 214-215, 236, 242

ABOUT THE AUTHORS

Henry David Crockett, Ph.D., C.S.P

Professor of Management Information Systems (MIS)
School of Business Administration
Portland State University, Portland, Oregon

Gillian R. Hall, B.S. **Mark E. Wheeler, B.S.**

Graduate Students of Management Information Systems (MIS)
School of Business Administration
Portland State University, Portland, Oregon

Winners of the
1991 International Excelerator Student Project Competition